University of St. Francis Library
D0876292

COMPLETE HANDBOOK of SPORTS SCORING and RECORD KEEPING

COMPLETE HANDBOOK of SPORTS SCORING and RECORD KEEPING

Jack Richards and Danny Hill

Parker Publishing Co., Inc. West Nyack, N.Y.

PARKER PUBLISHING COMPANY, INC.

West Nyack, N. Y.

Library of Congress Cataloging in Publication Data

Richards, Jack W.
Complete handbook of sports scoring and record keeping.

1. Sports—Statistics. 2. Sports—Records. 3. Sports officiating. I. Hill, Danny, joint author. II. Title.
GV741.R47 796'.021'2 73-14815
ISBN 0-13-161257-3

Printed in the United States of America

How This Book Will Help You

This book has a dual mission. First, it is intended as a complete statistical manual for 13 sports. Here for the first time in one book is a comprehensive summary of statistical interpretations for all major sports.

The interpretations are authentic and may be used as references by the experienced statistician, yet the explanations and examples are painstakingly fundamental so they should be clearly understandable to the novice.

Examples also are given of unusual situations, a detail often lacking in statistician's manuals for individual sports. It should be noted that in a number of sports, there is no other available instructional material (other than Rules of Scoring) on statistics or record-keeping. Thus, this is the *only* place in which statistical and scoring instructions may be found for those sports.

The second intended purpose of these pages is to serve as a coaches' crutch, to satisfy either desire or necessity.

The home team is charged with statistical responsibility and the coach, as the school's representative, often must select and train a student in the elements of statistics and record-keeping.

It is a time-consuming and constant activity. It is hoped this book will not only save valuable time for coaches, but result in more accurate and reliable statistics of their games.

In many cases, coaches want special statistical studies for use as coaching aids (such as "turnover" charts or "shot" charts in basketball). This material can be compiled accurately by the statistician familiar with this text.

Herein also is a basis for understanding the nuances of scoring and record-keeping for a coach who is assigned to a sport with which he is not entirely familiar. At the same time, it provides for the experienced coach a ready reference in these areas.

Because statistics and records have become an integral part of modern sports, most physical educators feel a professional obligation

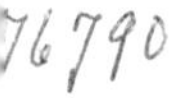

to be familiar with the techniques and methods of scoring and record-keeping. The writers believe this compendium is so comprehensive and valid that it can be a bona fide text for physical education students.

Dedicated coaches devote inordinate time to reading written material, attending clinics and exchanging ideas with other coaches on techniques and mode of play. They (particularly in high schools and small colleges) also learn all they can about first-aid procedures for trainers, equipment purchasing and maintenance, publicity, travel arrangements, ticket printing and distribution, ticket selling, gate and crowd controls, dressing room facilities, *ad infinitum* (of such things are athletic directors made).

With the knowledge obtained, they have been able to instruct aides or students to handle these functions. Heretofore, there has been little or no instructional material available for this purpose in statistics, scoring or record-keeping for all sports. We hope this book will serve that function.

Jack Richards
Danny Hill

Dedication

To Homer F. Cooke, Jr., Steve Boda,
Henry Chadwick, Irving Howe,
Walter and Al Munro Elias

Contents

Chapter 1

What the Sports Statistician Does

As progenitor of interpretative football statistics, Homer F. Cooke, Jr., in a succinct foreword to the NCAA's *Football Statistician's Manual*, offers a superb introduction for those charged with recording and maintaining statistics on any level.

"The essential purpose of football statistics," Cooke wrote, "is to broaden the base of interest in the sport for players and fans, alike. Although the primary goal of all competition properly is victory, interest in a sport need not and should not be confined exclusively to the victor. Statistics, without detracting from the primary goal, do more than anything else to focus attention on 'how they played the game' in addition to the fundamental 'who won or lost.'

"So, the role of statistics in football is not that of 'proving anything,' nor of supporting victory—an attainment seldom in need of statistical verification. Rather, it is that of broadening interest to include the noteworthy feats of both sides."

Cooke's admonition that statistics are not cast in the role of proving anything is, perhaps, the best starting point for the budding statistician.

The Sports Statistician

A statistician is a record-keeper; he records what happened on the field in an objective manner. A good statistician makes all entries exactly as they occur on the field or arena, without regard to whether it is his team or an opponent. He is not trying to "prove anything," but only to record what actually happened on the field.

In addition to complete objectivity, the practical philosophy of a good statistician should embody the concepts of total accuracy and concentration. Accuracy is of vital importance on every single play because the complete game statistics are only as valid as the sum of the statistics recorded for each individual play.

Accurate identification of players involved and precise recording of "what happened" are essential on *every* play. In every sport, there are devices that can be utilized to cross-check figures for accuracy. Before he learns one rule or interpretation, a statistician should be indoctrinated thoroughly in the importance of accuracy.

Accurate statistics are of importance and interest to news media, coaches, players and fans, and they provide a means of continuity and comparison that increases their value. But, without accuracy, they are of little value.

A statistician, therefore, should recognize the significance of his task and should be thoroughly acquainted with the scoring and statistical rules, interpretations and procedures. This knowledge, along with dedication to accuracy, should result in reliable and respected statistics.

The ability to concentrate is a vital asset for the good statistician. He always will face the temptation to follow the play as an excited spectator, neglecting to make important notations until it is too late.

For instance, in football, on a pass interception, if the statistician waits until he watches the play to its conclusion, it is too late to determine *where* the ball was intercepted, thus too late to record accurately *how many* yards it was returned by the interceptor. Or, on a punt return, the statistician must note the exact spot where the player started his return *before* he starts enjoying the actual runback itself. If he does not, there will be no way to *accurately* record either the distance of the punt or the yardage of the return.

As time goes on, the statistician learns to quickly note the essential information of a play (such as yardage and player identity in football), *then* to enjoy the play to its conclusion. But to reach this point, he must make a continuous and conscious effort to keep his primary concentration on statistical information.

Responsibilities of the Statistician

Those charged with compiling statistics actually wear four different hats—scorer, statistician, historian and play-by-play recorder. Often, because of necessity, they all are worn by one man.

The statistician of the *home* team is the official scorer and statistician, unless otherwise appointed by a league or conference. He has the responsibility and authority to make decisions involving judgment (i.e. yardage gained on all plays, whether a man reaches base by hit or error, who is credited with a rebound, and so forth) and communicates such decisions, where appropriate, to others in the press box.

In a league that requires a statistical report, the home statistician (unless otherwise designated by league regulation) is responsible for providing this information to the league office on whatever form is designated by the league.

The official statistician should have all working forms and game report forms (samples for each sport are shown in corresponding chapters of this book) ready for use well in advance of the game. He should verify team rosters to insure accuracy of identification by uniform numbers.

The depth and extent of statistical information used will vary, depending upon the level of play and the emphasis by those directing the program. However, basic working charts should provide all the information needed to maintain whatever statistics are desired.

All work sheets should be saved in a permanent file. This provides a reference when researching records or other material which may not have been compiled in the final game statistics report.

If he uses proper working forms, a competent and experienced statistician or scorer can handle the chores alone. But, in some sports, because of the rapid action or because the recording of statistics is more complex, it is highly desirable that two or more be assigned for each game.

If the home team has only one statistician, he may recruit assistance from the visiting team's statistician. Help from a representative of the visiting team is always welcome, particularly to confirm identification of unfamiliar players.

When there are two statisticians, in football, the head statistician should be responsible for determining yardage on each play; the other should note the identity of players handling the ball. When more than two persons are available, duties can be divided. For instance, one man can keep defensive statistics, others play-by-play.

Many major colleges and professional football teams have a staff of at least five statisticians—the head statistician, two who compile the offensive statistics, one for defensive statistics and one for play-by-play. However, unless there is a demand for special or unusual statistics, a competent two-man team can adequately cover football statistical responsibilities.

Additional help should be used if a play-by-play chart (examples included in *Football* chapter) is desired. Play-by-play records are of help to coaches and news media and provide an excellent reference and cross-check for statistical purposes.

In basketball, because of the fast pace and varied responsibilities, as many as seven statisticians are used by some teams. In addition to the official scorer, two are assigned shooting statistics, two more for rebounding, assists and turnovers, and another pair for play-by-play summaries.

Obviously, every team cannot assign seven men for statistics. If only one statistician is available, he likely will have time for only simple numerical recording and may not be able to keep up with much else except the number of shots attempted and made, rebounds, assists and turnovers. And he will be hard pressed to keep pace with all of that in a high-scoring game. As others may be available, more detail and other categories may be added to the statistical report of the game.

In other sports one man comfortably can record all the statistics normally required. Responsibilities that are unique to each sport will be covered in the subsequent chapters on those sports.

The First Sports Statistics

Statistics have been an ancillary product of competitive sports for at least 100 years. In the early days, simple won-lost records were utilized for comparative or record purposes.

Henry Chadwick, called the Father of Baseball by sports historian Frank G. Menke, was generally credited with devising, in the 1860s, the first box score and batting averages.

The first baseball statistics were confined to runs and hits, and within a decade (1876), simple statistical champions were recorded in batting averages, pitcher's won-lost records, home runs and stolen bases.

However, it was well into the 20th Century before more sophisticated baseball statistics were initiated. Just prior to World War I, a Chicago printing salesman, Irving Howe, established a statistical service that today is known as the Howe News Bureau and provides the American League with its official statistics.

A grocery clerk, Al Munro Elias, who started dabbling with figures in his mother's kitchen, founded, with his brother, Walter, the Elias Sports Bureau in 1916 in New York. It now serves both the National Baseball League and the National Football League.

Today, the abundance of baseball records is limited only by the energy and imagination of the statistician. The World Series Record Book, alone, lists more than 400 pages of records. And there is an almost limitless number of variations for each standard—such as the record for left-handers and for right-handers, or against right-handers or left-handers, or records made in games at home and away, etc.

Football statistics have not reached the extent of detail of baseball (yet), but the gridiron figure filberts are not far behind. Football record books bulge with the numerical testimony of the nation's pigskin heroes. But, for the first 63 years of this great American game, statistics (other than scoring) rarely were recorded.

When used they were sporadic and unreliable. Probably the most comprehensive and objective statistical record research in football history was completed by Steve Boda of the National Collegiate Sports Service. His productive investigations revealed that a number of hallowed and hoary records attributed to football immortals were totally inaccurate.

It was not until 1932, when Homer F. Cooke, Jr. initiated a statistics program in the unlikely hamlet of Enumclaw, Wash., that football statistics and record-keeping were accorded significant analytical study and development.

Cooke devised and cultivated football statistics out of desperation. As owner and editor of a weekly newspaper in Enumclaw, he constantly was frustrated when writing advance stories for games in a league of town teams. There were no real facts available to support praise of a player generally described as "a great runner," or an "outstanding passer," or the "best kicker in the league."

A fastidious advocate of accuracy, Cooke wondered "how great?" and "how outstanding?" So he devised a system which enabled him to keep personal statistics on the teams and individuals in the league. He soon transferred his attention to the University of Washington and in 1936 established the first national statistics service in Seattle.

Circa World War II, he moved the National Collegiate Athletic Bureau (now known as the National Collegiate Sports Service) to New York. As the service arm of the National Collegiate Athletic Association (NCAA), it became the fountainhead of all football statistics.

Recognizing the attention gained for baseball and football through the use of statistics, other sports have become more attuned to the comparison of quality performances, whether time, distance or number. But baseball and football paved the numerical way.

Chapter 2

Baseball

In no sport is complete statistical objectivity more important than in baseball, where the scoring rules require key decisions based chiefly on the *scorer's judgment.*

The rules call for the *scorer's judgment* in determining whether a batter is credited with a hit, or a fielder an error; whether the pitcher is charged with a wild pitch, or the catcher a passed ball; which relief pitcher is credited with a win, and which player is charged with an error when two or more players are involved in a misplay.

In addition, the scorer's *opinion* is required to determine what is considered "ordinary effort" and whether a pitcher pitches "effectively."

This provides more latitude for scorers, but it also involves greater responsibility. The statistician must maintain rigid objectivity; he must score every play on the basis of considered and, hopefully, experienced judgment without regard to the individual player or team for which he plays.

There is a practical yardstick which may help you to be impartial and objective. In determining whether a play should be scored as a hit or an error, for instance, if the batter involved is on *your* team, ask yourself how you would have scored it had he been on the opposing team. Score it the same, whether he's on your team or is an opponent.

Although the scorer is permitted to change decisions within a reasonable time limit, reliable statisticians seldom make changes once a scoring decision is made. Changes should be made only if additional information becomes available from an authoritative source.

For instance, you will find that from the press box or grandstand, it is sometimes difficult to make accurate judgments, i.e. did the shortstop misplay a batted ball (error) or did it take a bad hope at the last instant (base hit)?

In such cases, it can be helpful to consult the umpire nearest the play (between innings or after the game). He usually will be in position to provide an accurate report on what happened. This would be a valid reason for changing a scoring decision.

Another example might be on a stolen base attempt, when no one covers second and the catcher's throw sails into center field, enabling the runner to take an extra base. You may have to consult the coach or manager to determine who was responsible for covering the base before charging an error.

In any case, make decisions impartially and stick to them unless subsequent information dictates a change.

Because of the great variety of situations in baseball, scoring rules are necessarily detailed to cover every possible circumstance. The instructions here are intended to cover basic situations (and should be adequate for nearly all situations).

For complete baseball scoring instructions, consult the *Official Baseball Rules,* available at a nominal sum from *The Sporting News,* 1212 N. Lindbergh Blvd., St. Louis, Mo. 63166.

Official Scorer

In professional baseball, the official scorers for each league, usually baseball writers who cover the league, are appointed by the league president. For baseball in high school or college, this is not often practical, so the statistician for the home team is the official scorer. The official scorer has sole authority to make decisions involving judgment.

If reports or box scores are required for league play or for use by the press, the official scorer is responsible for preparation and distribution of the forms. Such forms may be supplied by the league, or the scorer may obtain or devise forms such as those shown at the end of this chapter.

The scorebook of the official scorer must at all times reflect the exact status of the game. For instance, on a suspended or protested game, the official scorebook should show the exact situation at the moment of protest or suspension (i.e. number of outs, position of any runners, ball and strike count on the batter, and any runs scored thus far in the inning).

When a game is called after it becomes a "regulation" game (i.e. at least five innings have been completed, or at least four and one-half innings if the home team is ahead), include all team and individual records up to the time the game was called. If it is a tie game, do not enter a winning or losing pitcher, but record all other statistics.

This also applies for forfeited games which are regulation games. If the team winning by forfeit is ahead at the time of the forfeit, the winning and losing pitchers are those who would have been designated if the game had been called (by rain, etc.) at the time of the forfeit. If the team winning by forfeit was behind, or the score was tied at the time of the forfeit, there is no winning or losing pitcher. If a game is forfeited before it becomes a regulation game, include no records. Report only the fact of the forfeit.

Under *no* circumstances should the scorer make any decision that conflicts with official playing rules or with an umpire's decision. In the case of an apparent conflict, the chief umpire should be consulted at the earliest practical moment.

Batting

Times at Bat

A player is charged with a time at bat each time he makes an official appearance as a batter and hits safely, is safe on an error, strikes out, flies out, grounds out, hits a ball that results in a runner being forced out, or is called out for an infraction before reaching first base (interference with catcher, etc.).

1. A batter is not charged with a time at bat when credited with a sacrifice bunt or sacrifice fly, when he is awarded first base on four called balls, on being hit by a pitched ball or because of interference or obstruction, or when he is replaced by a pinch-hitter before completing his turn at bat.
2. No time at bat is charged if, during a player's batting turn, a baserunner is put out for the third out of the inning before the batter can complete his time at bat.

Runs

This requires no judgment on the part of the scorer. Credit a baserunner with one run each time his team is credited with a run after he crosses home plate safely.

Base Hits

A batter is charged with a time at bat and credited with a base hit when he reaches first base (or any succeeding base) safely on a fair ball:

1. Which touches the ground or fence before being touched by a fielder or which clears a fence;
2. Hit with such force, or so slowly, that a fielder has no opportunity to make a play (even if the fielder deflects the ball from or cuts off another fielder who could have put out the runner);
3. Which takes an unnatural bounce (bad hop) so that a fielder cannot handle it with ordinary effort, or which touches the pitcher's plate or any base before being touched by a fielder and bounces so that a fielder cannot handle it with ordinary effort;
4. Which has not been touched by a fielder and which is in fair territory when it reaches the outfield unless in the *scorer's judgment* it could have been handled with *ordinary effort.*

Example: A ground ball which goes between the legs of an infielder, even though he doesn't touch it, normally would be charged as an error, not a base hit, unless covered by Number 2 above (hit with such force, etc.).

5. Which has not been touched by a fielder and touches a runner or an umpire.

Exception: Do not score a hit when a runner is touched (and called out) by a batted ball on which the infield fly rule is invoked.

6. When a fielder *unsuccessfully* attempts to put out a preceding runner and, in the *scorer's judgment,* the batter would not have been put out at first base by perfect fielding.

Note: Always give the batter the benefit of the doubt. In general, score a hit when exceptionally good fielding fails to result in a putout.

A batter who reaches base safely is charged with a time at bat but is not credited with a base hit:

1. When a runner is forced out by a batted ball, or would have been forced out except for a fielding error.

Note: If, with a man or men on base, the batter hits a ball which falls to the ground in the outfield for an apparent hit, but the outfielder throws to a base in time to *force out* a preceding runner, the batter *is not* credited with a hit.

Note: If a preceding runner, who is forced to advance because the batter becomes a runner, fails to touch the first base to which he is advancing and is called out on appeal, it is a force out and not a base hit.

2. When the pitcher, catcher or any infielder handles a batted ball and puts out a preceding runner who is attempting to advance one base or

to return to his original base, or would have put out such runner with *ordinary effort* except for a fielding error. It is a fielder's choice.
3. When a fielder fails in an attempt to put out a preceding runner, and in the *scorer's judgment* the batter could have been put out at first base. It is a fielder's choice.

Note: If a fielder merely looks toward or feints toward another base before attempting to make the putout at first base, this is not considered "an attempt" to put out the preceding runner.

4. When a runner is called out for interference with a fielder attempting to field a batted ball, unless in the *scorer's judgment* the batter would have been safe had there been no interference.

In determining whether a safe hit should be scored as a one-base hit, two- or three-base hit, or home run, a general rule is to credit the batter with as many bases as he advances and would have advanced without error and with *ordinary effort* on the part of the fielding team.

1. With a runner or runners on base, when the batter advances more than one base on a safe hit and the fielding team makes an effort to put out a preceding runner, the *scorer shall determine* whether the batter made a legitimate two- or three-base hit or whether he advanced beyond first on a fielder's choice.
2. Do not credit the batter with a three-base hit when a preceding runner is put out at the plate, or would have been out but for an error.
3. Do not credit the batter with a two-base hit when a preceding runner trying to advance from first base is put out at third, or would have been except for an error.
4. With the exception of Numbers 2 & 3 above, do not determine the value of a base hit by the number of bases advanced by a preceding runner.

Example: Runner on first, batter hits safely to right fielder, who throws to third base in unsuccessful attempt to put out runner. Batter advances to second base on the throw. Credit batter with a single.

Example: Runner on second, batter hits fair fly ball. Runner holds up to see if ball is caught, and when it drops to ground, advances only to third, while batter takes second. Credit batter with a double.

Example: Runner on third. Batter hits high fair fly. Runner takes lead, then runs back to tag up, thinking ball will be caught. Ball falls safe, but runner cannot score, although batter has reached second. Credit batter with a double.

5. When batter *overslides* in an attempt to make a two- or three-base hit, and is tagged out before getting back to base safely, he is credited

only with as many bases as he reached safely. (i.e. if he *overslides* third base and is tagged out, he is credited only with a double.)

6. However, if the batter *overruns* second or third base and is tagged out trying to return, he is credited with the last base he touched (i.e. if he *overruns* third base after reaching that base *on his feet* and is tagged out attempting to return, he is credited with a triple.)

7. If a batter, after making a safe hit, is called out for failing to touch a base, the last base he reached safely shall determine whether it should be a one-, two-, or three-base hit (i.e. if he is called out for missing third, he is credited with a double.)

8. When a batter is awarded two or three bases or a home run because of an umpire's ruling (ground-rule double, obstruction, etc.) he shall be credited with two or three bases or a home run, as the case may be.

9. On a safe hit which ends a game by driving in the winning run, credit the batter with only as many bases on his hit as are advanced by the runner who scores the winning run. However, to receive credit for the same number of bases (as advanced by the runner who scores the winning run), the batter must run out his hit for the same number of bases.

Example: Score tied, runner on second, batter hits line drive into left center on which runner scores winning run. But batter holds up, as run scores, after crossing first. Credit him only with single.

Example: Same situation, but as runner scores winning run, batter races to second base. Credit him with a double.

Exception: If the game-winning hit is a home run hit out of the playing field, the batter and all runners on base are entitled to score. Credit batter with a home run.

Batting Averages

The batting average of a player or team is computed by dividing the total *number* of safe hits (not total bases) by the total *official* times at bat.

Example: John Smith comes to the plate 10 times in a series. He is given two bases on balls, is hit by the pitcher, hits two singles, one three-base hit, and is put out the other four times. Thus, he has 7 *official* times at bat and hit safely 3 times. Dividing 3 by 7 gives a batting average of .429 (given in three decimals to the nearest figure).

Slugging Percentages

To compute the slugging percentage of a player or team divide the *total bases* of all safe hits by the total *official* times at bat.

Example: In the example under batting averages, John Smith hit two singles (two total bases) and one triple (three total bases) in seven official times at bat. Thus, divide his total bases, 5, by times at bat, 7, for a slugging percentage of .714.

Runs Batted In

A batter receives credit for a run-batted-in for every run which scores because of his safe hit, sacrifice (bunt or fly), infield out, fielder's choice or for a run which is scored because the batter, with the bases full, became a runner after a walk or being hit by a pitched ball, or was awarded first base for interference or obstruction.

1. When a batter hits a home run, he is credited with a run batted in for the run he scored, plus the run or runs of any batter who scores ahead of him on the home run.
2. Credit a run batted in for the run scored when, before two are out, an error is made on a play on which in the *scorer's judgment,* the runner would have scored even without the error.
3. Do not credit the batter with a run batted in when a run scores as he hits into a force double play or a reverse force double play, or when a fielder is charged with an error because he muffs a throw at first base which would have completed a force double play.
4. If a run scores when a fielder holds the ball or throws to the wrong base, the *scorer* must make a judgment on whether the batter is to be credited with a run batted in. (Ordinarily if the runner keeps going, credit a run batted in; if the runner stops, then starts running again when he notices the misplay, credit the run as scored on a fielder's choice).

Stolen Bases

Credit a runner with a stolen base whenever he advances one base unaided by a hit, a putout, an error, a force-out, a fielder's choice, a passed ball, a wild pitch or a balk.

1. If a runner starts for the next base before the pitcher delivers the ball, and the pitch results in what normally would be scored as a wild pitch or passed ball, credit the runner with a stolen base and do not score a wild pitch or passed ball.
2. When a catcher makes a wild throw attempting to prevent a stolen base, credit the runner (or runners) with a stolen base and do not charge catcher with an error unless the wild throw permits the stealing runner to advance one or more extra bases, or permits another runner to advance. In this case, credit a stolen base and charge the catcher with one error.
3. When a runner, attempting to steal or after being picked off base, evades being put out in a run-down play and advances to the next base without aid of an error, credit the runner with a stolen base. If another

runner also advances on the play, credit both runners with stolen bases.

4. If a runner advances while another runner, attempting to steal, evades being put out in a rundown play and returns safely, without error, to the base he originally occupied, credit a stolen base to the runner who advances.

5. On an attempted double or triple steal if any one runner is thrown out before reaching and holding the base he is attempting to steal, no other runner shall be credited with a stolen base.

6. On an attempted steal, when a runner is tagged out after oversliding a base, while attempting either to return to that base or to advance to the next base, do not credit him with a stolen base.

7. When, in the *scorer's judgment,* a runner attempting to steal is safe because of a muffed throw, do not credit a stolen base. Credit an assist to the player who made the throw, charge an error to the fielder who muffed the throw, and charge the runner with "caught stealing" (see below).

8. A runner is charged with "caught stealing" if he is put out, or would have been put out by errorless play, when he (a) tries to steal, (b) is picked off base and *tries to advance,* or (c) overslides while stealing.

Note: Do not charge a runner with "caught stealing" unless he has an opportunity to be credited with a stolen base when the play starts.

9. Credit a fielder's choice and *not a stolen base,* when a runner advances solely because of the defensive team's indifference to his advance.

Sacrifices

When a batter is credited with a sacrifice bunt or a sacrifice fly, do not charge him with a time at bat.

1. Score a sacrifice bunt when, before two are out, the batter advances one or more runners with a bunt and is put out at first base, or would have been put out except for a fielding error.

2. Score a sacrifice bunt when, before two are out, the fielders handle a bunted ball without error in an unsuccessful attempt to put out a preceding runner advancing one base.

3. Score a base hit, and not a sacrifice bunt, if the attempt to turn a bunt into a putout of a preceding runner fails, and in the *scorer's judgment,* perfect play would not have put out the batter at first base.

4. Charge the batter with a time at bat and do not credit him with a sacrifice bunt when any runner is put out attempting to advance one base on a bunt.

5. Charge the batter with a time at bat and do not credit him with a sacrifice bunt when, in the *scorer's judgment,* the batter is bunting primarily for a base hit and not for the purpose of advancing a runner or runners. However, the batter should be given the benefit of any doubt.

6. Credit the batter with a sacrifice fly when, before two are out, he hits a fly ball which (a) is caught and a runner scores after the catch, or (b) is dropped and a runner scores, if in the *scorer's judgment* the runner would have scored after the catch if the fly had been caught.

Note: In the case of (b) above, score a sacrifice fly even though another runner is forced out by reason of the batter becoming a baserunner.

Fielding

Putouts

Credit a player with a putout whenever he catches a fly ball or line drive, whether fair or foul, or catches a thrown ball which puts out the batter or runner, or tags a runner when the runner is off the base to which he is legally entitled.

There are a number of circumstances when there is an automatic putout credited to a defensive player. Credit the *catcher* with a putout when:

1. The batter is called out for an illegally batted ball;
2. The batter is called out for bunting foul for his third strike, unless the foul bunt is caught before it strikes the ground by a fielder other than the catcher. In that case, do not record a strikeout, but credit a putout to the fielder who catches the foul bunt;
3. The batter is called out for interfering with the catcher;
4. The batter is called out for failing to touch first base after receiving a base on balls or when a runner is called out for refusing to advance from third base to home with the winning run.

Other fielders are credited with automatic putouts (no assists unless specified) as described in the following:

1. When a batter is called out on an infield fly, which is not caught, credit the putout to the fielder who in the scorer's judgment could have made the catch;
2. Credit the putout to the fielder nearest the ball when a runner is called out for being touched by a fair ball (including an infield fly);
3. When a runner is called out for running out of the line to avoid being tagged, credit the putout to the fielder whom the runner avoided;
4. When a runner is called out for passing another runner, credit the putout to the fielder nearest the point of passing;
5. When a runner is called out for running the bases in reverse order, credit the putout to the fielder covering the base he left in starting his reverse run;

6. When a runner is called out for having interfered with a fielder, credit the putout to the fielder with whom the runner interfered, unless the fielder was in the act of throwing the ball when the interference occurred, in which case credit the putout to the fielder for whom the throw was intended. Credit an assist to the fielder whose throw was interfered with;
7. When the batter-runner is called out because of interference by a preceding runner, credit the putout to the first baseman. If the fielder interfered with was in the act of throwing the ball, credit him with an assist.

Assists

An assist is just what the name implies, an action which "assists" in making a putout. Credit an assist to each player who throws or deflects a batted or thrown ball in such a way that a putout results, or would have resulted in a putout except for a subsequent error.

1. Every player who assists in a putout by throwing (or deflecting) the ball is credited with an assist, but no player can be credited with more than one assist in a single play.

Example: In a rundown play, the ball may be thrown back and forth between two, three, or four players any number of times before the runner, caught in the rundown, is put out. Each player who threw the ball at least once during the rundown is given credit for an assist, but only one assist each.

2. When a runner is called out for interference or for running out of line, credit an assist to each player who throws or deflects the ball during the play.
3. Do not credit an assist to a pitcher on a strikeout (unless he fields an uncaught third strike and makes a throw which results in a putout).
4. A fielder is not credited with an assist when his wild throw permits a runner to advance, even though the runner is put out as a result of continuous play. (Unless the fielder takes part in the subsequent putout).

Double and Triple Plays

A player is credited with taking part in a double play or triple play if he makes a putout or an assist when two or three players are put out between the time a pitch is delivered and the time the ball next becomes dead or is next in possession of the pitcher in pitching position, unless an error or misplay occurs between the putouts.

If an additional putout results from an appeal play after the ball is in possession of the pitcher, credit this as part of a double or triple play.

Errors

An error shall be charged to a player for each misplay (fumble, muff or wild throw) which prolongs the time at bat of a batter or which prolongs the life of a runner, or which permits a runner to advance one or more bases.

1. There can be more than one error on one play, but charge only one error on any single wild throw or any muff regardless of the number of bases advanced by one or more runners.

Example: Batter grounds to shortstop, who throws to first in time for putout, but throws wild, batter-runner continuing on to second base. Charge one error to shortstop.

Example: Runner on second. Batter grounds to shortstop, who throws to first in time for putout, but throw skips off glove of first baseman. Batter-runner goes to second and man on second goes all the way home on muff. Charge one error to first baseman.

2. Mental mistakes or misjudgments are not to be scored as errors, unless specifically covered by the rules.
3. Slow handling of ball which does not involve a mechanical misplay is not considered an error.
4. It is not necessary that a player touch the ball to be charged with an error. If a ball goes through a fielder's legs untouched or a pop fly falls untouched, an error may be charged if, in the *scorer's judgment,* the fielder could have handled the ball with *ordinary effort.*
5. If a player muffs a foul fly, he is charged with an error, whether the batter subsequently reaches first base or is put out.
6. Charge a player with an error when he catches a thrown ball or a ground ball in time to put out the batter-runner at first base or any runner on a force play and fails to tag the base or the runner.
7. An error is charged against any player whose wild throw permits a runner to reach base safely (when in the *scorer's judgment* a good throw would have put out the runner) or whose wild throw permits any runner to advance one or more bases beyond the base he would have reached had the throw not been wild.
8. Charge a player with an error if his throw takes an unnatural bounce, or touches a base or the pitcher's plate, or touches a runner, a fielder or an umpire, thereby permitting any runner to advance.
9. An error is charged against a player whose failure to stop, or try to stop, an accurately thrown ball permits a runner to advance, providing there was occasion for the throw.
   (a.) If such a throw is made to second base, the *scorer shall determine* whether it was the duty of the second baseman or shortstop to stop the ball. Charge the error accordingly.

(b.) If in the *scorer's judgment* there was no occasion for the throw, an error should be charged to the player who threw the ball.

Note: It may be necessary for the scorer to consult the team manager or coach to make the determination in (a) or (b) above.

10. If a batter or runner is awarded one or more bases by an umpire because of interference or obstruction, charge one error to the player who committed the interference or obstruction, no matter how many bases the batter or runner may be advanced.

Note: If in the scorer's judgment the obstruction does not change the play, do not charge an error.

11. There are a number of instances when a player makes a misplay, but is not charged with an error. Do not charge a player with an error in any of the following situations.

(a.) No error is charged against the catcher if, after receiving a pitch, he makes a wild throw attempting to prevent a stolen base, unless the wild throw permits the stealing runner to advance one or more extra bases or permits any other runner to advance one or more bases.

(b.) Do not charge a player with an error when he makes a wild throw, if in the *scorer's judgment* the runner would not have been put out with *ordinary effort* by a good throw, unless the wild throw permits any runner to advance beyond the base he would have reached without the wild throw.

(c.) A fielder is not charged with an error when he makes a wild throw in attempting to complete a double play or triple play, unless the wild throw enables any runner to advance beyond the base he would have reached had the throw not been wild.

(d.) However, if a fielder muffs a thrown ball which, if held, would have completed a double or triple play, charge an error to the fielder who drops the ball (and credit an assist to the fielder who made the throw).

(e.) If a fielder fumbles a ground ball or drops a fly ball, a line drive or thrown ball, but recovers in time to *force out* a runner at any base, do not charge him with an error.

(f.) If a fielder permits a foul fly to fall safely with a runner on third base and before two are out, do not charge an error, if in the *scorer's judgment* he deliberately refused the catch to prevent the runner from scoring after the catch.

(g.) No error is charged on a wild pitch or passed ball. These are commonly called "battery errors" (not fielding errors) and are recorded, respectively, only under "wild pitch" or "passed ball."

Note: No error is charged when the batter is given a base on balls, is hit by a pitched ball, or when he reaches first base as a result of a wild pitch or passed ball.

Note: Do not charge an error when a runner or runners advance as the result of a wild pitch, passed ball or balk.

1. When the *fourth called ball* is a wild pitch or passed ball, and as a result (a) the batter-runner advances to a base beyond first base, or (b) any runner forced to advance because of the base on balls advances more than one base, or (c) any runner, not forced to advance, advances one or more bases, score the base on balls and charge the extra bases advanced to the wild pitch or passed ball. There is no error charged.
2. When the catcher recovers the ball after a wild pitch or passed ball *on the third strike,* and throws out the batter-runner at first base or tags him out, but another runner or runners advance, score the strikeout, putout and assists, if any, and credit the advance of the other runner or runners as having been made on the play. There is no wild pitch or passed ball.

Fielding Averages

To compute the fielding average of a player, divide the total putouts and assists made by the player by the total of putouts, assists and errors made by him.

Example: During a series, a player makes 13 putouts, 18 assists and is charged with 2 errors. Divide the total putouts (13) and assists (18) by the total of putouts (13) and assists (18) and errors (2). Thus, 31 divided by 33 gives him a fielding average of .939.

Wild Pitches and Passed Balls

A pitcher is charged with a wild pitch when a legally delivered ball is so high, or so wide, or so low that the catcher does not stop and control the ball by *ordinary effort,* thereby permitting a runner or runners to advance.

Note: It is a wild pitch, and not a passed ball, if a legally delivered ball *touches the ground before reaching home plate* and is not handled by the catcher, permitting a runner or runners to advance.

A catcher is charged with a passed ball when he fails to stop or control a pitched ball, when he should have been able to do so by ordinary effort, and which enables a runner or runners other than the batter to advance.

Note: It is an error, not a passed ball, if a batter reaches first base following a third strike dropped or missed by the catcher.

Base on Balls

Credit the batter and charge the pitcher with a base on balls whenever a batter is awarded first base because of four balls having been pitched outside the strike zone. The batter is not charged with an official time at bat.

Note: If the fourth ball hits the batter, it should be scored as a hit batter instead of a base on balls.

Strikeouts

A strikeout is charged to the batter and credited to the pitcher whenever (a) a batter is put out by a third strike caught by the catcher, (b) a batter is put out by a third strike not caught when there is a runner on first base before two are out, (c) a batter becomes a runner because a third strike is not caught, or (d) a batter bunts foul on the third strike.

Note: If a bunt on third strike results in a foul fly caught by any infielder, do not score a strikeout. Credit the fielder who catches the foul fly with a putout.

If a batter leaves the game with two strikes against him, and the substitute batter completes the strikeout, charge the strikeout and the time at bat to the first batter. However, if the substitute batter completes the turn at bat in any other manner, score the action as having been that of the substitute batter.

Pitching

Games

A pitcher is credited with appearing in a game whenever he is announced as the starting pitcher or comes in as a relief pitcher.

Note: The starting pitcher is required to pitch to one batter (unless this requirement is waived by the umpire because of injury or illness) and a relief pitcher is required to pitch to one batter (or until the offensive team is put out). Thus, any time a pitcher is announced as starting pitcher or comes into the game as a relief pitcher, he is credited with playing in that game.

Innings Pitched

Credit a pitcher with a full inning of play whenever he is on the mound when all three outs are made in the inning. If a player pitches only part of an inning, credit him with one-third of an inning for each putout that is made while he is in the game.

Note: In this determination, it does not matter whether the player put out is a batter or a runner who may have reached base while a different pitcher was on the mound. The pitcher is credited with one-third of an inning for each putout made while *he* is on the mound.

Hits

A pitcher is charged with a hit for each safe hit made while he is in the game.

Note: If a relief pitcher enters the game when the batter already has a ball and strike count from the previous pitcher and the batter hits safely, charge the hit to the relief pitcher.

Runs

Charge a run to a pitcher for each run scored by an opposing player who becomes a runner while he was pitching. When pitchers are changed during an inning, the relief pitcher should not be charged with any run scored by a runner who was on base at the time he entered the game, nor for runs scored by any runner who reaches base on a fielder's choice which puts out a runner left on base by the preceding pitcher.

Example: Smith of Team A is pitching. He gives up a single to Brown of Team B and Smith is replaced by relief pitcher Green. While Green is pitching, Black of Team B grounds to shortstop, resulting in forceout of Brown at second base. Should Black subsequently score, the run is charged to Smith.

Earned Runs

Earned runs often are used as a measure of the effectiveness of a pitcher, for they reflect the number of runs scored primarily against the efforts of the pitcher, without penalizing him for runs scored by lack of fielding support by his team. Earned runs are relatively easy to determine if each inning is reconstructed to see what runs would have scored without errors or passed balls.

An earned run is charged every time a runner reaches home base by the aid of safe hits, sacrifice bunts, a sacrifice fly, stolen bases, putouts, fielder's choices, bases on balls, hit batters, *balks or wild pitches* (including a wild pitch on third strike which permits a batter to reach first) *before fielding chances have been offered to put out* the defensive team.

Note: For the purpose of this rule, defensive interference penalty is considered to be a fielding chance.

Note: In computing earned runs, a wild pitch or a balk is solely the pitcher's fault and contributes to an earned run just as a base on balls. No run shall be charged to a pitcher as earned:

1. When scored by a runner who reaches first base (a) on a hit or otherwise after his time at bat is prolonged by a muffed foul fly; or (b) because of interference or obstruction; or (c) because of any fielding error.
2. When scored by a runner whose life is prolonged by an error, if such runner would have been put out by errorless play.
3. When the runner's advance is aided by an error, a passed ball, defensive interference or obstruction, if in the *scorer's judgment* the run would not have been scored without the aid of such misplay.

An error by a pitcher is treated exactly the same as an error by any other fielder in computing earned runs.

Whenever there is a fielding error, give the pitcher the benefit of the doubt in determining to which bases any runners would have advanced had there been errorless play.

When more than one pitcher is used during an inning, relief pitchers shall not be charged with any earned run scored by a runner who was on base at the time he entered the game, nor for earned runs scored by any runner who reaches base on a fielder's choice which puts out a runner left on base by a preceding pitcher.

Note: A pitcher should be charged with the *number* of runners he put on base, rather than the runners as *individuals*. When a pitcher is relieved, he should be charged with all runs subsequently scored up to and including the *number* of runners he left on base when he left the game, unless such runners are put out without action by the batter (i.e. caught stealing, picked off base or called out for interference when a batter-runner does not reach first base on the play).

However, when more than one pitcher is used in an inning, the relief pitcher is not given the benefit of previous chances for putouts not accepted (errors) in determining the earned runs scored off his efforts.

Example: With two out, Pitcher Brown walks Smith. Jones reaches base on an error. Brown is relieved by Green, and the next batter, Wilson, hits a home run. Charge two *unearned* runs (Smith, Jones) to Brown, one *earned* run (Wilson) to Green.

Example: With none out, Brown walks Smith and Jones reaches base on an error. Green relieves Brown and Wilson hits a home run, scoring three runs. Green then strikes out Hall and Dunn. Morgan reaches base on an error, then Allen hits a home run, scoring two runs. Charge

Brown with two runs (Jones, Smith), one *earned* (Smith). Charge Green with three runs (Wilson, Morgan, Allen), with one earned (Wilson).

When more than one pitcher is used in an inning, a relief pitcher is not charged with the first batter to whom he pitches if the batter reaches first base on four called balls if the batter had a decided advantage when pitchers were changed.

1. If, when pitchers are changed, the count is 2 balls and 0 or 1 strike, or 3 balls, and 0, 1, or 2 strikes, and the batter walks, charge the batter and the base on balls to the preceding pitcher.

Note: Any other action by the batter (i.e. base hit, error, fielder's choice, force out, hit by pitcher) shall be charged to the relief pitcher.

2. If, when pitchers are changed, the count is 0 balls and 1 or 2 strikes, 1 ball and 0, 1 or 2 strikes, or 2 balls and 2 strikes, charge that batter and his actions to the relief pitcher.

Earned Run Average

To compute a pitcher's earned run average (ERA), multiply the total earned runs charged against him by 9, and divide the result by the total number of innings he pitched.

Example: A player pitches a total of 162 1/3 innings, giving up 51 runs, of which 48 runs are earned. Multiply the total *earned* runs (48) by 9. The result (432) is divided by the total innings pitched (162 1/3) to give him an average of 2.66 earned runs per game (nine innings).

Winning and Losing Pitcher

The starting pitcher is credited with a game won only if he pitches at least *five complete innings* (of a game that goes six innings or more) and his team not only is in the lead when he is replaced, but remains in the lead the remainder of the game.

In a five-inning game, the starting pitcher must go four complete innings (and his team stays in the lead) to receive credit for the win.

Note: There is one exception to the "starting pitcher" rule. In some non-championship games (such as all-star games) several pitchers will divide the pitching chores by throwing two or three innings each. In such cases, it is customary to credit the victory to the pitcher of record, whether starter or reliever, when the winning treams takes the lead it maintains until the end of the game. However, in regular season games, even if the coach or manager decides in advance to split up the pitching assignments among three of four pitchers, the five-inning minimum still applies.

When the starting pitcher has not remained in the game the required number of innings and more than one relief pitcher is used, the winning pitcher shall be determined by the following criteria:

1. If the winning team assumes the lead while the starting pitcher is in the game (or does so in the inning that he is removed for a pinch-hitter or runner), and that lead is maintained to the end of the game, the winning pitcher is the relief pitcher who in the *scorer's judgment* was the most effective.
2. When the score is tied, the game becomes a new contest insofar as the winning and losing pitcher is concerned.
3. Once the opposing team assumes the lead, all pitchers who have pitched up to that point are excluded from being credited with the victory except that if the pitcher against whose pitching the opposing team gained the lead, continues to pitch until his team regains the lead (or does so in the inning he is removed for a pinch-hitter or runner), which it holds until the end of the game, he is the winning pitcher.
4. In most cases, the winning relief pitcher is the one who is the pitcher of record when his team assumes the lead (or does so in the inning he is removed for a pinch-hitter or runner) and maintains it to the end of the game.

Exception: Do not credit a victory to a relief pitcher who in the scorer's judgment pitches briefly or *ineffectively* if a succeeding relief pitcher pitches *effectively* in helping his team to maintain the lead. In such a situation, credit the succeeding relief pitcher with the victory.

5. The starting pitcher is charged with a loss, regardless of how many innings he has pitched, if he is replaced when his team is behind or falls behind because of runs charged to him after he is replaced, and his team stays behind for the remainder of the game.

Won-Lost Percentage

To determine the won-lost record of a pitcher, divide the total number of games won by the total of games won and lost.

Example: Smith appears in 18 games, receives credit for the victory in 11, is charged with the loss in 5 and is not involved in the won-lost decision in the other 2 games. Divide the games won (11) by the total of games won (11) and lost (5); the won-lost percentage, then, is 11 divided by 16, or .688.

Saves for Relief Pitchers

In modern times, the increasing use of relief pitchers has led to a statistic that helps reflect the effective efforts of a pitcher who goes into a game with his team already in the lead and thus has no chance to be credited with a victory.

This statistic is called "saves" and records the number of times a relief pitcher does pitch effectively in holding a lead.

1. A relief pitcher is credited with a "save" when he enters the game with his team in the lead and holds the lead the remainder of the game but does not receive credit for the victory.

Shutouts

A statistical entry should be made in the record of each pitcher who pitches a shutout.

No pitcher is credited with a shutout unless he pitches the complete game, or unless he enters the game with none out in the first inning before the opposing team has scored, puts out the side without a run scoring and pitches all the rest of the game.

When two or more pitchers combine to pitch a shutout, a notation may be made in the pitching records, but no individual pitcher is credited with the shutout.

Baseball Records

Baseball statistics and records have become so detailed that there is almost no limit to the number of categories in which records may be kept. The *Sporting News* record book for the World Series, alone, lists more than 400 pages of records.

For practical purposes, however, basic records for team and individuals should include the statistical entries previously covered in this chapter. Cumulative records should be maintained for each individual and team and prepared during the season as often as desired for use by the manager or coach or for publicity purposes.

If there are no other requirements for cumulative records, they should be prepared at the end of each season to show the season's performance of each player and to provide a basis for all-time records for each team.

Batting

Cumulative statistics should include these categories for each player and team (the total for all individual players on a team should equal the team totals):

Games (G), official times at bat (AB), runs scored (R), safe hits (H), two-base hits (2B), three-base hits (3B), home runs (HR), total bases (TB), number of runs batted in (RBI), stolen bases (SB), sacrifice bunts (SH), sacrifice flies (SF), number of bases on balls received (BB), number of times struck out (SO) and batting average (Avg.). To review, the batting average is computed by dividing the total number of safe hits by the total number of official times at bat.

The season's record of a player might look like this:

Player, Team	G	AB	R	H	2B	3B	HR	TB	RBI	SB	SH	SF	BB	SO	Avg.
Jim Smith, Panthers	20	82	14	26	4	1	5	47	18	3	1	3	9	14	.317

Optional entries might be the number of times hit by pitcher (HBP), number of times caught stealing (CS) and slugging percentage (Slg. Pct.). In the example above, Smith's slugging percentage would be .573, dividing total bases (47) by times at bat (82).

Championship Requirements

To be eligible for a league batting championship, a player must be credited with as many or more *total appearances* at the plate in league games as the number of games *scheduled* for each club in his league that season, *multiplied by 3.1*.

Example: If a league schedules 20 games for each team, a player must make a total of 62 (20 times 3.1) appearances at the plate to be eligible for the batting championship. If a league schedules 45 games for each team, a player must make a total of 140 (45 times 3.1) appearances at the plate to be eligible.

Note: Total appearances include all *official* times at bat plus bases on balls, times hit by pitcher, sacrifices and times awarded first base because of interference or obstruction.

If there is any player with fewer than the required number of total plate appearances whose average would be highest even if he were charged with the required number of plate appearances or official times at bat, then that player is the league batting champion.

Example: In a league with a schedule of 20 games, we have seen that 62 total appearances is the minimum to qualify for the batting championship. Of those with 62 or more appearances, Player A has 88 total plate appearances with a batting average of .367 based on 29 hits in 79 "official" times at bat. Player B has only 58 total appearances with a batting average of .408, based on 20 hits in 49 "official" times at bat. Even if Player B were charged with 62 total appearances (four more than his actual 58), and thus 53 "official" times at bat (four more than his actual 49), his batting average of .377 still would be the highest, so Player B would be awarded the batting championship (at .408).

Fielding

Cumulative statistics should include these categories for each player and team (the total for all individual players on a team should equal the team totals):

Games (G), putouts made (PO), assists made (A), errors committed (E), double plays in which the player participated (DP), and fielding percentage (Pct.). To review, fielding percentage is computed by dividing the total number of putouts and assists by total number of putouts, assists and errors.

The season's record of a player might look like this:

Player, Team	G	PO	A	E	DP	Pct.
Jim Smith, Panthers,	22	50	54	4	10	.963

For catchers add a column for passed balls (PB). An optional entry for catchers might be the number of times he threw out men attempting to steal. This category is "caught stealing" (CS).

Championship Requirements

To be eligible for the fielding championship, a player must have the highest fielding record at his position and have participated at that position in the minimum number of games or innings prescribed in the following:

1. If an infielder or outfielder, he must have participated at his position in at least *two-thirds* of the number of games scheduled for each club in his league that season.
2. If a catcher, he must have participated as a catcher in at least *one-half* the number of games scheduled for each club in his league that season.
3. If a pitcher, he must have pitched at least *as many innings* as the number of games scheduled for each club in his league that season.

Note: However, if another pitcher has a fielding average as high or higher, and has handled more total chances in a lesser number of innings, he shall be the fielding champion.

Pitching

Cumulative statistics should include these categories for each player and team (the total for all individual players on a team should equal the team totals):

Games (G), games started (GS), complete games (CG), games won (W), games lost (L), games saved (Sv), won-lost percentage (Pct.), shutouts (SHO), number of innings pitched (IP), hits allowed (H), runs allowed (R), earned runs allowed (ER), bases on balls issued (BB), number of batters struck out (SO), and earned run average (ERA).

To review, won-lost percentage is computed by dividing the total number of games won by the total of games won and lost, and the earned run average is computed by multiplying the total number of earned runs charged against him by 9, then dividing the result by the total number of innings he pitched.

The seasons' record of a pitcher might look like this:

Player, Team	G	GS	CG	W	L	Sv	Pct.	Sho	IP	H	R	ER	BB	SO	ERA
Bob Clark, Panthers	14	11	8	7	4	2	.636	2	98	71	41	35	39	65	3.22

Optional entries could be total number of home runs given up by the pitcher, total number of official at-bats against the pitcher, balks committed, sacrifice bunts and sacrifice flies by opposing batters, and hit batsmen and wild pitches charged to him.

In general, pitchers are ranked by the highest won-lost percentage or the lowest earned run average. In the major leagues, the champion is the pitcher (who has pitched the required number of innings) with the lowest ERA.

Championship Requirements

To be eligible for a league championship, a pitcher must pitch at least as many innings as the number of games scheduled for each team in his league that season.

Box Scores

In reporting the results of games to the news media, a form should be used to summarize the game in an easily-read style. The format will depend upon the style desired by the news media. For most newspapers, a box score (Form 2-A) or a line score (Form 2-B) is desirable. Form A duplicator masters are available from Ned West, 2660 Acorn Ave., N.E., Atlanta, Ga. 30305.

A boxscore reflects the pertinent statistics of a game and a knowledgeable statistician can almost reconstruct the entire game by a study of the box score.

The format of the box score will depend upon the style used by

Form 2-A

Stats Form 105. Order Masters from Ned West, 2660 Acorn Ave., N.E., Atlanta, Ga. 30305

OFFICIAL BASEBALL BOX

PANTHERS	AB	R	H	RBI
MORGAN, 3b	5	0	0	0
HENRY, 1f	5	1	2	0
CALLAHAN, rf	5	1	2	1
CARTER, 2b	4	1	1	0
MILLER, ss	2	0	1	1
HILLER, 1b	4	0	3	2
PERRY, c	4	0	1	0
HALL, cf	2	0	0	0
THOMAS, cf	1	0	0	0
TALBOT, p	3	1	1	0
WILLIAMS, p	0	0	0	0
GARVEY, p	0	0	0	0
THOMPSON, -b	1	0	1	0
DANA, p	0	0	0	0
TOTALS	36	4	12	4

SPARTANS	AB	R	H	RBI
PATTERSON, ss	4	1	0	0
ROLAND, 2b	2	2	1	0
OLIVER, cf	5	1	1	3
HARRIS, 1b	3	0	1	1
PAINTER, 1f	4	1	2	1
SCHULTZ, 3b	3	1	0	0
R. SMITH, rf	3	0	2	2
J. SMITH, c	4	0	0	0
NELSON, p	1	0	0	0
BUTLER, p	0	0	0	0
AKIN, p	1	0	1	0
LLOYD, -a	1	1	1	0
HUNTER, p	1	0	0	0
TOTALS	32	7	9	7

a-tripled for AKIN in 7th. b-singled for Garvey in 8th.

SCORE BY INNINGS	1	2	3	4	5	6	7	8	9	10	11	12	13	14	TOTALS
PANTHERS	0	1	2	1	0	0	0	0	0						4
SPARTANS	1	0	0	1	0	1	4	0	X						7

E – CARTER, PATTERSON, HARRIS

DP – CARTER TO MILLER TO HILLER; SCHULTZ TO POLAND TO HARRIS

PO–A – PANTHERS 24-12; SPARTANS 27-13

LOB – PANTHERS 9; SPARTANS 8

2B – CARTER, PERRY, PAINTER, R. SMITH, OLIVER

3B – PAINTER, LLOYD HR –

SB – HILLER, PATTERSON

S – MILLER SF – MILLER, R. SMITH

	IP	H	R	ER	BB	SO
TALBOT	6 1/3	5	4	3	4	5
WILLIAMS (L, 10-2)	0	1	3	3	1	0
GARVEY	2/3	2	0	0	0	0
DANA	1	1	0	0	0	1
NELSON	3	6	3	3	2	3
BUTLER	1	3	1	1	0	0
AKIN (W, 3-4)	3	2	0	0	0	3
HUNTER	2	1	0	0	0	0

HBP – PATTERSON by WILLIAMS

WP – NELSON

BK – PB –

SAVE – HUNTER T – 2:40 A – 9,255

the news media. Where space is available, a paper may use a box score such as Form 2-A, which details the basic batting and pitching performances.

The designated hitter rule has no bearing on the basic format of the box score, except that some papers, to save space, may omit the names of pitchers in the batting section (Form 2-A) and include them only in the pitchers' section of the box. In the box score, the designated hitter is referred to as "dh."

For more important games, the papers may use a more complete box score, with additional columns for fielding statistics. When the game commands less attention, newspapers often will use a variation of the linescore shown in Form 2-B.

Panthers	012	100	000 – 4
Spartans	100	101	40x – 7

Form 2-B

Talbot, Williams (7), Garvey (7), Dana (8), and Perry. Nelson, Butler (4), Akin (5), Hunter (8), and J. Smith. W— Akin (3-4). L—Williams (10-2).

Proving a Box Score

A box score always should be checked for accuracy. It is absolutely essential that the box score be in balance or proved.

To prove a box score, add the total of each team's official times at bat, bases on balls received, hit batters, sacrifice bunts, sacrifice flies and batters awarded first base because of interference or obstruction. This total *must* equal the total of the team's runs, players left on base and the opposing team's putouts.

In the boxscore Form 2-A, the Panthers have 36 official times at bat, were issued 2 bases on balls and they had 1 sacrifice bunt and 1 sacrifice fly for a total of 40. This equals the total of the Panthers' runs (4), left on base (9) and the Spartans' putouts (27).

The Spartans had 32 times at bat, 5 bases on balls, 1 sacrifice fly and 1 hit batter for a total of 39. This matches the total of Spartan runs (7), left on base (8) and Panther putouts (24).

How to Keep Score

The rules of scoring have shown in detail how to interpret any

CENTRAL HIGH vs. EAST TECH

PLAYERS	Pos.	1	2	3	4	5	6
SMITH	8	6-3 ①		5-3 ①	L-7 ③		
FORTONE	5	3		1-6 ②		SH	
LOGUE	3	SB 7		F-7 ③		SB	
ROLIN	7	1B			4	1-3 ① SAC	
HARRIS	6	K ②			F-8 ①	K ②	
KING	9	F-8 ③			2	5-3 ③	
LANE / Sub. MOORE	4 / 4		F-9 ①		2 1B		K ①
BRYAN	2		4-6 ② BB		2 HR		4-3 ②
BARRETT / Sub. KEEBLE	1 / 2		DP 6-3 ③		K ②		
CONRAD	1						K ③
SUMMARY		2/3	0/0	0/1	4/4	0/1	0/0

WINNING PITCHER CONRAD LOSING PITCHER HUNTER INNINGS PITCH

AT BAT OFF BARRETT 14 OFF CONRAD 24 HITS OFF BA

RUNS OFF BARRETT 3 OFF CONRAD 1 BASE ON BALLS

STRUCK OUT BY BARRETT 2 BY CONRAD 6 HIT BY PITCHEI

DOUBLE PLAY HARRIS TO LANE TO LOGUE

PASSED BALLS NONE LEFT ON BASE CENTRAL 6 EAST

Scoremaster 739 N. FAIRFAX AVE., HOLLYWOOD, CALIF. 90046

Form 2-C

given play, but it is necessary to keep an accurate, permanent record of each game so that all statistics are available for (a) rapid summarization in box score form at the end of the game, and (b) for reference to permanent records.

There are many different kinds of scorebooks used for this purpose, with the most complete probably C.S. Peterson's *Scoremaster,* which is published by Scoremaster, Inc., Box 46038, Hollywood, Ca. 90046.

This book compactly includes space for every pitch made in a game (and what happened to it). If properly used, the book enables a scorer to completely re-create the game, pitch by pitch, at any time in the future. See Form 2-C for sample of partial *Scoremaster* page.

In this scorebook, there is a box (Form 2-D) in each inning for each player. Each of these boxes includes smaller boxes for recording each ball and strike, a quick notation for how a batter reaches base, and the diamond in the center provides space to mark the progress of a batter-runner around the bases.

The numbers around the diamond are designations of fielding positions—pitcher (1), catcher (2), first base (3), second base (4), third base (5), shortstop (6), left field (7), center field (8), and right field (9).

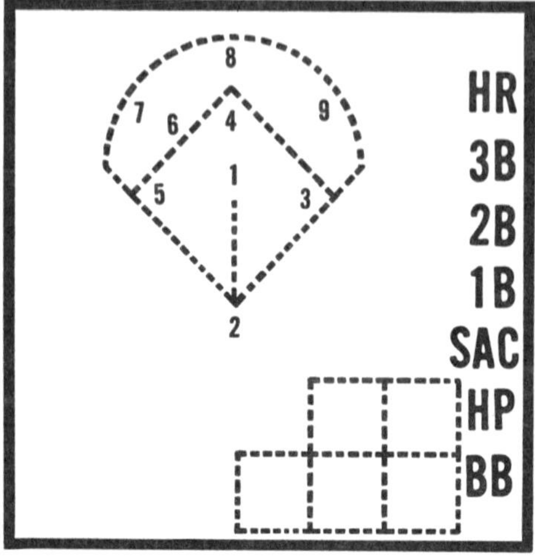

Form 2-D

When a batter or runner is put out, the number or numbers which designate the positions of the defensive players handling the ball are inserted in the box opposite the batter's name.

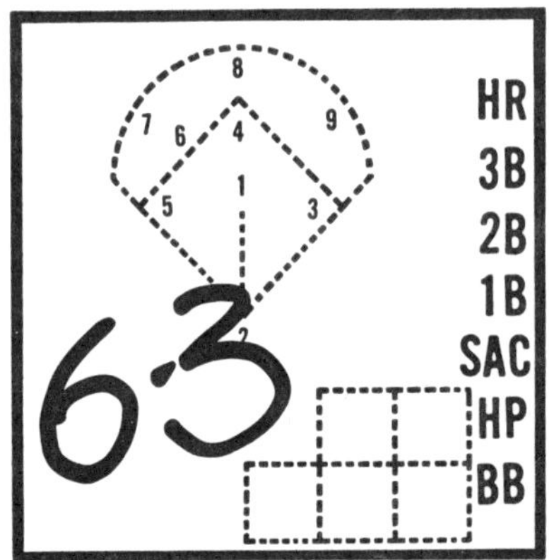

Form 2-E-1

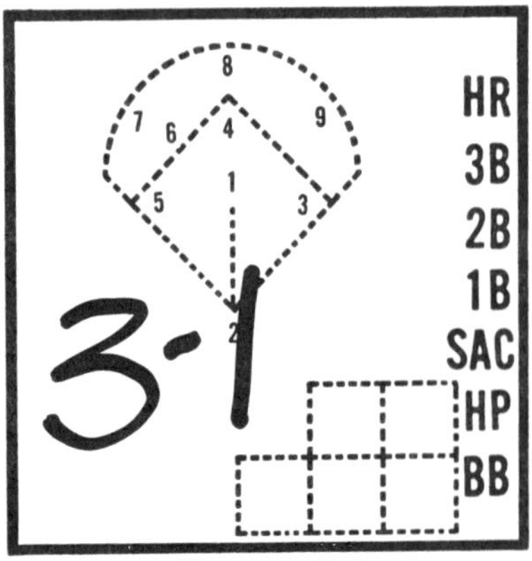

Form 2-E-2

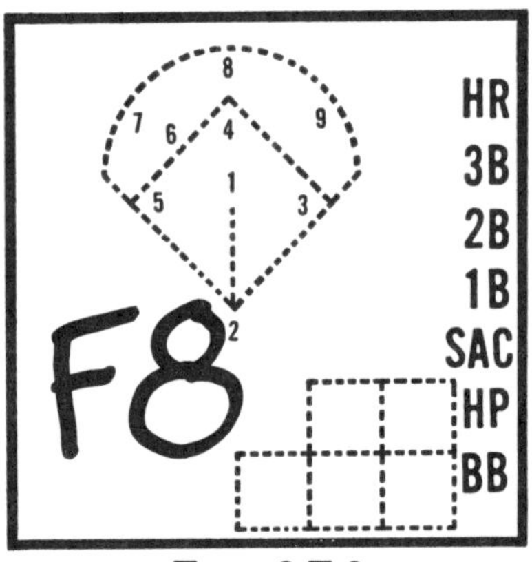

Form 2-E-3

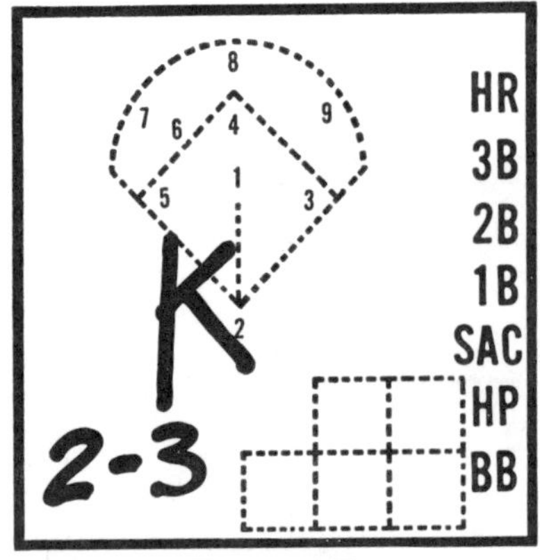

Form 2-E-4

Form 2-E-5

For instance, if a batter grounds out to the shortstop, the ball goes from the shortstop (6) to first base (3), and a simple entry, 6-3, is made in the box. (Form 2-E-1)

If the batter hits a grounder to the first baseman (3), who throws to the pitcher (1), covering first base, the entry is 3-1. (Form 2-E-2)

If a player flies out to center field (8), a notation would be made F-8. Some scorers show the difference between a fly ball (F-8) and a line drive (L-8). (Form 2-E-3)

If a player strikes out, the standard notation is a "K." Some scorers enter "Kc" when the third strike is called. The catcher is credited with the putout. If the catcher (2) drops a third strike, then throws out the batter at first (3), a "K" is entered, with a 2-3 entry indicating the throw. (Form 2-E-4)

Most scorers add a circled number to show the number of outs

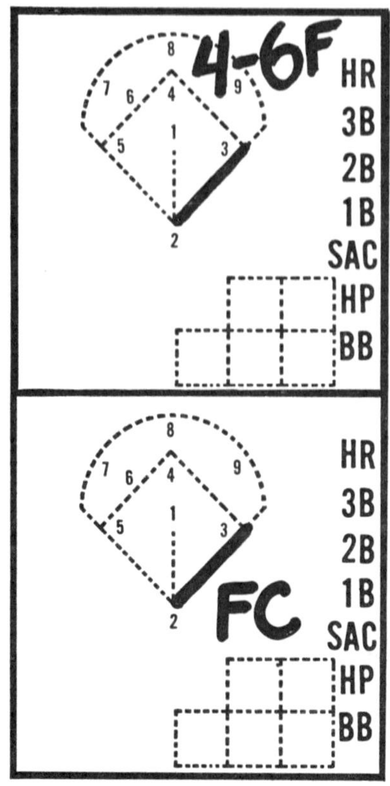

Form 2-E-6

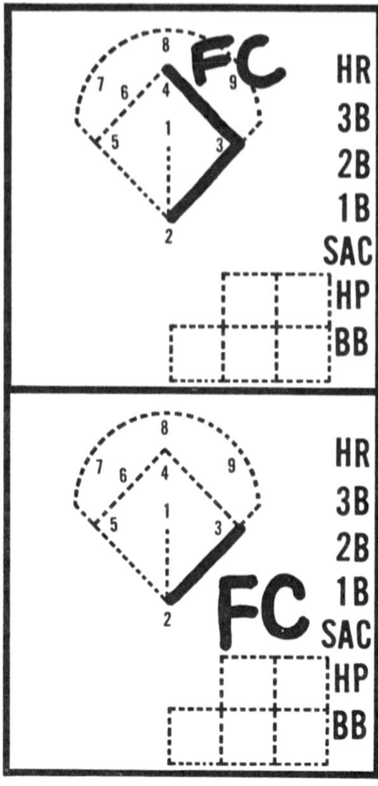

Form 2-E-7

in an inning. In Form 2-E-5, the batter grounded out to third base (5-3) and it was the second out of the inning.

The examples in Form 2-E-6 show how to score a fielder's choice. Player A, who was on first base, is forced at second when Player B grounds to the second baseman, who throws to the shortstop for the force play. In Player A's box, show 4-6f, and in Player B's box, FC.

On a fielder's choice where no one is put out (and the batter is not credited with a hit), show the letters FC for both the runner and batter in place of the 4-6f of the previous example. (Form 2-E-7)

On double plays (or triple plays), note the appropriate putouts in the box for each player, then connect the boxes with a line or bracket, and note "DP" or "TP" to show what transpired. In this example, Player A singled to left field. Then Player B hit a ground ball to the second baseman, who threw to the shortstop to retire Player A, and the shortstop relayed to first base in time to put out Player B. The double play is scored 4-6-3, but broken down between the two boxes, as noted. (Form 2-E-8)

When a batter or runner is safe on an error, the progress on the bases is so indicated by the use of the letter "E" and the number of the fielder who made the misplay. In the example in Form 2-E-9, the batter grounded to shortstop (6), who fumbled the ball, enabling the batter to reach first. Some scorers indicate the kind of error, by added notations. Instead of just "E6," indicating error by the shortstop, they will show "E6F" for a fumble, "E6Th" for a bad throw or "E6D" when a player drops a throw for an error. In the latter case, the assist can be inserted, "E6D (A4)."

When a player (or players) advances on a wild pitch (WP) or passed ball (PB), this progress should be appropriately recorded, such as for this instance when the player doubled to right-center, moved to third on a passed ball and scored on a wild pitch. (Form 2-E-10)

When a player (or players) steals a base, this should be indicated with the notation "SB." In this example, the batter singled, then stole second base. (Form 2-E-11)

The small boxes at the lower right-hand corner of each individual box provide space to record balls and strikes. This can be done with a simple dot or dash or, if the scorer wants to record the actual sequence, they can be entered in numerical order.

If an entry for foul balls is desired, enter "f" in the appropriate strike box and if the foul (or fouls) came with two strikes on the batter, mark "F" on the left of the two strike boxes for each additional foul ball. To differentiate between a called strike and a swinging strike, the letter "c" can be entered for a called strike in the appropriate box.

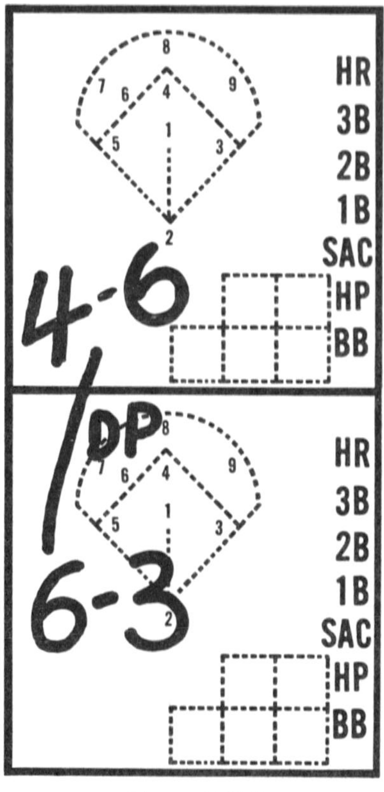

Form 2-E-8

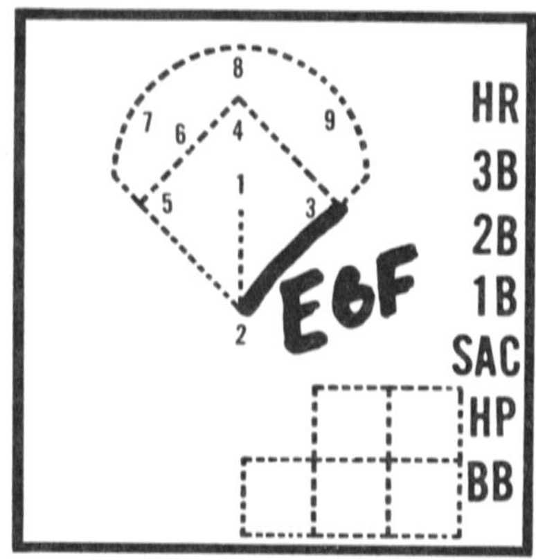

Form 2-E-9

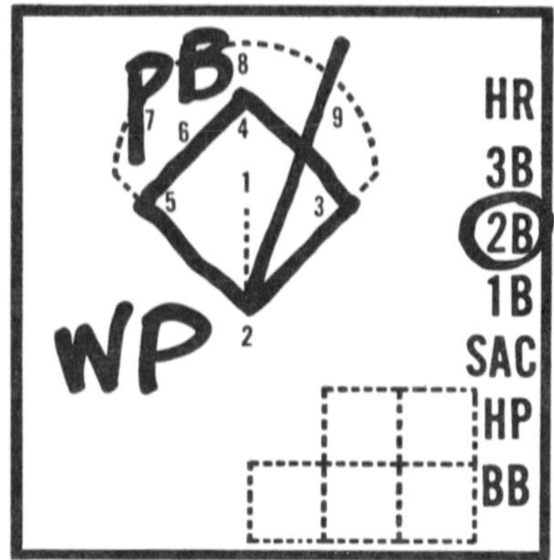

Form 2-E-10

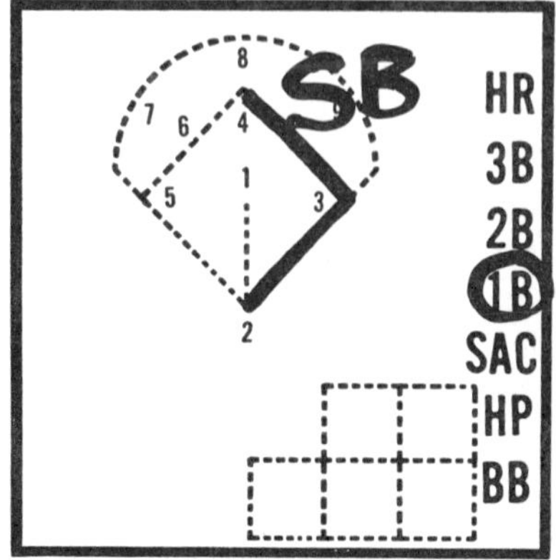

Form 2-E-11

Form 2-E-12

In the example in Form 2-E-12, the batter swung and missed the first pitch, the next two were called balls, the fourth pitch was a called strike, the fifth was a called ball, the next two were fouled off and on the eighth pitch, the batter flied out to the third baseman.

When a batter reaches first base, the manner in which he reached base should be indicated by circling the appropriate abbreviation in the column at the right-hand side of the box. Then, his progress around the bases should be charted until he reaches home or is left on base.

For instance, if a batter reaches first base on four balls, Form 2-E-13 shows the proper entry.

If a player is credited with a sacrifice, indicate this in the box opposite his name and show the same information in the box of the runner or runners advancing on the sacrifice. In the example in Form 2-E-14, Player B bunted to the pitcher (1) and was thrown out at first base (3) as Player A (who had walked) advanced to second base.

When an attempted sacrifice is turned into a force-out, score it in the same manner as any other fielder's choice. In the example in Form 2-E-15, Player A went to first on a walk, then was forced at second (1-6) when Player B bunted to the pitcher.

If a player hits safely, indicate how many bases he made on the hit by marking the appropriate entry in the right-hand column of the box. Show the direction the ball was hit by a line from a home plate. In the example in Form 2-E-16, the batter made a two-base hit on a drive to left-centerfield.

When a batter attempts a sacrifice bunt and beats it out for a hit, it is scored as any other one-base hit. Some scorers indicate that the hit was made on a bunt. (Form 2-E-17)

Show the complete progress of a player around the bases. For purposes of this example, the box is divided into four boxes to show how his progress is recorded for each base advanced (Forms 2-E-18, 2-E-19, 2-E-20, 2-E-21). The player singled to right, stole second, went to third on a wild pitch and scored on a sacrifice fly by the next batter.

Runs batted in are noted by adding (below home plate) for each runner who scores, the fielding position number of the player who is credited with the run batted in. In the previous example, the batter scored on a sacrifice fly by the second baseman (4). Thus, at home plate in the box of the scoring runner, a "4" is inserted to show that the second baseman batted in the run. (Form 2-E-22)

If, while Player A was on third base, the second baseman (Player B) had hit a home run (instead of a sacrifice fly), "4" would have been inserted at home plate in the box of *both* players to show both runs batted in for Player B. (Form 2-E-23)

Form 2-E-13

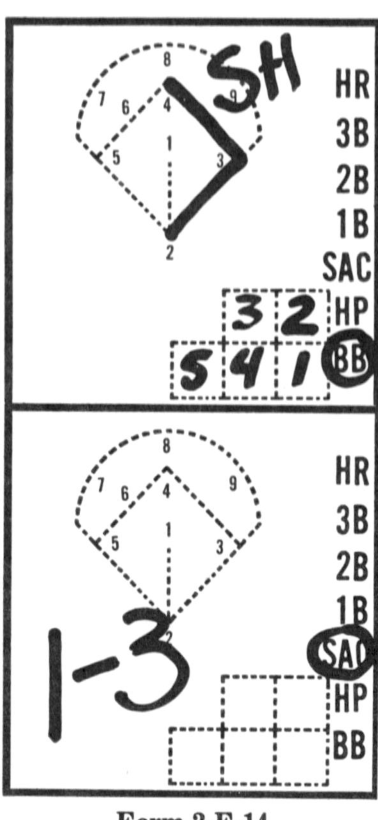

Form 2-E-14

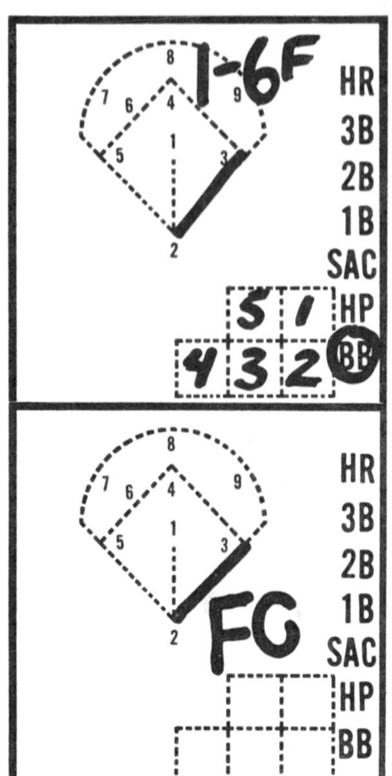

Form 2-E-15

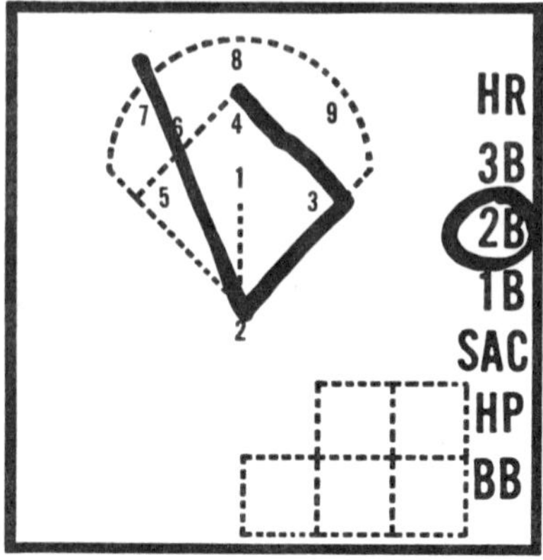

Form 2-E-16

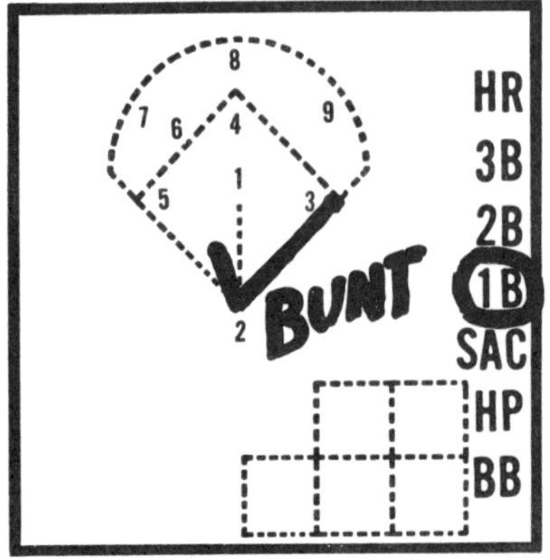

Form 2-E-17

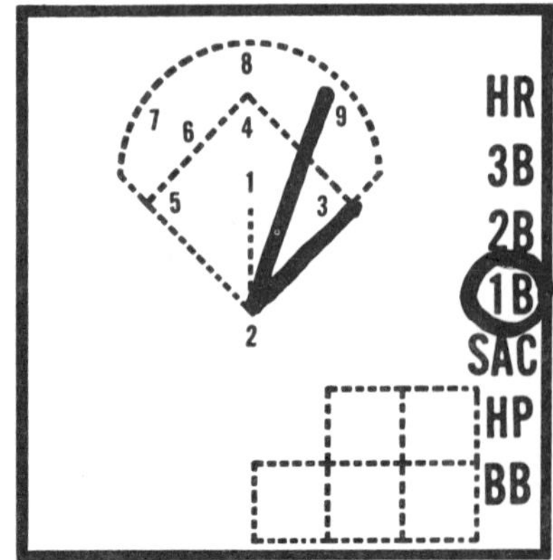

Form 2-E-18

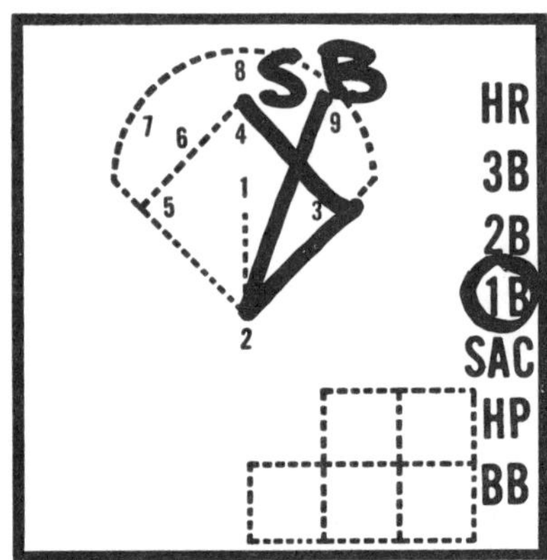

Form 2-E-19

Form 2-E-20

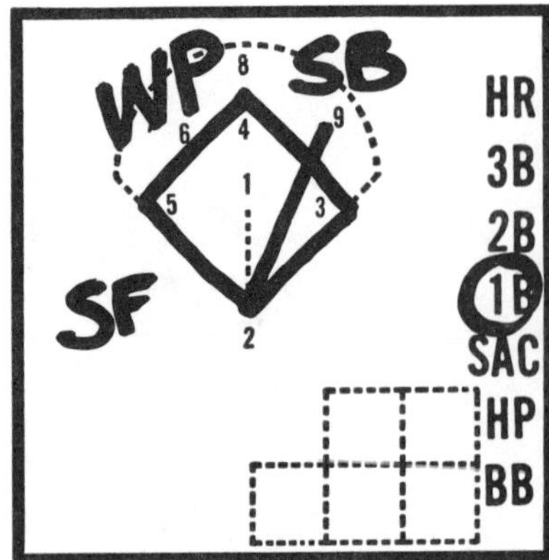

Form 2-E-21

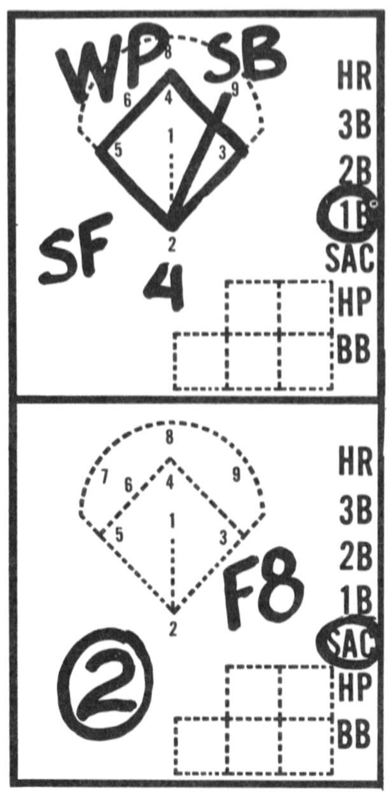

Form 2-E-22

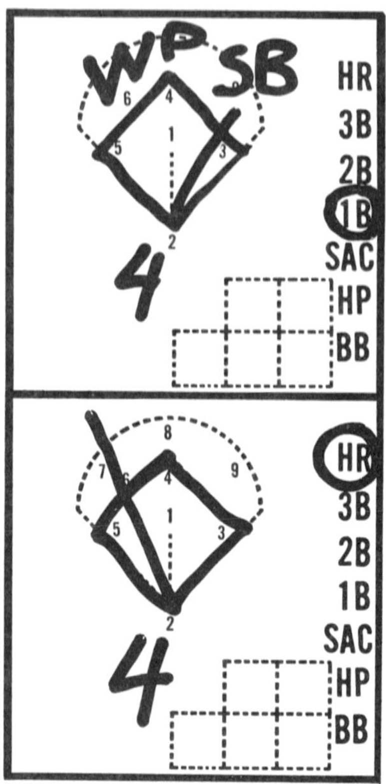

Form 2-E-23

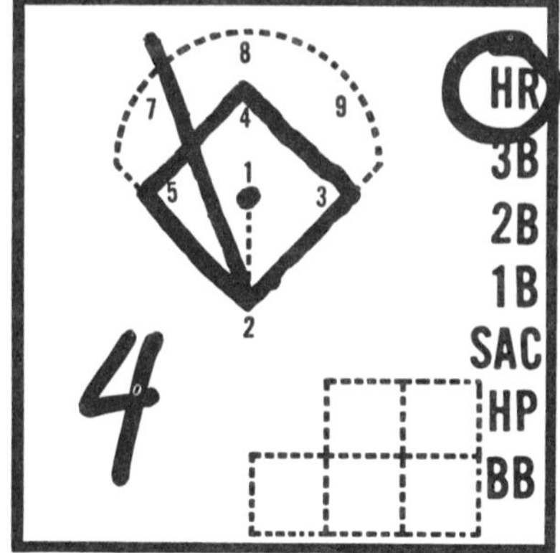

Form 2-E-24

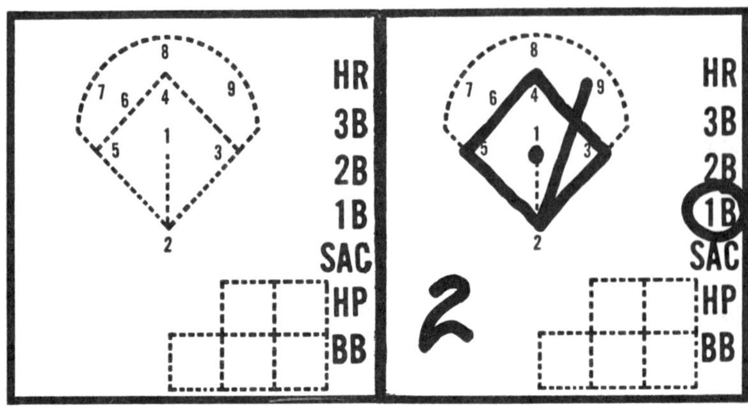

Form 2-E-25

As a device for a quick visual check, insert a dot or some other readily apparent symbol in the middle of the box of each player scoring a run. Thus, for Player B in the previous example, his box should appear like the one in Form 2-E-24.

When substitutions are made, be certain that an entry is made to show the proper inning the substitution was made. One method is to draw a heavy black line on the right-hand margin of his batting box following the last inning in which his team was at bat while he was in the game, as shown in Form 2-E-25. (Note other examples for players Lane, Barrett and Keeble in Form 2-C.)

Proving a Scorebook

The scorebook should be checked for accuracy exactly in the same manner as proving the box score, in the procedure shown in that earlier section.

When transcribing statistics from a scorebook to a box score, do not rely on the balance of the scorebook to prove the box score. To insure accuracy (an error could be made in transferring the statistics) prove *both* the scorebook and the box score.

Chapter 3

Basketball

It should be stressed again that, when possible, a minimum of two statisticians be assigned to each game. Perhaps this is most important in basketball because the Official Scorer is technically a member of the officiating team.

A competent and experienced statistician can handle the functions of both the scorer and the statistician, but the pace of the game is so fast that complete accuracy becomes questionable under these conditions. For this reason, it is preferable that the Official Scorer concentrate only on the scorebook and his other duties, and be freed from the responsibilities of the statistician.

This is a precaution taken to avoid mistakes under the pressure of having one man do too many things. An error in statistics can be remedied by a later cross-check, but an error either in procedure or in scorebook entries by the Official Scorer can affect the conduct or the outcome of the game.

In recognition of the importance of the Official Scorer, and to insure accuracy during the fast action of basketball, major colleges usually assign one man as Official Scorer, two to keep statistics on shooting, two for rebounding, and two for play-by-play charts.

When two men are paired in shooting statistics, for example, one will keep a shot chart for both teams while the second man identifies the player or players taking shots and making assists. When desired, they can switch roles at halftime.

Whether there is one statistician or seven, the duties of the Official Scorer remain the same. He shall:

1. Record the field goals made.
2. Record the free throws made and missed.
3. Keep a running summary of the points scored.

4. Record the personal and technical fouls called on each player and on the team.
5. Record the time-outs charged to each team.
6. Keep a record of the names and numbers of players who are to start the game and all substitutes who enter the game.
7. Summarize the game totals.

In addition to these official recordings, he is also required to:

1. Notify a team and its coach through an official whenever that team takes a fifth charged time out.
2. Signal the nearer official each time a team is granted a charged time out in excess of the legal number and in each half when a player commits a common foul beginning with his team's fifth personal foul (for a game played in quarters), or seventh personal foul (for a game played in halves).
3. Notify the nearer official when there is an infraction of the rules pertaining to submission of the roster, substitutions, or number of players.

Statistics

As in other sports, basketball statistics are recorded for three purposes: (a) for preparing reports for the news media, (b) for permanent records, and (c) for coaching aids. For the latter, each coach will instruct the statistician as to which types of statistical forms or summaries he desires. The interpretations and instructions in this chapter should enable the statistician to prepare any of the report forms commonly used as coaching aids.

However, these basic statistics should be maintained in all categories for news media and for purposes of keeping records:

1. Field Goals Attempted (FGA)
2. Field Goals Made (FG)
3. Field Goal Percentage (Pct.)
4. Free Throws Attempted (FTA)
5. Free Throws Made (FT)
6. Free Throw Percentage (Pct.)
7. Total Points (PTS)
8. Rebounds (Reb.)
9. Assists (A)
10. Turnovers (usually broken down into types, i.e. bad passes, traveling, 3-second violations, etc.)
11. Minutes Played (MP)

Field Goals

Charge a player with a Field Goal Attempt (FGA) whenever he shoots, throws, or taps the ball at the basket in an attempt to score. Credit him with a Field Goal (FG) and two points if the referee signifies a score.

Exception: Do not charge a player with a FGA when he is fouled in the act of shooting and the goal is *not* made. If the goal is made, of course he should be charged with both a FGA and a FG.

It is the scorer's judgment whether a player is "attempting to score," and thus is charged with a FGA.

When a FGA is missed and on the subsequent rebound(s), another player or players of the offensive team attempt to tap the ball back into the basket, charge a FGA for each tip-up because the player(s) is attempting to score a goal.

Example: Green of Team A attempts a field goal with a jump shot. The ball misses, but his teammate, Horton, taps the rebound back toward the basket. He misses, but another teammate, Smith, tips the rebounding ball up and in. Charge Green with one FGA. Charge Horton with one FGA (and credit him with a Rebound). Charge Smith with a FGA, credit him with a FG, two points and one Rebound.

Example: Green of Team A attempts one free throw, but misses. His teammate, Horton, taps the rebound at the basket, but misses. Parker of Team B grabs the rebound and passes the ball up court to a teammate. Charge Horton with one FGA (and credit him with one Rebound). Credit Parker with one Rebound. Of course, Green is charged with one FTA.

Example: Green of Team A attempts a field goal with a jump shot, but the ball falls short of the basket. His teammate, Horton, grabs the ball in the air and jumps up to put the ball in the basket. Charge Green with one FGA. Credit Horton with one Rebound, one FG, and charge him with one FGA.

If a player shoots and then fouls a player from the opposing team by charging into him after the ball leaves his hands, he is to be charged with a FGA (and a FG if the basket is made). If the foul is called before the ball leaves the shooter's hands, the ball is dead before the shot and there is no FGA.

If a defensive player inadvertently tips the ball into the wrong basket, charge a FGA to the offensive player credited with the field goal.

When a defensive player is called for goal-tending, charge a FGA to the offensive player credited with the field goal.

When an offensive player attempts to tap in a teammate's wayward shot and is called for offensive goal-tending, charge the teammate with a FGA and credit the defensive team with a "team" Rebound.

If the offensive player is charged with goal-tending while "dunking" the ball, charge the player with a FGA and credit the defensive team with a "team" Rebound.

Field Goal Percentage

To compute a player's or team's Field Goal Percentage, divide the number of Field Goals made by the number of Field Goals Attempted.

Example: Player A is charged with 14 FGA and is credited with successfully making 8 FGs. His Field Goal Percentage is .571 (8 divided by 14).

Leaders in Field Goal Percentage are ranked in order of the highest percentage. A minimum should be determined to qualify for the championship. It depends upon the number of games played by the teams of the ranked players, but normally a player should be required to score field goals at the rate of four to six times the number of games scheduled.

Example: In a league where each team plays 14 games, a player should be required to score at least 56 (4 x 14) Field Goals to qualify for the Field Goal Percentage championship.

Minimums are not rigid, but determined in a manner designed to insure that the champion be a true one. For instance, if Player A participated in all of his team's 20 games and scored 120 Field Goals while compiling a Field Goal Percentage of .536, it would not be equitable to compare his record with Player B, who recorded a .561 Field Goal Percentage, but who scored only 60 Field Goals in eleven games.

It's possible that if Player A had scored only 60 Field Goals, his Percentage would have been higher, and conversely, if Player B had taken enough shots to score 120 Field Goals, his rate of accuracy might have diminished. To make proper comparisons, players should be ranked on performances as nearly comparable as possible.

In Field Goal Percentages, as in other basketball statistics, teams are ranked on their totals in the same manner as individual players.

Worksheets

There are many types of worksheets for use in basketball statistics. The scorebook can be, in effect, a work sheet. If only numerical totals are wanted for individual statistics, a simple chart (Form 3-A) can be prepared easily with ruler and pen or pencil. With this form, simply insert one tally each time a player makes a FG and/or a FGA.

CENTRAL HIGH	FGA	FG	FTA	FT	REB OFF	REB DEF	A
SMITH	𝍸 𝍸 𝍸 ||	𝍸 ||||					
HORTON	𝍸 |||	||					
JONES	||||						
MATHER	𝍸 𝍸	𝍸 |					
JOHNSON	𝍸 ||	||					
RICHARDS	𝍸 𝍸 |	||||					
TEAM							
TOTALS	57	23					

Form 3-A

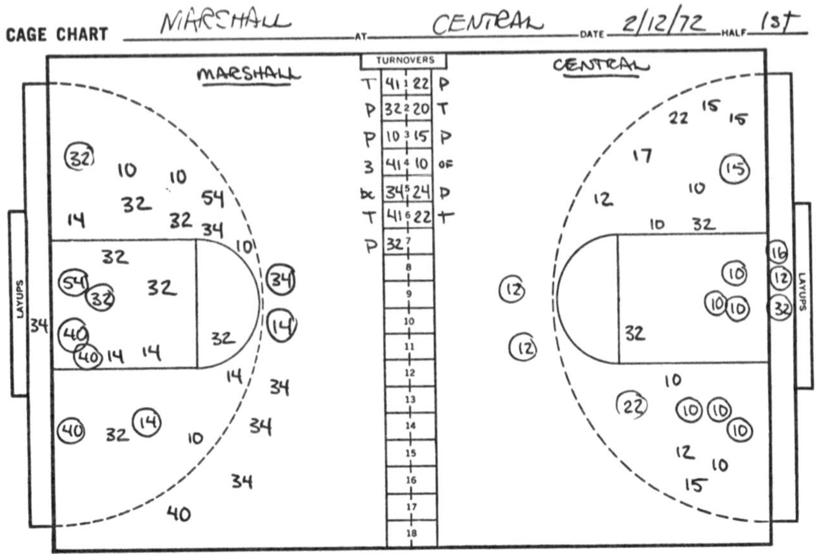

Form 3-B

Perhaps the most efficient workchart is a shot chart (Form 3-B) because information included can be used both by the statistician and the coach.

With a shot chart, each time a player is charged with a FGA, write his uniform number at the approximate spot on the court from which he attempted the shot. If the shot is successful, circle the number.

Because there are so many shots made close to the basket, a separate spot is provided to list layups, tip-ins, and other shots made from within a few feet of the basket (see Form 3-B). Master duplicator stencils of shot charts, combined with scoring summaries, are available from Fred Casotti & Co., 320-31st St., Boulder, Colo. 80302.

Free Throws

No scorer's judgment is required in recording free throws. An entry is made for each Free Throw Attempted (FTA) and each successful Free Throw (FT).

If using simplified work sheets (Form 3-C), these statistics can be entered in a numerical tally on the same sheet used for other statistics. Some shot charts include space for recording Free Throws.

CENTRAL HIGH	FGA	FG	FTA	FT	REB		A
					OFF	DEF	
SMITH	卌 卌 卌 ||	卌 ||||	||||	||||			
HORTON	卌 |||	||	|||	|			
JONES	||||						
MATHER	卌 卌	卌 |	||||	||			
JOHNSON	卌 ||	||	|	|			
RICHARDS	卌 卌 |	||||	||||	|||			
TEAM							
TOTALS	57	23	16	11			

Form 3-C

Free Throw Percentage

To compute the Free Throw Percentage for a player or team, divide the number of Free Throws made by the number of Free Throw Attempts.

Example: Roosevelt High attempted 17 Free Throws and made

11. The team Field Goal Percentage is .647 (11 divided by 17). As in Field Goal Percentage, leaders in Free Throw Percentage are ranked in order of the highest percentage. Because players usually take fewer free throws than field goal attempts, the minimum Free Throws scored to qualify for the championship should be from three to five times the number of scheduled games. Again, keep in mind that the minimum should be established in a way to insure a true champion.

Rebounds

A Rebound is credited to the player who *gains control* of the ball after a missed shot.

On *every missed* field goal and free throw attempt, a rebound *must* be credited to a player or to a team.

Example: Green of Team A shoots at the basket, but misses. As the ball comes off the backboard, his teammate, Horton, grabs the ball and throws it out to another teammate. Credit Horton with one Rebound (and Green with a FGA).

Example: Green of Team A takes a shot at the basket, but misses. As the ball comes off the backboard, his teammate, Horton, leaps and tries to tap the ball into the basket. His tip misses and his teammate, Smith, tips the ball up and into the basket. Charge Green with one FGA. Credit Horton with one Rebound and one FGA. Credit Smith with one Rebound, one FGA and one FG. (Team totals will be 3 FGA, 1 FG, and 2 Rebounds.)

Example: Green of Team A shoots at the basket, but misses and the ball does not touch the rim or backboard. Green's teammate, Smith, grabs the ball out of the air and passes the ball back to Green, who shoots again, this time making the basket. Charge Green with *two* FGA and credit him with one FG. Credit Smith with one Rebound.

If a player does not catch a rebound, but tips it out to a teammate, he is judged to have controlled it and is credited with a Rebound. However, if when he tips it out, the ball goes to a player from the opposing team, the opponent who catches the ball is credited with the Rebound.

On a blocked shot, if the blocker's teammate recovers the ball, the blocker is credited with the Rebound. If an opposing player recovers the ball, he gets the Rebound. If the blocked shot goes out of bounds, it is a team Rebound. Of course the player whose shot is blocked is charged with a FGA.

When two players from opposing teams retrieve a rebound *simultaneously* and a "held ball" is called, the Rebound is credited to the player whose team gains control of the ensuing jump ball.

Note: This rule does not apply when a player gains clear control of a rebound and is *then* tied up by an opponent so that a "held ball" is called.

When a team gains technical possession of the ball, and it is not controlled by an individual, credit a Team Rebound to that team which gains possession.

Example: Green of Team A attempts a field goal (or free throw) and the missed shot goes out of bounds (whether or not it touched the rim or backboard) before any individual touches or controls the ball. Team B thus gains possession (a throw-in from where the ball went out of bounds) and Team B is credited with a Team Rebound.

Example: Green of Team A attempts a free throw (or field goal) and the missed shot strikes the rim of the basket and is touched (but not controlled) by a player of Team B before it goes out of bounds. Team A thus regains possession (a throw-in) and Team A is credited with a Team Rebound.

Example: Green of Team A is awarded two free throws. He misses the first but (because he has a second free throw) his team retains possession and is credited with a Team Rebound.

Note: The same ruling applies on a missed free throw after a technical foul.

There is an excellent means of cross-checking in basketball statistics. The total of all *missed* Field Goal and Free Throw Attempts for both teams, plus the Team Rebounds for both teams, *must* equal the total Rebounds for both teams.

Example: Team A made 33 Field Goals in 68 Attempts, made 17 of 26 Free Throws, was credited with 6 Team Rebounds, and Team A's total Rebounds were 47. Team B made 31 of 69 Field Goals, 26 of 40 Free Throws, was credited with 4 Team Rebounds and a total of 59 Rebounds. Thus, Team A missed 44 shots (35 FGA and 9 FTA) and Team B missed 52 (38 FGA and 14 FTA) for a total of 96. Team A had 6 Team Rebounds, Team B had 4, for a total of 10. Adding 96 and 10 gives a total of 106, which equals the total team Rebounds (47 plus 59) for both teams.

Note: There may be some confusion between the terms "Team Rebounds" and "total team." Team Rebounds refers to those Rebounds not controlled by an individual and technically credited to the "team" gaining possession. They are listed as "team" in a summary of individuals. The total team Rebounds refers to the total for each team of all individual rebounds plus the Team Rebounds.

Rebounding statistics can be recorded on a cumulative work sheet

CENTRAL HIGH	FGA	FG	FTA	FT	REB OFF	DEF	A
SMITH	卌 卌 卌 ||	卌 ||||	||||	||||	卌	卌 ||	
HORTON	卌 |||	||	|||	|	||	|||	
JONES	||||					||	
MATHER	卌 卌	卌 |	||||	||	|||	|||	
JOHNSON	卌 ||	||	|	|	卌 |	卌 ||	
RICHARDS	卌 卌 |	||||	||||	|||	||	|	
TEAM					|	||	
TOTALS	57	23	16	11	19	25	

Form 3-D

(Form D) along with summaries in other categories, or they can be maintained separately. Some statisticians and coaches prefer to separate rebounds off the offensive board from those off the defensive backboard. This is reflected in Form 3-D.

Statistical rankings in Rebounds are based on *average number* of Rebounds per game. In some leagues or conferences, where teams play the same number of games, rankings are based on the most total rebounds.

Average Per Game is derived by dividing the total number of Rebounds by the number of games played.

Example: Green of Central High played in 22 games and was credited with 196 Rebounds. His Average Per Game was 8.9 (196 divided by 22) Rebounds Per Game.

In establishing minimums for Rebound championship qualifications, the least complicated method would be to require a player to play in at least 75 percent of his team's games. In computing averages, a player is considered to have played a game if he is in it for at least one play.

Assists

A player is credited with making an Assist when he makes a pass that *contributes directly* to a field goal.

The scorer must make the judgment on whether a pass "contributes directly" to the scoring of a field goal. It is *not* the intent to record an Assist on *every* pass that precedes a scoring play, but to provide credit only to those passes which by their execution make the scoring play possible.

Example: Player A cuts past his man for the basket and Player B passes to him in time for Player A to receive the pass and make a lay-up for a field goal. Credit Player B with an Assist.

Example: Player A passes the ball outside to Player B, who then dribbles to drive past his man for a lay-up field goal. Do not credit an Assist to Player A. The pass merely put the ball in Player B's possession. His drive, *not* the pass, was the contributing factor in the scoring play.

Note: This does not mean that an Assist cannot be credited if the scorer dribbles before shooting. In the first example above, Player B may have made a perfect pass to the cutting Player A, but the latter was far enough from the basket that he was forced to dribble once, or even several times, before making the lay-up. The pass still *contributed directly* to the scoring play and Player B should be credited with an Assist.

Only one assist can be credited for any single field goal scored, regardless of how many times the ball was handled prior to the score.

Example: On a fast break, three players of Team A pass the ball back and forth as they race down the court. Only one Assist can be credited if a field goal is scored, normally to the player who made the last pass to the one scoring the field goal.

Generally, an Assist is credited to the last man who made a pass to the scoring player, but the Assist may be credited to a player who made an earlier pass that, in the scorer's judgment, was more vital to the scoring play.

Example: Player A grabs a defensive rebound as two of his teammates, Players B and C, race downcourt. Player A makes a full-court pass to where both of his teammates are near their own basket, with no defenders nearby. Player B takes the pass and shovels off the ball to Player C, who makes the lay-up. If, in the scorer's opinion, the long pass contributed more to the scoring play than the short pass by Player B, the Assist may be given to Player A.

Players are ranked on the most Assists per game. Again, there should be championship minimums, probably about two or three times the number of games scheduled. If a player's team had 20 games scheduled, he should be credited with at least 40 to 50 Assists to qualify for the championship. Again, the minimum should be established to insure a true champion.

Recording of Assists is usually a simple cumulative numerical procedure and the work sheet used for other statistics can be utilized for this purpose (See Form 3-E).

CENTRAL HIGH	FGA	FG	FTA	FT	REB OFF	REB DEF	A
SMITH	卌 卌 卌 II	卌 IIII	IIII	IIII	卌	卌 II	I
HORTON	卌 III	II	III	I	II	III	
JONES	IIII					II	I
MATHER	卌 卌	卌 I	IIII	II	III	III	
JOHNSON	卌 II	II	I	I	卌 I	卌 II	卌
RICHARDS	卌 卌 I	卌	IIII	III	II	I	III
TEAM					I	II	
TOTALS	57	23	16	11	19	25	10

Form 3-E

Scoring

Scoring statistics are taken directly from the scorebook and, of course, a player is credited with two points for each successful Field Goal and one point for each successful Free Throw. In the American Basketball League, field goals shot from outside a designated line (30 feet from the basket) count three points.

Scoring championship is normally determined by the highest number of Points Per Game, with the champion required to play at least 75 percent of his team's games.

Some leagues, where the teams play the same number of games, award the championship to the player scoring the most total points. This determination avoids the necessity for establishing a minimum.

Turnovers

Turnovers may be defined as the loss of the ball to the opponent before an attempt at the basket is made. This may occur in several ways:

a. Bad pass (P)
b. Traveling (T)
c. 3 second lane violation (3)
d. Back court violation (bc)
e. Offensive foul (OF)

Example: A space usually is provided in shot charts (Form 3-F) for turnovers in a form similar to this partial two-team record of turnovers.

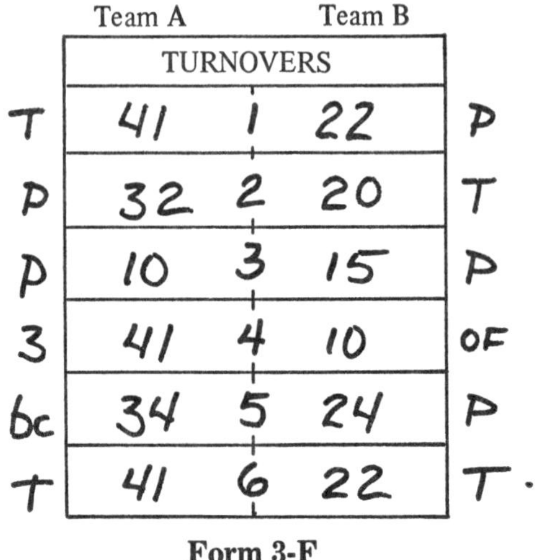

	Team A	TURNOVERS	Team B	
T	41	1	22	P
P	32	2	20	T
P	10	3	15	P
3	41	4	10	OF
bc	34	5	24	P
T	41	6	22	T.

Form 3-F

Records

Records should be maintained for individuals and teams in all of the basketball statistical categories.

As time and available material permits, records should be catalogued in each category for single games, for season, and for either one-half or one-quarter periods, depending upon whether it is high school or college.

In addition, other records may be useful, such as for individuals, best career records, most consecutive Free Throws made, and most consecutive Field Goals made. For teams, most consecutive wins, most wins in a season, best winning percentage, etc. For a complete season, an entire team's cumulative statistics can be maintained in the same format as for a single game (Form 3-G shows actual season's statistics for University of Santa Clara in the 1972-1973 season).

How to Keep Score

There are several types of basketball scorebooks, but the same basic procedure can be used with each. Perhaps the most complete is the Official NCAA Basketball Scorebook, available at the National Collegiate Sports Service, Box 757, Grand Central Station, New York, N.Y., 10017. (See Form 3-H) Entries are somewhat standardized, with spaces

FINAL 1972-73 VARSITY BASKETBALL STATISTICS

NAME	G	FGA-FGM	PCT	FTA-FTM	PCT	REB	AVG	A	PTS	AVG
STEWART, C	26	291-186	63.4	161-115	71.4	235	9.0	11	487	18.7
WINKLER	19	198-104	52.5	78-62	79.5	60	3.2	50	270	14.2
LAVARONI, F	26	319-155	48.6	93-46	49.5	275	10.6	74	356	13.7
DIGGS, F	26	221-119	53.8	77-40	51.9	148	5.7	36	278	10.7
BELLOTTI, G	25	228-91	39.9	46-36	78.3	105	4.2	61	218	8.7
PIRO, G	25	129-55	42.6	52-42	80.0	48	1.9	52	152	6.1
HALE, G	26	110-52	47.3	58-43	74.1	44	1.7	82	147	5.7
HUBBARD, F	15	66-31	47.0	31-20	64.5	30	2.0	2	82	5.5
MILES, G	24	94-37	39.4	44-23	52.3	70	2.9	51	97	4.0
HELMAN, G	13	23-7	30.4	8-4	50.0	26	2.0	2	18	1.4
ROMEY, G	2	1-0	0.0	2-1	50.0	0	0.0	0	1	0.5
COWARD, G	9	4-1	25.0	5-1	20.0	7	0.8	5	3	0.3
AYCOX, G	4	8-2	25.0	2-0	0.0	2	0.5	0	4	1.0
MCFALL, F	1	0-0	0.0	0-0	0.0	1	1.5	0	0	0.0
TEAM REBOUNDS						145				
TOTALS:		1692-840	49.6	657-433	65.9	1196	46.0	426	2113	81.3

G–GAMES PLAYED, FGA-FGM–FIELD GOALS ATTEMPTED-MADE; PCT.–PERCENTAGE OF SUCCESSFUL FIELD GOALS MADE; FTA-FTM–FREE THROWS ATTEMPTED-MADE, PCT.–PERCENTAGE OF SUCCESSFUL FREE THROWS, REB.–NUMBER OF REBOUNDS, AVG–AVERAGE NUMBER OF REBOUNDS PER GAME, A–ASSISTS, PTS. TOTAL NUMBER OF POINTS SCORED, AVG.–NUMBER OF POINTS SCORED PER GAME.

Form 3-G

TEAM	Central	PLACE OF GAME	Riverton
COACH	Bill Davis	REFEREE Brownell	UMPIRE Harrison

POINTS SCORED EACH PERIOD						
FIRST HALF	SECOND HALF	OVERTIME	OVERTIME	OVERTIME	HALF SCORE	FINAL SCORE
35	27	8			35	70

OFFICIAL SCORER'S RESPONSIBILITY — DATE 2/21 — ATTENDANCE 8764

POS	NO.	FOULS	PLAYER	FIRST HALF FIELD GOALS	FIRST HALF FREE THROWS	SECOND HALF FIELD GOALS	SECOND HALF FREE THROWS	OVERTIMES FG	OVERTIMES FT	FIELD GOAL ATTEMPTS	REBOUNDS	ASSISTS	TIME PLAYED	FG	FGA	FT	FTA	SM	RB	A	PF	TP
F	11	P1 P2 P3 P4 P5	Franks	222	●●●●	22	●○●			卌 III / 卌 III	卌 II / 卌	/ I	44¾	5	16	6	7	12	12	1	3	16
F	21	P1 P2 P3 P4 P5	Hudson	2	●●	2	●●	2	●●●	III / 卌 I	III / 卌	I /	20¾	3	9	7	7	6	8	1	4	13
F	23	P1 P2 P3 P4 P5	Greene	2	●●	2	●● ○○			I / IIII	II / III	I /	22	2	5	4	6	5	5	1	3	8
F	22	P1 P2 P3 P4 P5	Tomkovich										½	0	0	0	0	0	0	0	0	0
C	15	P1 P2 P3 P4 P5	Monroe	2	●● ●● ●			2	●●	卌 IIII / 卌 III	卌 III / 卌 I	I /	31½	2	17	6	7	16	14	1	4	10
C	24	P1 P2 P3 P4 P5	Carson		○○		●			I / I	/ 卌	/ III	[illegible]	0	0	0	2	2	1	0	0	0
G	10	P1 P2 P3 P4 P5	Slade	2	●● ● ●●	22	○ ●●			卌 II / IIII	I /	II / I	25½	3	11	6	8	10	1	3	5	12
G	14	P1 P2 P3 P4 P5	Thomas			222				/ 卌	I / IIII	/ I	19½	3	5	0	0	2	5	1	2	6
		P1 P2 P3 P4 P5																				
		P1 P2 P3 P4 P5									(Team) I / 卌								6			
			TOTALS	9	22-17	9	13-9	2	5-4	76	67	15	225	20	76	30	40	66	67	15	27	70

TEAM FOULS: FIRST HALF 1 2 3 4 5 6 — SECOND HALF 1 2 3 4 5 6

RUNNING SCORE

TIME OUTS 1 2 3 4 5 6

SCORE	1	2	3	4	5	6	7	8	9	10	11	12	13	14	15	16	17	18	19	20	21	22	23	24	25	26	27	28	29	30	31	32	33	34	35	36	37	38	39
PLAYER SCORING		10	11	15	15	10	10	15	15		3		11	10	10		15	15	11	11		11		21	21	21		11	11		23		20	23	23		14	11	
TIME OF SCORING		16¾	15	14	14	13½	13½	12¾	12¾		12½		12	11½	11		10½	10½	7½	7½		6¼		5½	5	5		2	2		1½		1	¼	¼		17¼	16½	
OTHER DATA																																							

SCORE	40	41	42	43	44	45	46	47	48	49	50	51	52	53	54	55	56	57	58	59	60	61	62	63	64	65	66	67	68	69	70	71	72	73	74	75	76	77	78
PLAYER SCORING	14	20		23	23	23		10	11		11		11	10	10		10		21	21	21		14		15	15	21	21	21		21								
TIME OF SCORING	16	14¾		14	13½	13½		11	10½		8¾		5¾	5¼	5¼		4½		3¾	2½	2½		1¼		4	4	3¼	2¼	2¼		0								
OTHER DATA																																							

SCORE	79	80	81	82	83	84	85	86	87	88	89	90	91	92	93	94	95	96	97	98	99	100	101	102	103	104	105	106	107	108	109	110	111	112	113	114	115	116	117
PLAYER SCORING																																							
TIME OF SCORING																																							
OTHER DATA																																							

Form 3-H

provided for each player's name, jersey number (NO.) and position (POS) such as G for guard, C for Center, and F for forward.

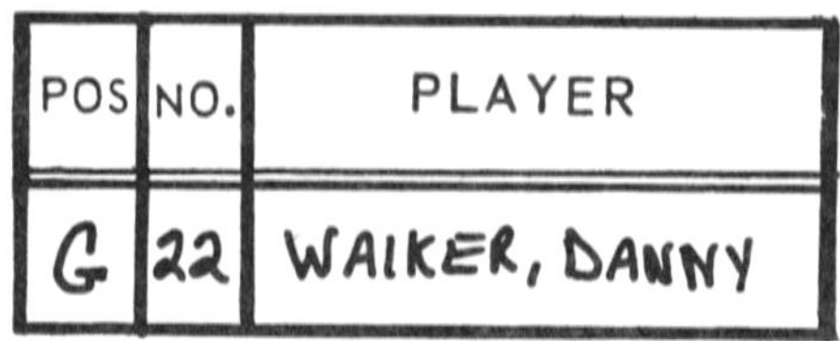

POS	NO.	PLAYER
G	22	WALKER, DANNY

Form 3-I

Fouls

When a player is charged with a personal foul, draw a line through the number (in sequence) of the foul committed. When a player is charged with a technical foul, insert the letter "T" in the empty square.

Example: Form 3-J shows how the scorebook would be marked for a player who has been charged with two personal fouls and one technical foul.

FOULS		
P1	P2	P3
P4	P5	

Form 3-J

A notation should be made in the scorebook for the total personal fouls charged to a team in order to readily determine the bonus free throw situations. Each time a player is charged with a personal foul, draw a line through the numbered box for Team Fouls.

Example: In the first half of a game, a team has been charged with four personal fouls, as shown in Form 3-K.

TEAM FOULS FIRST HALF 1 2 3 4 5 6

Form 3-K

Field Goals

Enter a "2" or an "x" in the column opposite the player's name for each field goal he scores.

Example: Form 3-L shows optional entries for a player who has scored four field goals.

Form 3-L

FIELD GOALS
2222

FIELD GOALS
XXXX

Free Throws

Both free throw attempts and free throws scored are recorded. A single free throw attempt is indicated by a circle . When the free throw is made, fill in the circle with an "x" .

When two shots are awarded, the attempts are indicated by joining the circles . The first attempt of a possible bonus is indicated by a circle with a line attached . When the second attempt is awarded, a second circle is added .

Example: In one game, this player made his first free throw, was then awarded two shots, missing his first and making the second; his next free throw was under a bonus situation and he made the first, missed the second; then he was awarded a single free throw, which he missed. (See Form 3-M)

Form 3-M

Running Summary

All scorebooks have space provided to maintain a running score so that at any time in the game, the exact score can be noted.

Periodically (during a time-out, for instance) a cross-check should be made by quickly adding all individual scoring for each team to make sure the sum of points for all individuals equals the team total as noted in the Running Summary.

A diagonal line drawn through the correct number (corresponding to the total number of points) for each team should be inserted after each score.

The NCAA Scorebook, and some others, provide additional space to indicate the uniform number of the player making the point(s), the time in the game the score was made, and "other data."

"Other data" could be the uniform number of the defensive player against whom the shot was made; a notation to indicate the type of shot (i.e. "H" for hook shot, "J" for jump shot or "R" for Rebound); a "T" for technical foul converted, or whatever the statistician or coach would like for further detail. (See Form 3-N)

SCORE	1	2	3	4	5	6	7	8	9	10	11	12	13	14	15	16	17
PLAYER SCORING		14		15		10	14		10		22		10	15		22	10
TIME OF SCORING		8^{17}		6^{58}		6^{20}	5^{45}		4^{50}		3^{10}		2^{15}	1^{50}		:32	9^{40}
OTHER DATA		J		H		J	FT		J		R		J	T		R	FT

Form 3-N

A heavy vertical line should be drawn through the Running Summary box at the end of each quarter or half. In the previous example, the team had scored 16 points at the end of the first quarter.

Time-Outs

Draw a diagonal line through the proper numbered box each time a team is charged with a time-out. Put additional numbers in empty boxes if more than five time-outs are called. (See Form 3-O)

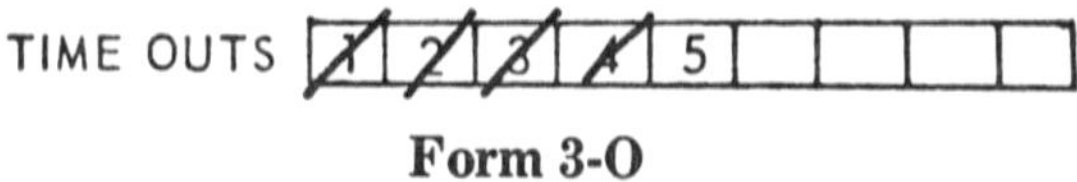

Form 3-O

Summary Column

Add the game totals for each player, including the statistical non-scoring entries. (See Form 3-P)

SUMMARY									
TIME PLAYED	FG	FGA	FT	FTA	SM	RB	A	PF	TP
35	6	12	3	7	10	10	4	3	15

Form 3-P

Note: SM in the Summary Column is a total of field goal and free throw shots missed. This column is provided for a cross-check on Rebounds. The total of all shots missed, for both teams, *must* equal the total number of rebounds for both teams (see example in section on Rebounds).

Box Scores

Each game may be summarized in a box score to show the statistical performance of each player. The box score form used may vary, but is normally devised to conform to the style of the newspaper which may publish the game results.

The emphasis placed on the game by the newspapers will determine how detailed the box score should be, but the statistician should include at least enough material to provide the newspaper with all the information it desires.

Included at the minimum should be the name of each player, the number of FGA and FG, the number of FTA and FT, and total Points. Depending upon the newspaper's space limitations, additional entries may be made for Rebounds, Assists, Personal Fouls, Turnovers, and Minutes Played.

Below the individual team entries should be listed the team's totals for the game, including field goal percentages in the first half, the second half, and for the game. Also included is the total number of shots missed, the team rebounds and the score by periods.

Form 3-Q is a sample of a complete box score, for which duplicator master stencils are available for a modest cost from Ned West, 2660 Acorn Ave., N.E., Atlanta, Ga. 30305.

From a practical standpoint, most newspapers will use a simplified box score to conserve space. Most common is one like the sample below used by wire services and many newspapers:

CENTRAL	FG	FT	PTS	MARSHALL	FG	FT	PTS
Frazee	4	2	10	Radetich	3	0	6
Chancellor	3	0	6	Brandeburg, R	3	1	7
Ogden	11	5	27	Brandeburg, D	0	0	0
Errington	2	0	4	Emery	7	3	17
Seeger	1	0	2	Buickerood	5	3	13
Rodriquez	4	2	10	Covey	5	0	10
Hernandez	0	0	0	Chell	0	0	0
TOTALS	25	9	59	TOTALS	23	7	53

Halftime Score: Central 27, Marshall 23 Fouls: Central 7, Marshall 12.

A real space-saver is an abbreviated box score that reports only points and halftime score, and normally requires less than an inch of newspaper space.

Stats Form 103-A—Order Masters from Ned West, 2660 Acorn Avenue, N.E., Atlanta, Georgia 30305

OFFICIAL BASKETBALL BOX

CENTRAL	FIELD GOALS MADE	FIELD GOALS ATT'D.	FREE THROWS MADE	FREE THROWS ATT'D.	RE-BOUNDS	ASS'TS	PER. FOULS	TOTAL POINTS	TURN-OVERS	MINS. PLAYED
JACKSON, C.	0	0	0	0	0	0	0	0	0	1
CICCARELLO, M.	0	0	0	0	0	0	0	0	0	1
GUIDO, J.	0	0	0	0	0	0	0	0	0	1
KING, H.	0	0	0	0	0	0	0	0	0	1
OGDEN, R.	11	20	5	8	19	1	3	27	1	31
SEEGER, B.	1	1	0	0	0	0	0	2	0	9
FRAZEE, J.	4	8	2	2	1	5	1	10	1	31
CHANCELLOR, D.	3	4	0	0	1	0	0	6	3	17
ERRINGTON, K.	2	4	0	1	5	0	2	4	1	23
RODRIGUEZ, N.	4	8	2	4	4	2	1	10	1	31
HERNANDEZ, R.	0	2	0	0	3	1	0	0	3	14
TEAM					1					
TOTALS	25	47	9	15	34	9	7	59	10	160

PERCENTAGES: FGs: 1st H .481 2nd H .600 Game .532 Shots Missed 28
FTs: 1st H .500 2nd H .615 Game .600 Team Rebounds 1

MARSHALL	FIELD GOALS MADE	FIELD GOALS ATT'D.	FREE THROWS MADE	FREE THROWS ATT'D.	RE-BOUNDS	ASS'TS	PER. FOULS	TOTAL POINTS	TURN-OVERS	MINS. PLAYED
BRANDEBURG, D.	0	5	0	0	1	5	0	0	3	32
BRANDEBURG, R.	3	11	1	2	4	2	5	7	4	31
CHELL, L.	0	0	0	0	0	0	0	0	0	1
EMERY, B.	7	19	3	3	5	1	3	17	2	32
BUICKERIOD, K.	5	10	3	4	7	0	3	13	3	32
COVEY, D.	5	10	0	0	11	2	1	10	1	16
RADETICH, J.	3	4	0	0	0	0	0	6	0	16
TEAM					4					
TOTALS	23	59	7	9	32	10	12	53	13	160

PERCENTAGES: FGs: 1st H .333 2nd H .448 Game .390 Shots Missed 38
FTs: 1st H .750 2nd H .800 Game .778 Team Rebounds 4

OFFICIALS REYNOLDS & MITCHELL
CROWD 3250
DATE 2/12/72

SCORE BY PERIODS	1	2	3	4	EP	EP	G
CENTRAL	13	27	43	59			59
MARSHALL	13	23	40	53			53

Form 3-Q

CENTRAL (59)	MARSHALL (53)
Frazee (10)	Radetich (6)
Chancellor (6)	Brandeburg, R. (7)
Ogden (27)	Buickerood (13)
Errington (4)	Emery (17)
Seeger (2)	Covey (10)

Halftime score: Central 27, Marshall 23. Subs: C—Rodriquez (10), Hernandez. M—D. Brandeburg, Chell.

Depending upon the demand by news media or coaches, statisticians may prepare an abbreviated half-time box, which is used to summarize important information for both teams at the half-way point in the game.

The form provides space for team statistics in FGA, FG and FG Percentage; FTA, FT and FT Percentage; total Rebounds plus individual Scoring leaders, individual Rebound leaders and a listing of players with three fouls or more. There also is space for additional information of special interest. Form 3-R is a sample of an Abbreviated Halftime Box Score, also available from Ned West.

Scoring Sequence Report

Many teams keep a scoring sequence or play-by-play report (see Form 3-S). It provides information on the details of scoring for both teams. Included should be the time remaining when the score occurred, the score for both teams at that point, the name of the player who scored, and the manner in which he scored (set shot, jump shot, hook, lay-up, etc.).

In the event of a foul shot, insert the name of the player who committed the foul. Give the names of substitutes and the time they enter the game. Usually, the scoring of one team is described all in caps, while the other team's scoring is detailed in small letters. This is done to visually separate the scoring details for both teams. The same visual distinction can be accomplished by using two different colors.

A full game box score can be recapped from the play-by-play. Its main purpose, however, is to aid sports writers with their preparation of reports on the game.

Stats Form 104. Order Masters from Ned West, 2660 Acorn Avenue, N.E., Atlanta 5, Georgia.

ABBREVIATED HALFTIME BOX

Date 2/12/72
Crowd 3250

	MARSHAL		CENTRAL	
Halftime Score	23		27	
Field Goals Attempted	30		27	
Field Goals Made	10		13	
Field Goal Percentage	.333		.481	
Free Throws Attempted	4		2	
Free Throws Made	3		1	
Free Throw Percentage	.750		.500	
Rebounds (Total Individual)	19		17	
Individual Scoring Leaders	K. BUICKERWOOD	6	Ogden	13
	COVEY	6	FRAZEE	6
	BRANDEBURG	5		
	EMERY	4		
Individual Rebounds Leaders	K. BUICKERWOOD	6	OGDEN	8
	COVEY	4	ERRINGTON	4
Players with three or more personal fouls				

Additional Information

Form 3-R

SCORING SEQUENCE REPORT

Game Central High vs. Marshall High Place Central Date 2/12/72

Time Left	Score C	Score M	Scoring Play
			FIRST QUARTER
			Central controls opening tip
6:39	2	0	Frazee on set shot, 20 feet top right of key
6:22	2	2	BUICKEROOD ON SET SHOT, 20 FT. TOP OF KEY
5:49	4	2	Chancellor on 15 foot jump shot right of key
5:34	4	4	R. BRANDEBURG JUMP SHOT TOP OF KEY
5:26	5	4	Ogden fouled by R. Brandeburg: 1 shot–good
5:20	5	6	BUICKEROOD FOULED BY ERRINGTON: 2 shots –1st good, 2nd good
4:51	7	6	Frazee drives from left side
4:19	9	6	Errington on reverse layup
3:53	9	7	R. BRANDEBURG FOULED BY OGDEN; 2 shots– 1st good, 2nd no good
2:38	11	7	Ogden drives baseline for 8 ft. jump shot.
2:24	11	9	RADETICH MUSCLES FROM UNDERNEATH
1:57			Errington fouled by Buickerood; 1 shot–no good
			COVEY REPLACES RADETICH: Hernandez for Chancellor
1:19	13	9	Ogden on followup
0:37	13	11	COVEY ON FOLLOWUP
0:05	13	13	R. BRANDEBURG ON 15 FOOT JUMPER LEFT OF KEY
			SECOND QUARTER
			Chancellor replaces Hernandez; Seeger replaces Errington
7:46	15	13	Seeger drives length of court for layup after steal
6:45			M. TIME OUT AFTER TRAVELLING NULLIFIES EMERY JUMP SHOT
			Errington replaces Chancellor
6:30	17	13	Frazee on 20 foot jumper
6:19	17	15	BUICKEROOD ON LAYUP;
5:51	19	15	Ogden on 10 foot jumper right side
5:34	19	17	COVEY ON 10 FOOT JUMP SHOT FROM BASELINE
4:43	19	19	COVEY ON FOLLOWUP
3:55	19	21	EMERY ON 15 FOOT JUMP SHOT FROM BASELINE
3:17	21	21	Ogden follows up his own missed jump shot
1:42	23	21	Ogden on jump shot from 15 feet, right side of low post
1:09	25	21	Ogden follows up his own missed shot
0:23	27	21	Rodriquez 12 foot jumper from baseline behind screen
0:03	27	23	EMERY FOLLOWS UP HIS OWN MISSED SHOT

Halftime: Central 27, Marshall 23

Form 3-S

Chapter 4

Football

Although football statistics have not reached the almost unending detail of baseball records, they have become increasingly sophisticated so that modern statisticians can provide information for a tremendous variety of material on "how they played the game."

This chapter will provide all the instructions necessary to record and maintain basic football statistics in any depth desired by the statistician or coach.

In the preceding section on statistician's responsibility, it was suggested that at least two statisticians be assigned to record football statistics. If additional personnel is available, one or two should be assigned to keep a play-by-play (see forms later in this chapter) chart of the game.

If statistics are not needed immediately after the game for release to news media, and there is only one statistician, the coach or statistician may prefer to keep *only* a play-by-play. He then can record statistics leisurely after the game from the complete play-by-play record. However, when possible, record both the complete statistics and play-by-play because the two can be cross-checked for accuracy.

General Interpretations

The statistical procedures outlined in this chapter are basically for college and high school football. Statistics for professional football differ in some areas, and these differences will be noted in the applicable sections of the statistics instructions.

Comparative statistical rankings in football are generally based on "average per game" or "average per play."

Statistics should be used *only* for regular-season games. Some teams do not play in playoff or bowl games, so players should be compared only on their regularly scheduled games. Statistics for bowl or playoff games should be compiled separately for comparison only against other performances in those games.

However, for league records, many leagues or conferences use statistics from regular season league games, only to reflect performances of each player and team in an equal number of games. Whichever system is used, it is important that all teams in one league use the same standards.

There is a statistical entry to cover every single play in a football game. In each category where there is an individual entry, there is a corresponding entry for the team. The totals for all individuals on a play or plays must equal the team totals for the same play or plays.

Note: There is no individual entry, but there is a team entry for each first down, each penalty, and each fumble and fumble recovery.

• **Pro Ruling:** Individuals are charged with fumbles and credited with fumble recoveries. Many high school and college statisticians now also record unofficial statistics in this category for record purposes.

There can be only one "attempt" charged to any player and his team on any one play. Any other player who gains or loses ground in a play started by another player is not charged with an "attempt," but *is* credited with yardage gained or lost.

Example: Team A has ball at Team B's 40-yard line. Hall of Team A takes handoff and runs to Team B's 30-yard line, where he laterals to teammate Cooke, who runs to the 25 before he is tackled. Hall is charged with *one* Rushing "attempt," and credited with 10 yards gained under Rushing, Cooke is charged with *no* Rushing attempt and credited with five yards under Rushing. Team A is charged with *one* Rushing attempt and 15 yards under Rushing.

Note: Full explanation of yardage gained or lost on lateral passes will be detailed later in this section.

Fractional yardage is eliminated in statistics. It is the judgment of the official scorer whether a distance between yard-lines is recorded as the greater or lesser number. However, the determination must be consistent so that overall yardage exactly equals the progress of the ball (i.e. on a drive that covers 60 yards, the yardage recorded for individual plays in that drive should total 60 yards. Also, if a play ends between, for instance, the 36 and 37-yard lines, and the statistician rules the ball advanced to the 37, the next play, statistically, must start from the 37).

Also, on a *first down* play, if a team gains between 9 and 10 yards, it must be recorded as nine because first down sticks are not advanced.

At the end of each game, all individual totals must equal the team totals in each category.

Example: For Team A, Brown rushes 8 times for 60 yards; Allen rushes 2 times for 3 yards; Smith rushes 11 times for 98 yards. Team A totals in Rushing then *must* be 21 rushes for 161 yards.

Generally, only the yardage from goal line to goal line is recorded statistically. The single exception is on field goal attempts, when the 10 yards from the goal line to the goal posts is added.

• **Pro ruling:** Punt, kickoff and interception returns are measured from the point of reception, including end zone yardage. Many high school and college statisticians unofficially record the total return yardage, including end zone yardage, for record purposes. Field goal yardage is measured only to the goal line, where the goal posts are located in professional games.

Basic Statistical Categories

In football (and every other sport), statistical entries for record purposes can be in as many categories as the statistician has imagination to devise. Basically, however, practical statistics are recorded for individuals and for teams in Rushing, Passing, Total Offense, Pass Receiving, Pass Interceptions, Punt Returns, Kickoff Returns, Punting, and Scoring.

First Downs

First downs are registered only on plays originating from the line of scrimmage and are recorded whenever the yardsticks are ordered moved forward, or when a touchdown is scored from scrimmage within a series of downs starting ten yards or more from the goal line.

• **Pro ruling:** A first down is credited on each *scoring* play resulting from rushing or passing, regardless of the distance covered.

A first down is recorded when the offensive team is awarded a first down because of a penalty. This is true even though the yardsticks might be moved backwards.

There can be only one first down on a given play. There are instances where, after the whistle has blown and a first down signified, a penalty moves the yardsticks an additional ten or more yards. In this case the continuity is broken and the scorer should credit the team with a penalty first down over and above the first down previously achieved. In all cases, the official scorer should be guided by the action of the officials.

Example: Team A starts a rushing play on Team B's 45-yard line and it carries 12 yards to Team B's 33, where Team B is penalized for a personal foul and officials mark off 15 more yards to Team B's

18-yard line. Team A should be credited with a first down by rushing *and* a first down by a penalty.

The final play of a series which gains the required yardage for a first down determines whether the first down is credited to Rushing, Passing or Penalty.

Example: Team A has the ball at midfield. On the first play, Green runs off tackle for four yards and on the second he runs over guard for five yards. On the next play, Team B is penalized five yards for offside, advancing the ball to Team B's 36. The yardsticks are moved forward and Team A is credited with a first down by *penalty*.

Example: Team A has ball at midfield. On first play, Team A's quarterback, Stone, passes to his teammate, Black, who is tackled at Team B's 41. On the next play, Green runs over guard for two yards to Team B's 39. The yardsticks are moved forward and Team A is credited with a first down by Rushing.

On broken plays where there is a fumble and subsequent recovery, and the advance results in a first down, it shall be considered a first down by rushing.

Example: Passer attempting to pass fumbles. Teammate recovers and advances to first down. Credit team with a first down by rushing.

Example: Punting situation and punter fumbles. He or teammate recovers and advances to first down. Credit first down by rushing.

No first down is recorded on any kickoff, punt, or interception runback, regardless of the distance.

Rushing

All offensive running plays from scrimmage are termed "Rushing" plays.

Rushing yardage gained or lost is measured from the *line of scrimmage* to the point where the ball is declared dead or recovered by an opponent in the case of a fumble.

Example: Ball is at midfield. Green of Team A takes handoff from quarterback and runs off tackle to Team B's 38-yard line, where he is tackled (or run out of bounds). Credit Green (and Team A) with one Rushing attempt and 12 yards under "Rushing." Team A is credited with a first down by Rushing.

Example: Ball is at midfield. Green of Team A takes handoff from quarterback and runs off tackle to Team B's 38-yard line, where he fumbles and the ball bounces to the 35 where it is recovered by Green's teammate (or an opponent). Credit Green (and Team A) with one Rushing attempt and 15 yards under "Rushing." Charge Team A with one fumble and with a fumble recovery. (If the fumble is recovered by an opponent, credit Team B with the fumble recovery.) If the fumble had bounced backwards to the 40-yard line, Green (and Team A) would be credited only with 10 yards under Rushing. Team A is credited with first down by Rushing.

Example: Same situation, but when Green fumbles at Team B's 38, his teammate, Black, picks up the fumble at the 35 and runs to Team B's 30 before he is tackled. Credit Green with *one* Rushing attempt and 15 yards under Rushing. Credit Black with *no* Rushing attempt and 5 yards under Rushing. Credit Team A with *one* Rushing attempt, 20 yards under Rushing and a first down by Rushing. Charge Team A with one fumble and one fumble recovery.

• **Pro ruling:** In the case of a fumble, yardage is measured to where it is fumbled or the point of recovery, whichever is *less,* regardless of which team recovers the fumble. (See Pro Rulings under "Fumbles" in a later section.)

Rushing totals for a player or team is a *net* figure. All rushing losses must be recorded so that rushing totals for a player or team is a net figure (i.e. total yardage gained minus total yardage lost).

Example: In one game, Russell of Team A carries the ball 8 times. In 6 of the attempts, he gains 4,5,8,32,1, and 17 yards for a gross gain of 67 yards. In one other attempt he is held for no gain and in the eighth carry he is thrown for a 3-yard loss. For the game he has 8 carries for a total (net) gain of 64 yards.

Note: The ball carrier is charged for the lost yardage regardless of the reason (fumble, loss of footing, missed block by a teammate, etc.) except in the case of a wild pass from center (charged to team) or on some incomplete laterals (charged to player responsible for incompletion). These exceptions are covered later in this chapter.

Any gain or loss from a lateral pass which started from a rushing play is recorded under rushing yardage.

Example: Ball is at midfield. Brown of Team A takes handoff from his quarterback and runs through guard to the 40-yard line, where he laterals to teammate, Strong, who carries to the 35 before he is tackled. Charge Brown with one Rushing Attempt and 10 yards under Rushing. Charge Strong with *no* Rushing Attempt and 5 yards under Rushing. Team A is credited with one Rushing Attempt and 15 yards under Rushing and a First Down by Rushing.

Example: Same situation, but when Brown reaches the 40, he laterals to Strong, who catches the ball at the 43, where he is tackled.

Charge Brown with one Rushing Attempt and 7 yards under Rushing. Charge Strong with no Rushing Attempts and no yards (Brown threw the ball back to the 37, so he is responsible for the backward movement). Team totals are the same as Brown's.

Example: Same situation. When Brown reaches the 40, he laterals to Strong, who catches the ball on the 43, runs to the 38, then, in trying to avoid a tackler, circles back to the 42 where he is tackled. Charge Brown with one Rushing Attempt and 10 yards under Rushing. Charge Strong with no Rushing Attempt and *minus* two yards under Rushing. (Strong's action was responsible for the backward movement, so he is charged). The total for the two individuals is the same as the team total for the one play—one Rushing Attempt for 8 Rushing yards.

A run from a fake field goal or punt formation is considered a Rushing play.

Rushing statistics tables or rankings include Times Carried Ball (TCB or Plays) or Number of Carries (No.); Gross Yards Gained (YDS or GAIN); Yards Lost (YL); Net Yards Gained (NET or YDS); Average Yards Per Game (Yd.PG); and Touchdowns (TDs). Entries may also be included to show Average Yards Per Carry (Avg.) and the Longest Gain (LG) made on a single play.

Average yards per game is derived by dividing the number of total net yards by the number of games played. Average yards per carry is computed by dividing the total net gain by the number of times the ball was carried.

Players are ranked on Average Net Yards gained Per Game for the number of games actually played.

Example: Smith, in one game, carries the ball six times. He gains 18, 4, 13, and 7 yards in four carries (he scores a touchdown on the fourth carry), fails to gain on the fifth and loses 3 yards on the sixth attempt. He has gained 42 gross yards, with 3 yards lost, for a net gain of 39 yards. His average gain per carry is 6.5 (39 yards divided by 6 plays).

Player, Team	TCB	GAIN	LOST	NET	AVG.	TDs	LG
Smith, Central	6	42	3	39	6.5	1	18

The preceding example is for one game. On a cumulative basis (for two or more games), a column should be added for Games (G) and Average Yards Per Game (Yd.PG).

Example: For the season, Smith plays in eight of his team's ten games. These figures might represent his season's performance.

Player, Team	G	TCB	GAIN	LOST	NET	TDs	LG	Yd.PG
Smith, Central	8	87	513	19	494	6	31	61.8*

*The 61.8 Yards Per Game average derived from dividing 494 (yards) by 8 (games).

Note: For purposes of statistics rankings, a player is charged with a game if he is in the game for at least one play. Thus, if a player misses two games in a 10-game season, he is charged with only 8 games in the statistics rankings. Normally, to qualify for the rankings or statistical championships, a player is expected to be in the lineup for a minimum of 75 percent of his team's games.

The examples listed show the style for maintaining permanent records of a player and team in Rushing. When listing Rushing statistics for distribution to news media, it is usually practical to provide only abbreviated statistics (special forms for summarizing statistics will be shown later in this chapter).

Space available by the newspaper will dictate how abbreviated to make the report, but the columns in the following example should be included when possible.

Player, Team	G	NET	Yd.PG
Smith, Central High	8	494	61.8

As space allows, add, in order, TDs (6), TCB (87), and LG (31). The statistics for Gross Yardage Gained and Yards Lost are of interest mostly in compiling a list of the season's "highs" and in compiling all-time records.

• **Pro Ruling:** Rushing leaders in professional football are ranked on Total Number of Net Yards Gained, regardless of the number of games played by the individual. Professional players are ranked only against other players in their own league, thus each team plays the same number of games. Some college conferences still retain this ranking system; however, on a nationwide basis, Average Yards Per Game is a better comparison because of the wide disparity in number of games played each season by various teams.

Forward Passing

Forward passing gains or losses are measured from the *line of scrimmage* to the point where the ball is declared dead or recovered by an opponent in the event of a fumble.

Yardage includes the length of the pass plus or minus the yards gained or lost by the receiver after the completion. The total yardage credited to the passer and to the receiver(s) is identical.

Example: Team A has the ball at midfield. Smith of Team A passes to Brown, who catches the ball on Team B's 30-yard line and runs to the 15 before he is tackled. Smith is credited with one pass attempt, one completion and 35 yards under Passing. Brown is credited with one Pass Reception and 35 yards under Pass Receiving. Team totals are one attempt, one completion, 35 yards under Passing and one First Down by Passing.

Example: Same situation. Smith of Team A passes from midfield to Brown, who catches the ball on Team B's 30, circles back to avoid a tackler, and is downed on the 35. Smith (and Team A) is credited with one pass attempt, one completion and 15 yards under Passing. Brown is credited with one pass reception and 15 yards under Pass Receiving. Team totals include one First Down by Passing.

If a forward pass is completed and the receiver is downed behind the line the scrimmage, the passer is credited with an attempt and completion and *minus* yardage under Passing. The receiver is credited with one pass reception and *minus* yardage under Pass Receiving.

Example: Team A has the ball on Team B's 30-yard line. Mobley drops back to the 40 and passes to King, who is downed on the 35. Credit Mobley (and Team A) with one pass attempted, one pass completed and *minus* 5 yards under Passing. Credit King with one pass reception and *minus* 5 yards under Pass Receiving.

If a deflected or batted pass by a defender is caught by the passer, credit the passer with one pass attempt, one completion (to himself) and passing yardage gained or lost.

Example: Ball on Team B's 30. Mobley of Team A passes, but it is batted back by Team B and caught by Mobley on Team B's 35 where he is downed. Credit Mobley (and Team A) with one pass attempt, one completion and minus 5 yards under passing.

On pass interference penalties, there are *no* statistics recorded under Passing or Receiving. It is a *penalty* charged against the defending team and yardage and first down are credited under Penalties. The passer is *not* charged with an attempt, a completion, or yards gained, and the receiver, or player interfered with, is *not* credited with a pass reception or yardage.

The passing team is credited only with a first down by penalty, the defensive team is charged with one penalty, and the distance from the line of scrimmage to the spot of the infraction is recorded under Yards Penalized. (In most high school leagues, the penalty for pass interference is 15 yards from the line of scrimmage.)

Note: Occasionally, an official signals an interference penalty, but the receiver still catches the ball. In this case, the play takes precedence over the penalty and both individual and team statistics are recorded under Passing and Pass Receiving. In such cases where the distance gained is not sufficient for a first down, the passing team may take the option of the penalty because it includes the first down at the spot of the infraction. In this case, do *not* record passing statistics.

A passer is charged with a pass attempt (no completion and no yards) when it is ruled he intentionally grounded the ball (the penalty includes loss of down and the pass attempt accounts for this down). *Example:* Team A has ball on Team B's 30-yard line. Hall fades back to pass and at the 39, intentionally grounds a pass. A five-yard penalty is assessed against Team A (from Team B's 39 to the 44). Charge Hall with one pass attempted, no completions and no yardage. Charge Team A with one penalty and 14 yards Lost by Penalty (the penalty is from the spot of the foul, but penalty yardage is measured from the line of scrimmage, from the 30 to the 44).

When a player apparently is planning to pass, but is downed behind the line of scrimmage before he throws the ball, the play is recorded as a *Rushing* play and the loss is entered as loss by Rushing. He is not a passer *until* he throws the ball; thus he is charged with a rushing attempt and the yardage lost by Rushing.

• **Pro Ruling:** This is a separate, special category in professional statistics: Yards Lost Attempting to Pass (YLAP). The individual passer is *not* charged with the attempted pass, nor for yardage lost. However, the yardage lost on such plays *must* be deducted from his *team's* gross passing yardage to reflect the actual net yards gained from Passing plays.

Thus, in listing individual passers, an entry must be made for "Team" to reflect Yards Lost Attempting to Pass. In this way, the total of the individual entries will equal the team totals.

Example: These are the actual statistics for the Dallas Cowboys in the 1972 NFL season.

PASSER	ATT	COMP	YARDS	YLAP	NET YDS
Morton	339	185	2,396	–	2,396
Staubach	20	9	98	–	98
Hill	3	1	55	–	55
Montgomery	3	1	31	–	31
Reeves	2	0	0	–	0
Team				31/238##	–238
Totals	367	196	2,580	31/238##	2,342

##The Dallas passers were thrown 31 times and had a total of 238 Yards Lost Attempting to Pass.

Any gain or loss from a lateral pass which started from a passing play is recorded under Passing Yardage.

Example: Ball is midfield. Brown of Team A fades back and passes to his teammate, Strong, on Team B's 38-yard line. Strong runs to the 35, then laterals to another teammate, Harris, who runs to the Team B 30-yard line, where he runs out of bounds. Credit Brown (and Team A) with one pass attempt, one completion and 20 yards under Passing. Credit Strong with one pass reception and 15 yards under Pass Receiving. Credit Harris with *no* pass reception and 5 yards under Pass Receiving. Credit Team A with one First Down by Passing.

Passing statistics include Attempts (ATT), Completions (COMP), Interceptions (INT), Percentage of Completions (Pct), Net Yards Gained (YDS), Touchdown Passes (TDs), and Average Number of Completions Per Game (CM.PG). Longest Gain (LG) also is sometimes recorded.

To determine Percentage of Completions, divide the number of completions by the number of attempts. For instance, Smith attempts 22 passes and completes 14. The percentage of completions (14 divided by 22) is .636.

Passers are ranked by Average Number of Completions Per Game. To qualify for the Passing championship, a player normally should play in at least 75 percent of his team's games.

Example: Smith throws 22 passes, completes 14, has 2 intercepted, gains 180 yards and two of the completions go for touchdowns. Longest completed pass is for 38 yards.

Player, Team	ATT	COMP	INT	PCT	YDS	TDs	LG
Smith, Central	22	14	2	.636	180	2	38

On a cumulative basis, columns should be added for Games (G), and for Average Number of Completions Per Game (CM.PG). An example of final statistics for Smith might look like the following:

Player, Team	G	ATT	COMP	INT	PCT	YDS	TDs	LG	CM.PG
Smith, Central	9	233	121	12	.519	1481	14	64	13.4

This style provides complete statistics for maintaining permanent records. However, when listing Passing statistics for news media, it is usually practical to list only abbreviated figures, because of space limitations. (Special forms for summarizing statistics will be shown later in this chapter.)

Depending upon the space available and style used at the newspapers, these statistics should be provided at a minimum:

Player, Team	ATT	COMP	INT	CM. PG.
Smith, Central	233	121	12	13.4

As space permits, add TDs (14), YDS (1481), LG (64) and Pct. (.519)

• **Pro Ruling:** Also used are Percentage of Interceptions (number of interceptions divided by the number of passes), Percentage of TD passes (number of touchdown passes, divided by the number of passing attempts), and Average Gain Per Attempt (net passing yardage divided by total passes *attempted*).

• **Pro Ruling:** Rather than on number of completions per game, pros rank passers on an involved formula combining the comparative rankings in four categories—Percentage of Completions, Percentage of TD Passes, Percentage of Interceptions and Average Yards Gained Per Attempt.

Prior to 1973, each NFL passer was ranked numerically in comparison with other passers in the league in each of these four categories. On that basis, the passer with the fewest points was the champion.

In 1973, the method of ranking passers was changed to a tabular system in which each passer is awarded rating points (devised from arbitrary tables) on his exact statistical performance in each of these categories, and the player with the *most* points is the champion.

The arbitrary tables are much like decathlon tables, with an absolute value assigned for every practical statistical performance. The major advantage of the new system is that it provides a means to readily compare passing performances with those of other years, or those in other league divisions.

In this system, each passer is *rated individually against a pre-fixed standard performance* in each of the four categories. The base standard approximates very closely the *average statistical performances* of all passers in the National and American Football Leagues for the 13-year period from 1960 through 1972. The base performance represents a 1.000 rating in any category.

Illustration A	Pct. Comp.	Pct. TD	Pct. Int.	Avg. Yds.
13-year Average, 160-172	50.2	4.97	5.67	7.01
Base Performance (1.000 rating)	50.0	5.0	5.5	7.00

To earn a 2.000 rating in any category, a passer must perform to *approximately record levels*, as Illustration B will show:

Illustration B	Pct. Comp.	Pct. TD	Pct. Int.	Avg. Yds.
Record Season Performance	70.3	10.2	1.2	11.17
Performance to earn 2,000 rating	70.0	10.0	1.5	11.00

The *highest point rating* that can be earned *in any category* is 2.375. In the percentage of interceptions category, this would occur if a passer had a 0.0 interception percentage. In the other three categories, this point rating may be earned by a performance *well in excess of the record* for a full season as the following table will show.

Illustration C	Pct. Comp.	Pct. TD	Pct. Int.	Avg. Gain/Pass
Record Season Performance	70.3	10.2	1.2	11.17
Performance to earn 2.375 rating	77.5	11.9	0.0	12.50

Conversely, the *lowest point rating* that can be assessed *in any category* is 0.0000. In the percentage of touchdowns category, this would occur if a passer had a 0.0 percentage of touchdowns. In the other three categories, this will occur when a passer reaches a standard far below the normal range of performance as the following table will show.

Illustration D	Pct. Comp.	Pct. TD	Pct. Int.	Avg. Gain/Pass
Performance to earn 0.000 rating	30.0	0.0	9.5	3.00

Summary of Illustrations A Through D

Category	Season Record	12-year Average	2.375 Perfor	2.000 Perfor	1.000 Perfor	0.000 Perfor
Pct. Comp.	70.3	50.2	77.5	70.0	50.0	30.0
Pct. TD	10.2	4.97	11.9	10.0	5.0	0.0
Pct. Int.	1.2	5.67	0.0	1.5	5.5	9.5
Avg. Gain	11.17	7.01	12.50	11.00	7.0	3.0

Computing the Point Rating Upon Which Leaders Will Be Determined

To compute the final point rating under the new system, the points earned in each of the four categories *are totalled and then converted to a 1.000 scale*. To do this, divide the sum of the points in the four categories by 6.000.

For instance, a passer performing to exact base standards in each of the four categories would earn a total of 4.000 points (1.000+1.000+1.000+1.000). A 6.000 total on the conversion scale converts to 100.0 points. Thus, a passer with a 4.000 rating total would have a converted final rating of 66.7 (4.000÷6.000=66.7).

It is possible to go over 100.0 points on the scale, particularly in short-term situations. Checking back through the NFL and AFL leaders starting in 1932, however, there have been only six players who have surpassed a 100.0 point rating score for a full season's plaay.

The NFL has tables showing the exact point rating for any specific performance in any of the four categories. A fifth table enables the statistician to convert the rating point totals to a scale of 100.0. However, if rating tables are not available, rating points can be computed by the statistician using the partial tables in Forms FB-1 through FB-4.

These tables show the first progression of points, then points at various intervals. The arithmetic progression in each table is consistent throughout the table, so that one can easily compute the actual point ratings for any performance. Then, the points for each division are added and the sum divided by 6.000 to determine the rating score.

Example: In 1972, Earl Morrall of Miami had a 55.3 percentage of completions, 7.3 percentage of TD's, 4.7 percentage of interceptions, and his passes averaged 9.07 yards per attempt. Consulting the forms, the rating points can be determined by extrapolation.

For percentage of completions, the 55.3 of Morrall should be broken down into components that will correspond to those in Form FB-1. This would be 55.0 plus 0.3.

In computing the progressions of points 0.3 actually is 30.3 in the table because the progressions start at 30.0 and not at 00.0. Thus, adding 1.250 (for 55%) plus .015 (0.3%) gives a total of 1.265 rating points for percentage of completions.

Morrall's percentage of TD's was 7.3, and consulting Form FB-2, we see that 7.0 is 1.400 and 0.3 is 0.060 for a total of 1.460 rating points in this category.

Percentage of Interceptions must be handled differently. It will be noted in Form FB-3 that the rating decreases 0.025 for each 0.1 increase in percentage. Thus Morrall's 4.7% (4.0 and 0.7) is coverted to 1.375 rating points (4.0) *minus* 0.175 (7 x 0.25). Thus, he has 1.200 rating points.

Morrall's average gain per pass was 9.07. Form FB-4 shows that his rating points are 1.500 (for 9.0) plus .018 (for .07) for a total of 1.518 in this category. Because the rating table starts at 3.0, in actual progressions 3.07 in the table is considered 0.7 for purposes of computation.

To recap, Morrall was credited with 1.265 plus 1.460 plus 1.200 for 1.518, respectively, for the four categories. The sum of these four (5.443) is divided by 6.000 to give the rating score of 90.7 for his season's performance.

Form FB-1

Percentage of Completions	
30.0	0.000
30.1	0.005
30.2	0.010
30.3	0.015
30.4	0.020
30.5	0.025
30.6	0.030
30.7	0.035
30.8	0.040
30.9	0.045
31.0	0.050
35.0	0.250
40.0	0.500
45.0	0.750
50.0	1.000
55.0	1.250
60.0	1.500
65.0	1.750
70.0	2.000
75.0	2.250
77.5 and over	2.375

Form FB-2

Percentage of Completions	
0.0	0.000
0.1	0.020
0.2	0.040
0.3	0.060
0.4	0.080
0.5	0.100
0.6	0.120
0.7	0.140
0.8	0.160
0.9	0.180
1.0	0.200
2.0	0.400
3.0	0.600
4.0	0.800
5.0	1.000
6.0	1.200
7.0	1.400
8.0	1.600
9.0	1.800
10.0	2.000
11.0	2.200
11.9 and over	2.375

Form FB-3

Percentage of Compeltions	
0.0	2.375
0.1	2.350
0.2	2.325
0.3	2.300
0.4	2.275
0.5	2.250
0.6	2.225
0.7	2.200
0.8	2.175
0.9	2.150
1.0	2.125
2.0	1.875
3.0	1.625
4.0	1.375
5.0	1.125
5.5	1.000
6.0	0.875
7.0	0.625
8.0	0.375
9.0	0.125
9.5 and over	0.000

Form FB-4

Average Gain Per Pass	
3.00	0.000
3.01	0.003
3.02	0.005
3.03	0.008
3.04	0.010
3.05	0.013
3.06	0.015
3.07	0.018
3.08	0.020
3.09	0.023
3.10	0.025
3.20	0.050
3.30	0.075
3.40	0.100
3.50	0.125
3.60	0.150
3.70	0.175
3.80	0.200
3.90	0.225
4.00	0.250
5.00	0.500
6.00	0.750
7.00	1.000
8.00	1.250
9.00	1.750
10.00	1.750
11.00	2.000
12.00	2.250
12.50 and over	2.375

Example: At the end of the 1972 National Football League season, these were the actual statistics in the four categories involved for the National Conference leaders in passing:

	Pct. Comp.	Pct. TD	Pct. Int.	Avg. Yds. Gnd.	Points
Morral (AFC)	55.3	7.3	4.7	9.07	90.7
Kilmer (NFC)	54.3	8.4	4.9	7.32	84.6
Snead (NFC)	60.3	5.2	3.7	7.10	83.8
Lamonica (AFC)	53.0	6.4	4.3	7.00	79.3
Tarkenton (NFC)	58.0	4.9	3.5	7.15	82.0
Domres (AFC)	51.8	5.0	2.7	6.27	76.8
Spurrier (NFC)	54.6	6.7	5.9	7.37	76.1
Berry (NFC)	55.6	4.7	4.3	7.79	78.6

Pass Receiving

All statistics in Pass Receiving must correspond in number, yardage and touchdowns with statistics for Passing for either a game or season. That is, every time there is an individual (and team) entry for a pass completed, a Passing yard gained or lost or a touchdown scored by Passing, there must be a corresponding individual (and team) entry for a Pass Reception, a Pass Receiving yard gained or lost and touchdown by Pass Receiving.

The interpretations and examples in the preceding section of this chapter on Passing cover every situation governing Pass Receiving statistics. Pass Receiving statistics include Number of Games Played (G), Number of Passes Caught (NO. or CGHT), Yards Gained (YDS), Touchdown Passes Caught (TDs), and Number of Passes Caught Per Game (CT.PG). Longest Gain (LG) also is sometimes recorded.

Pass receivers are ranked on the Number of Passes Caught Per Game. To qualify for a league or national championship, a player should play in at least 75 percent of his team's games.

Example: Here is a typical season's record for a pass receiver:

Player, Team	G	CGHT	YDS	TDs	LG	CT.PG
Allen, Central High	9	48	699	4	72	5.3

• **Pro ruling:** Again, because professional teams have the same number of games scheduled for players being compared statistically, rankings are based on *total number* of passes caught for the season or for the period covered by the statistical ranking.

Interceptions

Interception returns are measured from the point where the player gains control of the ball after interception to the point where the ball is declared dead or recovered by an opponent in the case of a fumble.

If the interception is in the end zone, return yardage is measured from the goal line.

Example: Ross intercepts a pass on his own 40, circles to his 35 and is tackled. Charge passer (and his team) with one attempt and one interception under Passing. Credit Ross (and his team) with one pass interception and *minus* 5 yards under Interception Returns.

Example: Same situation, except that Ross, after circling back to his 35, then returns to the 45 before he is tackled. Same statistics, except Ross (and his team) is credited with 5 yards under Interception Returns.

Example: Ross of Team B intercepts a Team A pass in the end zone and does not attempt to run it out. The ball is put in play on Team B's 20. Charge passer (and Team A) with one pass attempt and one interception under Passing. Credit Ross (and Team B) with one interception and no yards under Interception Returns.

Example: Ross intercepts ball five yards into the end zone and runs it out to Team B's 15-yard line. Same statistics for Team A and its passer. Credit Ross (and Team B) with one interception and 15 yards (from goal line to where he is downed) under Interception Returns.

• **Pro Ruling:** If the interception occurs in the end zone, the yardage is measured from the point of interception, including end zone yardage.

Example: In a game between the San Francisco 49ers and the Minnesota Vikings, Taylor of the 49ers intercepts a pass (thrown by Tarkenton of the Vikings) four yards into the 49er end zone and runs it back to the 49er 23-yard line. Charge Tarkenton (and the Vikings) with one pass attempt and one interception under Passing. Credit Taylor (and the 49ers) with one pass interception and 27 yards under Interception Returns.

Any gain or loss from a lateral pass which started from an interception is recorded under Interception Return yardage.

Example: Ross intercepts a pass on the goal line and returns it 10 yards, where he laterals to Lane, who continues to the 18 before he is tackled. Ross is credited with one interception and 10 yards under Interception Returns. Lane is credited with *no* interception and 8 yards under Interception Returns. Their team is credited with one interception and 18 yards under Interception Returns.

Fumbles which are recovered in the air are considered interceptions and all attempts and yardage are recorded under Interceptions. This means, then, there can be more Interceptions *by* a team than the total number of Interceptions of forward passes thrown by its opponents.

•**Pro Ruling:** Fumbles recovered in air are recorded as "Fumbles" and any return yardage recorded as "Fumble Yardage."

Statistics for Interceptions show the Games (G), Number of Interceptions (NO); Yards Returned (YDS); number returned for Touchdowns (TDs) and Average Number of Interceptions Per Game (I.PG). The Longest Return or Gain (LG) also may be listed.

Example:

Player, Team	G	NO	YDS	TDs	LG	I.PG
Smith, Central	8	6	74	2	32	0.75

Players are ranked on the Average Number of Interceptions Per Game (I.PG).

• **Pro Ruling:** Players are ranked on the total *number* of interceptions. Again, this is practical, because all teams have the same number of games scheduled.

Lateral Passes

A lateral pass is a backward pass or one that travels parallel to the line of scrimmage.

A lateral pass is always considered an extension of the original play. Thus a lateral pass during a Rushing play is considered part of the original Rushing play; one which occurs during a Passing play is considered part of the Passing play, etc.

The receiver of a lateral is given credit for the yardage he gains, from the point where he *receives* the ball, but is *not* given an attempt, return or reception on the play (because only one individual and one team attempt can be recorded for one play).

Example: Ball is at midfield. Steele of Team A runs 15 yards to the 35 where he laterals to Morris, who takes the ball on the 39 and runs to Team B's 24 before he is downed. Credit Steele with one rushing attempt and 11 yards (50 to the 39) under Rushing. Credit Morris with *no* Rushing attempt and 15 yards (39 to the 24) under Rushing. Credit Team A with one rushing attempt, 26 yards under Rushing, and a first down by Rushing.

Example: Team A's ball at midfield. Hall passes to Steele at Team B's 33 where he laterals to Morris, who takes the ball on the 33 and runs to the 20. Credit Hall and Team A with one pass attempt. Credit Steele with one pass reception and 17 yards (50 to 33) under Pass Receiving. Credit Morris with *no* pass reception and 13 yards (33 to 20) under Pass Receiving. Credit Team A with one passing attempt, one completion, 30 yards under passing and one First Down By Passing.

Example: Team A's ball at Team B's 40. Hall drops back to midfield and passes to Steele at the 42, and he laterals to Morris, who takes the ball on the 43 and is tackled on the 45. Credit Hall (and Team A) with one pass attempt, one completion, and *minus* 5 yards by passing. Credit Steele with one pass reception for *minus* 3 yards. Credit Morris with *no* pass reception for *minus* 2 yards.

Example: Team B kicks off to Team A. Hall of Team A takes ball on his goal line, runs to the 10 where he hands off or laterals to Smith, who takes ball on the 10 and runs to the 30 before he is tackled. Credit Team A with one kickoff return and 30 yards under Kickoff Returns. Credit Hall with one kickoff return and 10 yards under Kickoff Returns. Credit Smith with *no* Kickoff Return and 20 yards under Kickoff Returns.

Example: Same situation. Hall runs to the 10, hands off or laterals to Smith, who takes the ball on the 10 and circles to the 8 where he is downed. Credit Team A with one kickoff return for 8 yards. Credit Hall with one kickoff return for 10 yards and credit Hall with *no* kickoff return for *minus* 2 yards.

A handoff or pitchout behind the line of scrimmage is not regarded, statistically, as a lateral pass. That is, there are no statistics recorded for the quarterback or other player who originated the handoff or pitchout. Similarly, when a player receives a kick and makes no real effort to advance before he laterals or hands off to a teammate, do not record any statistics for him. Charge the attempt and yardage to the player to whom he laterals or hands off the ball.

Example: Ball at midfield. Hall of Team A takes the snap from center and hands off to Steele, who runs over guard for two yards. There are *no* statistical entries for Hall. Credit Steele (and Team A) with one rushing attempt and two yards under Rushing.

Example: Team A's ball at midfield. As quarterback Hall starts to call signals, his fullback, Steele, goes in motion toward the sideline. Hall takes the snap and pitches out to Steele (still behind the line of scrimmage), who goes around end to the Team B 44. There are *no* statistical entries for Hall. Credit Steele (and Team A) with one rushing attempt and six yards under rushing.

Example: Team A's ball on Team B's 40-yard line. Quarterback Hall takes snap from center, and throws overhand lateral pass to his flanker, Green, who is standing on the Team B 47-yard line. Green then throws a pass to Steele on Team B's 30 yard line, where he is tackled. There are *no* statistics for Hall. Credit Green (and Team A) with one pass attempt, one completion and 10 yards (40 to 30) under Passing. Credit Steele with one pass reception and 10 yards under Pass Receiving.

When a pitchout occurs on an option play, the position of the player *receiving* the pitchout determines the manner of scoring. If he is still behind the line of scrimmage, ignore (statistically) the quarterback or other player making the pitchout lateral. If the quarterback has penetrated beyond the line of scrimmage, then *both* players are involved in the statistics on the play.

Example: Team A's ball on Team B's 40-yard line. Quarterback Hall takes the snap from center and runs parallel behind the line of scrimmage and as he is checked by the defense, pitches out to Steele, who takes the ball on the 43 and runs forward to Team B's 37-yard line. There are *no* statistics for Hall. Credit Steele (and Team A) with one rushing attempt and three yards Rushing.

Example: Team A's ball on Team B's 40-yard line. Quarterback Hall takes the snap from center and runs parallel behind the line of scrimmage, then turns downfield and runs to Team B's 36-yard line, where he pitches out to Steele at the 39. Steele runs to Team B's 32 before he is downed. In this case, because Steele was *beyond* the line of scrimmage when he received the pitchout lateral, credit Hall with one rushing attempt and *one* yard under Rushing (Hall gets credit only from line of scrimmage to the point where Steele *received* the pitchout lateral). Credit Steele with *no* rushing attempt and 7 yards under Rushing. Credit Team A with one rushing attempt for 8 yards under Rushing.

Incomplete laterals (including pitchouts) are scored as fumbles and yards lost are charged against the player who, in the scorer's judgment, was responsible for the failure of the pass.

Example: Team A's ball on its own 40. Hall pitches out to Smith, but throws over his head and Smith falls on the ball on A's 30. Record one rushing attempt and *minus* 10 yards for Hall under Rushing. Charge Team A with same statistics and also with one fumble, not lost.

Example: Same situation, but scorer rules the pitchout was accurate enough for Smith to handle, but he fumbled it. In this case, Smith is charged with the attempt and yards lost.

Intercepted lateral passes are treated as fumbles and any yardage gained or lost following the interception is credited under Interception Returns (see previous section on Interceptions).

Example: Team A's ball at midfield. Wilson runs off tackle to Team B's 42, where he laterals to a teammate, but Morgan of Team B intercepts on his own 45 and is downed at midfield. Credit Wilson (and Team A) with one rushing attempt and 5 yards (50 to 45) under Rushing. Charge Team A with one fumble lost. Credit Morgan with one interception (fumble) and 5 yards (45 to 50) under Interception Returns.

• **Pro Ruling:** Intercepted lateral passes are treated as Fumble Returns with yardage under Fumble Returns in the proper category (see professional football interpretations under ''Fumbles'' in later section).

The official statistician rules on whether a *completed* pass to a flanker or man in motion is a forward or lateral pass. If the pass is incomplete, the subsequent action of the officials will reveal whether it was a forward or lateral pass. (They will return the ball to the original line of scrimmage, if the incompleted pass was forward. If a lateral pass, the officials will do nothing, because the ball is live and still in play.)

However, if the pass is complete, the official statistician must rule whether it is a forward (Passing play) or lateral (Rushing play). He should be governed to some extent by the probable intent of the play and, as he becomes familiar with coaching styles, the statistician ordinarily will know whether it is designed to be a passing or running play. As a rule of thumb, in modern football, the pass toward the sidelines to the wide receiver or man in motion generally is interpreted, statistically, as a Passing play.

There are, of course, no statistical rankings under lateral passes because they all are components or extensions of the original play. These, then, are entered under the proper category—Rushing, Passing, etc.

Total Offense

Total offense is the total of net yards gained *Rushing and Passing* only, and does not include yardage gained by pass receiving or runbacks.

Example: In one game, halfback Wilson runs the ball 6 times for 42 net yards, passes 3 times (completing 2) for 23 net yards, catches 2 passes for 18 yards and returns one punt for 11 yards. His (and his team's) Total Offense is 9 plays (6 Rushing and 3 Passing) for 65 yards (42 plus 23). Plays and yardage for pass receiving and punt returns are not included.

Tables for Total Offense rankings include Rushing Plays (ATT. or NO. RUSH), Rushing Yards (RUSH), Passing plays (ATT or NO. PASS), Passing Yards (PASS), Total Yards (TOTAL), Touchdowns (TDs) or Touchdowns Responsible For—total of touchdowns scored and touchdown passes thrown (TDR), and Average Gain Per Game (Avg. Per Game or Yd.PG). For record purposes, keep an additional entry, Average Gain Per Play (Avg. Per Play).

A simplified form, however, is combined total of Rushing and Passing Plays (PLAYS), combined total of net Rushing and Passing Yards (YDS), and Touchdowns (TDs).

Example: Smith throws 14 passes, completes 10 for 108 yards and one touchdown and rushes 4 times for 46 yards, including one touchdown run.

	Rushing		Passing		Net	Avg.		
Name, Team	PLAYS	YDS	PLAYS	YDS	YDS.	GAIN	TDs or	TDR
Smith, Central	4	46	14	108	154	8.6	1	2

Simplified Version

Name, Team	PLAYS	YARDS	TDs
Smith, Central	18	154	1

Total Offense is ranked on average number of Total Offense Yards Per Game (Avg. PG). A player should play in at least 75 percent of his team's games to qualify for the championship.

Example: For a season, Smith's totals might look like this:

Player, Team	G	PLAYS	YDS	TDs	Yd.PG
Smith, Central	9	345	1687	11	187.4

Punts

Punts are measured from the *line of scrimmage* to the point where the receiving team first gains or loses *possession* of the ball or, if untouched by the receiving team, to the point where the ball is downed by the kicking team, is declared dead or goes out of bounds. (Note the word "possession." This is not necessarily the point where the receiving team first *touches* the ball, but where an individual gains physical control of the ball. Stated differently, it is where the impetus of the punt ends.)

Example: Ball at midfield. Arnold of Team A stands at his own 37, takes snap from center and punts to the Team B 15, where Rose catches the ball and runs to his 23 and is tackled. Credit Arnold (and Team A) with one punt of 35 yards (50 to the 15). Credit Rose (and Team B) with one punt return of 8 yards.

Example: Same situation. Rose takes the punt on the 15 and, in trying to elude tacklers, circles back to his own 8 yard line, then heads upfield and is tackled on the 12. Credit Arnold (and Team A) with one punt and 35 yards as before (Rose controlled the ball on the 15). Credit Rose (and Team B) with one punt return for *minus* 3 yards (15 to the 12).

Example: Same situation. This time Rose is standing on his own 25. When Arnold kicks, it goes over Rose's head. Rose retreats and gets one hand on the ball at the 15, but it bounces back to Team B's 8, where Rose picks it up and returns to the 12 before he is tackled. Credit Arnold (and Team A) with one punt for 42 yards (50 to the

8) and credit Rose (and Team B) with one punt return for 4 yards (8 to the 12).

Example: Same situation. Rose catches the punt on his own 10 and circles back to the end zone, where he is tackled for a safety (two points). Credit Arnold (and Team A) with one punt for 40 yards (50 to 10). Credit Rose (and Team B) with one punt return and *minus* 10 yards (10 to the goal line).

Note: In the event of a palpable fumble as the player attempts to catch the punt, the punt is measured to the point of the fumble, and the punt return is also measured from the point of the fumble.

Touchbacks are not deducted from the yardage of punts. If a punt goes over the goal line into the end zone, it is measured from the line of scrimmage to the goal line.

Loss from an unblocked punt that does not reach the line of scrimmage is *minus* yardage charged against the punter and the punting team.

A blocked punt is recorded as a "Team" entry and not charged against the individual punter. In the case of a blocked punt which does not pass the line of scrimmage, charge the *team* (not an individual) with one punt for *no* yards.

Example: In one game, Brown of Team A punts 3 times for 35, 38, and 40 yards. His fourth is blocked. Credit brown with 3 punts for 113 yards (37.7 average). Credit Team A (under the listing of individuals) with 1 punt for zero yards. For the Team Totals, Team A has 4 punts for a total of 113 yards (28.3 average).

• **Pro Ruling:** On a blocked punt, charge the *individual* (and team) kicker with a blocked punt and no yards.

If a kick is blocked and the ball travels toward the *kicker's* goal and is recovered by the *blocking* team, the yardage is treated as a punt return by the player who blocked the kick. Yardage for the punt return is measured from the line of scrimmage.

If the ball travels toward the kicker's goal and is recovered by the *kicking* team, the kicking *team* is charged with one punt for zero yardage. The yardage from the line of scrimmage to recovery is treated as a punt return by the player who blocked the kick, and the blocking team is charged with a fumble lost, except on fourth down (when possession reverts to Team B).

Example: Team A's ball on its own 40. Seymour's punt is blocked by Kay, who falls on the ball on Team A's 25. Charge Team A (not Seymour) with a blocked punt of zero yards. Credit Kay with one Punt Return of 15 yards.

Example: Same situation, but when Kay blocks the ball, his teammate, Richards, picks up the ball at the 25 and runs into the end zone for a touchdown. Again, charge Team A with one punt for zero yards and credit Kay with one punt return for 15 yards (40 to 25). Also, credit Richards with *no* punt return, but for 25 yards under Punt Returns, and a touchdown.

Example: Team A has the ball on its own 20 on third down. Seymour's punt is blocked by Kay of Team B, but Seymour (of Team A) falls on it at his own five-yard line. Charge Team A with one blocked punt; credit Kay with one return and 15 yards under Punt Returns. Charge Team B with one fumble lost.

• **Pro Ruling:** Players blocking punts are *not* credited with punt returns. The player and the yardage are noted only on the official score sheet under "remarks."

When a blocked punt is recovered by a player on the kicking team and the ball is advanced beyond the line of scrimmage, yardage gained is treated as "miscellaneous," for which there is no statistical entry except on Working Chart B (see later section on Work Sheets) or NFL official score sheets.

Exception: If the blocked punt is recovered by a player on the kicking team and he immediately punts again, charge the normal statistics of a blocked punt and credit a punt attempt and yardage to the player who punts.

Example: Team A has ball on its own 40-yard line. Seymour's punt is blocked by Kay and it bounds to Team A's 25-yard line, where Seymour picks it up and immediately punts again. Charge Team A (not Seymour) with a blocked punt of *no* yards. Credit Team B's Kay with a punt return of 15 yards and Team B with a fumble lost. Credit Seymour with one punt (from the 25) and the appropriate yardage under Punting.

When a player fumbles on an apparent punting play, then runs or passes (or if a teammate picks up the fumble and runs or passes), enter the attempt and yardage gained or lost under the appropriate category (Rushing or Passing).

• **Pro Ruling:** In this situation, any yardage gained or lost is scored as fumble yardage (see Pro Rulings under Fumbles).

Partially blocked punts are recorded as blocked punts if, in the scorer's opinion, the distance of the kick is materially affected.

• **Pro Ruling:** A partially blocked punt which travels beyond the line of scrimmage is *not* a blocked punt.

Punting statistics tables include Number of Punts (NO), Total Yardage of Punts (YDs), Average Yards Per Punt (AVG)—derived by dividing total punting yards by number of punts, Punts Blocked (Blkd), and, if desired, Longest Punt (Lng).

Players are ranked (for one game or a season) on highest average yards per punt.

Example: Seymour of Central High punts four times in one game. One is blocked and his other three go 35, 38, and 40 yards.

Player, Team	NO	YDS	AVG	Blkd	Lng
Seymour, Central	3	113	37.7	0	40
Team (or Central High)	1	0	0.0	1	0
Totals	4	113	28.3	1	40

Punt Returns

As noted in the section on punting, the distance of a Punt Return is measured from the point at which the impetus of the punt ends and the receiver is able to initiate forward progress.

It should be noted that when a receiver is required to run back toward his own goal line in order to field a punt, the point of measurement where the punt ends and the punt return starts is where he is able to *control* the ball and his body in order to initiate forward progress.

A player may be credited with minus yardage on a punt return when, in the opinion of the scorer, he moved backward on his own initiative and not because of the impetus of the punts. For examples of Punt Returns, see examples in previous section on Punting.

Only the number of punts which the receiving team actually attempts to return are included under Punt Returns (except, of course, blocked punts which travel toward the kicker's goal).

Under this ruling, there are *no* Punt Returns on fair catches or punts that go out of bounds, are touched down by the kicking team or roll dead. On a fair catch, if a player fumbles the ball, he is not charged with a Punt Return, but his team is charged with a fumble.

• **Pro Ruling:** A player who signals for, and safely makes, a fair catch is not credited with a Punt Return, but is credited with a Fair Catch. (In pro statistics, there is a special category for number of Fair Catches.) If, however, he fumbles or in another manner loses possession, he is charged with a Punt Return and a fumble.

The return of an attempted field goal, which is blocked or falls short and is returned by the defending team, is recorded as a Punt Return. The attempted field goal is not recorded as a punt, however (see Field Goals).

• **Pro Ruling:** Return by a defensive player of a blocked or unsuccessful field goal attempt is *not* recorded under Punt Returns, but listed only under "Remarks" on the pro score sheet.

Any gain or loss from a lateral pass which started from a Punt Return play is recorded under Punt Return yardage.

Punt Return statistical tables include Games (G), Number (NO), Yards (YDS), Average (Avg)—derived by dividing total punt return Yards by the total number of Punt Returns, Touchdowns (TDs), and, if desired, Longest (Lng.)

Player, Team	NO	YDS	AVG	TDs	LNG
Smith, Central High	3	42	14.0	0	21

Players are ranked by average yards per punt return. To qualify for championship, a player should have a minimum of 1.5 Punt Returns per game.

Kickoff Returns

Kickoff Returns are measured from the point where the receiver gains possession. On kickoffs that go over the goal line, the return is measured only from the goal line.

• **Pro Ruling:** On kickoffs that go into the end zone, the return is measured from the point the receiver gains possession, including end zone yardage.

A player is not credited with a kickoff return if he receives the ball in the end zone and grounds it. Kickoff returns are credited only on those kickoffs for which a return is attempted.

Note: There are no formal statistics for number or for yardage of kickoffs. Some statisticians keep a record of kickoff yardage for historical purposes.

Free kicks are recorded as kickoffs if made from placement and as punts if the ball is punted. The receiving player is credited with a kickoff return or a punt return, respectively.

• **Pro Ruling:** All free kicks, whether from placement or punted, are scored as kickoffs and the receiver is credited with a kickoff return in all cases.

Any gain or loss from a lateral pass (or handoff) which started from a kickoff return, is recorded under Kickoff Return yardage.

In all cases, where a player receiving a kickoff or punt makes no significant attempt to advance the ball upfield before he hands off or laterals to a teammate, the second player is credited with the attempt and yardage and the receiver is statistically ignored. Yardage is computed from the point nearest the receiving team's goal line where the second player gains control and is able to initiate forward progress.

Kickoff Return statistical tables include Games (G), Yards (YDS),

Average (Avg.)—derived by dividing total kickoff return yards by number of kickoff returns, Touchdowns (TDs) and, if desired, Longest (Lng).

Player, Team	NO	YDS	AVG	TDs	LNG
Smith, Central High	2	67	33.5	0	46

Players are ranked by average number of yards per kickoff return. To qualify for championship, players should have at least 1.5 kickoff returns per game.

Field Goals

Field goals are measured from the point where the ball is kicked to the goal *posts*.

Note: Field goal measurements in high school and college are 10 yards longer than in professional football, because in the former case, the goal posts are 10 yards behind the goal line.

Returns of attempted field goals that fall short are recorded as Punt Returns, as is the return yardage. See "Punt Returns."

• **Pro Ruling:** All yardage gained by a player in returning an unsuccessful field goal attempt is noted on the back of the official score blank under "Remarks."

The kicker is not charged with a field goal attempt if he does not actually kick the ball. If the player holding the ball juggles it long enough to prevent the kicker from making an attempt, a fumble is charged and the lost yardage recorded under Rushing.

• **Pro Ruling:** In this situation, the ball holder is charged with a fumble and yardage lost is listed as fumble yardage.

Field Goal statistics include Attempts (ATT), Made (MADE), Longest (Lng.) and Percentage (Pct.). Yardage of all attempts should be recorded, because some statisticians include the percentage of success of field goal attempts from various distances (i.e. 1 to 19 yards, 20 to 29 yards, 30 to 39, 40 to 49, and over 50 yards).

Player, Team	ATT	MADE	LNG	PCT
Smith, Central	8	5	37	.625

There is no accepted standard for ranking kickers. The National Collegiate Statistics Service ranks kickers by average number of points per game by kicking (field goals and conversions combined). The professional kickers are listed in order of the percentage of successful field goal attempts.

Points After Touchdown

Players attempting conversions are not charged with an extra point missed when a bad pass from center, or a muff by a ball holder, precludes an opportunity to kick. Charge such an attempt to the "team." However, if the ball is momentarily fumbled and then kicked, an attempt is charged to the individual kicker, whether successful or not.

Attempts at conversion which are blocked shall be scored as extra points missed.

• **Pro Ruling:** When, in the opinion of the official statistician, an error in the center snap or placement of the ball by the holder is the direct cause of a blocked conversion attempt, charge the attempt to the "team."

No fumble is charged on an attempted point-after-touchdown.

The try for point after touchdown is made while time is out and *is not* recorded as a rushing, passing or kicking play from scrimmage.

If the attempt is by rushing, the ball carrier is charged with the PAT attempt and, if successful, with the successful conversion and the point(s) scored.

If the attempt is by passing, the passer is charged with the attempt, and, if successful, with the conversion under *Passing*. However, the receiver is credited with a conversion and the point(s) scored under "Scoring." It is not recorded as a pass attempt, completion or reception.

Points after touchdown statistics can be maintained in many ways. The simplest is Attempts (ATT) and Made (MADE) and Points (PTS), and is included in the scoring tables. Where the two-point conversion is in vogue, it should be broken down to show Attempts and Made in each of the three categories.

Safeties

No individual credit is recorded for any player on either team when a safety is scored. The team benefiting from the score is credited with two points.

Note: However, on a scrimmage play that results in a safety, the ball carrier is charged with a rush attempt (or passing attempt and completion) and with yardage loss from the line of scrimmage to the goal line.

• **Pro Ruling:** Safeties *are* credited to the individual scoring statistics of a player who downs an opponent behind the goal line, blocks a kick which results in a safety, causes the intentional grounding of a forward pass behind the passer's goal line, or otherwise causes a safety through individual effort. However, on automatic safeties, no credit shall be given to an individual.

Example:

Player, Team	Kick	Run	Pass	Pts
Smith, Central High	6-5	2-1	2-1	9*

*Run and pass conversions worth two points each.

Other Statistics

All-Purpose Running

A relatively new statistical compilation is All-Purpose Running, which consists of the yardage a player totals by Rushing, Pass Receiving and Returns of Punts, Kickoffs and Interceptions. This category provides a comparison of versatile players who are proficient in all areas of ball carrying.

Statistics are obtained from those already recorded for the various categories involved. Statistics tables should show for each player the number of Games played (G), Rushing yardage (RUSH), Pass Receiving yardage (REC), total yards for all three types of Returns (RET), total yards from all five categories (YDS), and average Yards Per Game (YDPG).

Example: During the season, Smith of Central High rushed for 891 yards, gained 489 yards on pass receptions, returned punts for a total of 66 yards, returned kickoffs for a total of 141 yards and returned interceptions for 17 yards (total of returns, 66 + 141 +17 = 224).

Player, Team	G	RUSH	REC	RET	YDS	YDPG
Smith, Central High	9	891	489	224	1604	178.2

Players are ranked on Average Yards Per Game and should play in at least 75 percent of their team's games to qualify for the championship.

Fumbles

Note: Because the pro rulings on fumbles are considerably different than those for college and high schools, they are included in one grouping at the end of the section on fumbles, rather than after each fumble ruling or interpretation.

When a fumble terminates any play, the yards involved to the point of *recovery* are credited or charged to the player who fumbled, regardless of which team recovers the fumble.

Example: Team A's ball at midfield. Murphy runs through tackle to Team B's 42, where he fumbles and his teammate, Kline, falls on the ball on the 39. Credit Murphy with one Rushing Attempt and 11 yards rushing. Charge Team A with one fumble, not lost.

Example: Same situation, except when Murphy fumbles at the 42, a Team B player recovers the fumble at the 39. Credit Murphy with one Rushing Attempt and 11 yards rushing. Charge Team A with one fumble lost.

Example: Same situation, except when Murphy fumbles at the 42, his teammate, Kline, picks up the ball at the 39 and runs to Team B's 32 before he is tackled. Credit Murphy with one Rushing Attempt and 11 yards Rushing. Credit Kline with *no* Rushing attempt and 7 yards Rushing. Credit team with one Rushing attempt and 18 yards Rushing. Charge team with one fumble, not lost.

Example: Same situation, except when Murphy fumbles at the 42, the ball bounces backward to the 45, where it is recovered. Credit Murphy with one Rushing Attempt and 5 yards under Rushing. Charge team with one fumble.

A fumble which occurs near a sideline, whether or not it appears the player intended to fumble to get the ball out of bounds (to stop the clock), is recorded as a fumble.

Any gain or loss from a lateral pass that follows a fumble is recorded under the play (Rushing, Passing, etc.) in which the fumble occurred.

When a fumbled ball is *touched* by several players, only the player who lost possession and the player who ultimately gains possession shall be credited with yardage gained or lost. However, there can be more than one fumble and more than one recovery on a single play, but *only* if possession is clearly established following the original fumble (see Pro Ruling No. 8 under Fumbles).

On a fumble, where two players apparently contribute equally to a fumble (usually on a handoff or lateral), the player who, in the scorer's judgment, was in possession of the ball at the time of the fumble, is credited with the gain or charged with the loss.

A fumble caught by the opposing team before the ball touches the ground is an "intercepted fumble" and recorded under Interception Returns. Thus, the number of interceptions by a team can be greater than the number of passes intercepted by the opposing team. (See Pro Ruling No. 7 under Fumbles).

When a player on the offensive team recovers a teammate's fumble and advances, he is not charged with an attempt, but is credited with yardage under the category which initiated the play.

Example: Ball at midfield. Smith of Team A runs to Team B's 40, where he fumbles and ball rolls to 35, where his teammate, Green, picks up ball and advances to 30. Credit Smith with one rushing attempt for 15 yards; credit Green with *no* rushing attempts, but 5 yards under Rushing.

Example: Same situation. Mobley of Team A passes to Smith on 40, he runs to 35, where he fumbles and teammate, Green, picks up ball at 33 and runs to 30. Credit Mobley with one pass attempt, one completion and 20 yards under Passing. Credit Smith with one Pass Reception and 17 yards under Pass Receiving. Credit Green with *no* Reception and 3 yards under Pass Receiving.

There are no individual statistics under fumbles. In team statistics, normally there is a notation for each team for the number of fumbles and the number of fumbles lost.

• **Pro Rulings on Fumbles:** Any yardage gained or lost on a play in which a fumble occurs is recorded as follows:

1. When a player recovers his own fumble, he is credited with the net yardage gained or lost on the play in the category which initiated the action (i.e. rushing, passing, etc.). He is also charged with a fumble and credited with an "own recovery."
2. When a teammate or opponent recovers *behind* or *on* the line of scrimmage, the player who fumbled is charged with all yardage lost, if any, to the point of recovery or the new line of scrimmage, whichever is *less*.
3. When a teammate or opponent recovers *beyond* the line of scrimmage, the player who fumbled is credited with yardage gained to the point of his advance or to the point of recovery, whichever is *less*.
4. A teammate or opponent who recovers a fumble shall be credited with fumble yardage for any gain or loss from the point of recovery. If a teammate recovers behind the line and advances the ball, fumble yardage commences from the line of scrimmage. No minus yardage can be charged unless the teammate or opponent causes the minus yardage by running or throwing the ball after gaining possession.

Note: When a player fumbles behind the line of scrimmage and (a) the ball rolls or bounces beyond the line of scrimmage, or (b) a teammate recovers and advances the ball beyond the line of scrimmage, charge the original ball carrier with no (0) yards gained and treat the yardage beyond the line of scrimmage as fumble yardage.

5. When a fumbled ball rolls free and is recovered beyond the line of scrimmage by a teammate or opponent, any yardage between the point of fumble and point of recovery shall be treated as being the result of a loose ball.
6. If a fumbled ball goes out of bounds and remains in possession of the team fumbling or goes over the end line for a touchback or safety,

the play is scored as a fumble and is also noted as a "fumble out of bounds."

7. When a bobbled ball is recovered out of the air by a teammate or opponent, it is scored as a fumble and recovery. An exception is if a receiver juggles a pass, without establishing possession, and a teammate or opponent gains possession in the air. Then the play is scored as a completed pass or interception, as the case may be.

8. When a fumbled ball is *touched* by several players, only the player who lost possession originally shall be charged with a fumble and only the player who ultimately gains possession shall be credited with a recovery. However, there can be more than one fumble and more than one recovery on a single play, but only if possession is clearly established following the original fumble.

9. There must be a "recovery" for every fumble charged except for fumbles that go out of bounds. "Own recovery" designates a fumble recovered by any member of the team committing the fumble. "Opponent's recovery" designates a fumble recovered by any member of the team *not* committing the fumble.

10. In instances where the ball is clearly centered improperly, causing the ball handler to bobble the ball and obviously preventing him from carrying out his assignment properly, charge the *center* with a fumble, plus yards lost, if any, as fumble yardage. In non-kicking situations, also charge the intended ball handler with a rushing attempt. Should the original ball handler recover the fumble to advance the ball beyond the line of scrimmage, charge the center with a fumble and credit the ball carrier with rushing yardage. If a teammate recovers the fumble and advances beyond the line of scrimmage, credit yardage to "fumble yardage." If an opponent recovers the fumble, yardage lost to the point of recovery shall be charged to the center.

11. If the quarterback or other ball handler hands off improperly or laterals improperly behind the line of scrimmage, resulting in no gain or a loss on the play, he is charged with a rushing attempt, a fumble and any yardage lost is charged as fumble yardage. If a teammate recovers the ball and advances it for a gain, the ball handler shall be charged with a rushing attempt, a fumble and no yards gained, while the teammate shall be credited with fumble yardage for any gain beyond the line of scrimmage. If the fumble is recovered beyond the line of scrimmage, the advance to the point of recovery shall be treated as being the result of a loose ball.

12. When a passer fumbles on contact with the defense while attempting to pass, he is charged with a "tackled attempting to pass" and a fumble and with all yardage lost to the point of recovery as Yards Lost Attempting to Pass.

Exception: If the point of recovery is in advance of the original line of scrimmage or if the player recovering the fumble advances the ball beyond the line of scrimmage, the passer is charged with a "tackled attempting to pass" for no yards lost and also with a fumble, and the player who advanced the ball is credited with fumble yardage equal to the distance between the old and new lines of scrimmage.

13. When a player fumbles after catching or intercepting a pass or on a punt return or kickoff return, he is credited with a gain or loss to his original point of advance or the point of fumble recovery, whichever is *less*.

Exception: If the player recovers his own fumble, all yardage gained or lost is credited in the category initiating the action.

14. When a player who is to hold the ball on a field goal attempt juggles it long enough to prevent the kicker from making an attempt, charge the ball holder with a fumble and any yardage lost as fumble yardage. When a player fumbles on an attempted punt, preventing him from punting, charge him with any yardage lost as fumble yardage. In either case, if the player who fumbled or a teammate picks up the ball and attempts to run with it, any yardage gained or lost shall be scored as fumble yardage.

Exception: If a player recovering a fumble (on an aborted field goal or punt attempt) throws a forward pass, it shall be scored as a pass attempt and yardage shall be credited to the passing category if completed.

15. In professional football, fumble statistics include Number of Fumbles Made (NO.), Own Fumbles Recovered (OWN REC), Opponent's Fumbles Recovered (OPP. REC.), Yardaged Gained or Lost by Fumble Recovered (YDS) or Lost (YDS), and Total Fumbles Recovered (TOT REC).

		OWN			OPP			TOT
Player, Team	NO.	REC	YDS	LONG	REC	YDS	LNG	REC
Smith, Green Bay	1	1	3	3	2	0	0	3
Gray, Chicago	1	0	0	0	1	–4	–4	0

There is no ranking for individuals under fumbles.

Penalties

On any violation where a penalty nullifies the play and the penalty is assessed from the line of scrimmage, the penalty reflects the entire yardage on the play. In this instance, the play, whatever its nature, is not recorded; only the penalty yardage is recorded.

Example: Team A's ball at midfield, first down and 10 yards to go. Smith rushes for 18 yards to Team B's 32. However, Team A was offside and was penalized five yards from the line of scrimmage. Thus Team A has a first down and 15 from its own 45. The play was nullified and there are no rushing statistics for Smith of Team A. Charge Team A with one penalty and five yards lost by penalty.

If the penalty occurs within the framework of the play, and there is both yardage gained (or lost) as well as penalty yardage assessed, the offensive player(s) and team are credited with yardage gained (or lost) to the point of the infraction or to the farthest point of advance, whichever is less. The offending team, then, is charged with the penalty yardage assessed from that point.

Example: Team A has the ball at midfield. King rushes for 20 yards to Team B's 30, but a clipping penalty is called against Team A on Team B's 35 and Team A is penalized to midfield. King (and his team) is credited with a rushing attempt and with 15 yards (up to point of the infraction) Rushing. Charge Team A with a 15-yard penalty (from the 35 back to midfield).

Example: Team A has the ball at midfield. King rushes for 20 yards to Team B's 30, but a clipping penalty is called against Team A on Team B's 25-yard line. The penalty from the spot of the infraction places the ball on Team B's 40. Credit King (and his team) with a rushing attempt and 20 yards Rushing (to point of farthest advance). Charge Team A with a penalty of 10 yards (from the 30—point of farthest advance—back to the 40).

Example: Same situation, except penalty (at Team B's 25) is called after ball is declared dead. Thus Team A is penalized from where the ball is declared dead (Team B's 30) and is charged with 15-yard penalty (back to 45). Credit King (and Team A) with one Rushing attempt and 20 yards (50 to 30) Rushing. Charge Team A with one 15-yard penalty.

Example: Team A has the ball at midfield, King rushes for 10 yards to Team B's 40, but as he is tackled Team B is guilty of piling on and is penalized 15 yards to its own 25. Credit King (and Team A) with one rushing attempt and 10 yards. Charge Team B with one 15-yard penalty.

In any situation, when the offended team declines the penalty, the play and yardage *are* recorded and *no* penalty statistics are recorded.

As noted in the previous examples, there are a number of instances where the yardage actually lost by penalty is less, statistically, than the yardage stepped off by the referee.

It is also possible for the yardage lost by penalty to be greater than the actual yardage stepped off by the referee.

Example: Team A has ball at midfield. King rushes for 10 yards to Team B's 40, but Team B is charged with a personal foul at the 35 and a 15-yard penalty is marked off to Team B's 20-yard line. Although the penalty was 15 yards, Team B in actuality lost 20 yards (from the

40 to the 20) by the penalty. Credit King (and Team A) with one rushing attempt and 10 yards under Rushing. Charge Team B with 20 yards Lost by Penalty.

When a penalty occurs behind the point where a punt return, kickoff return, interception return or fumble return was initiated, disregard any yardage returned by the ball carrier. Credit him with one return for no yards.

When a passer throws a pass from a point beyond the line of scrimmage, any completion is nullified when an official calls the infraction. However, passer is charged with a pass attempt and team is charged with a penalty and loss of down.

On a roughing the passer penalty, if the pass is completed, credit the passer (and receiver) with the completion. Do not charge a pass attempt if pass is incomplete.

On an ineligible receiver penalty *that is accepted by the defense,* the play is nullified and penalty yardage assessed from the line of scrimmage. If the defense declines the penalty, treat the play as you would any passing play.

There are no individual or team passing statistics recorded when pass interference is charged. The play is nullified (see No. 3 under Passing).

Example: Team A's ball at midfield, first and 10. Hall throws a pass intended for Smith at Team B's 20-yard line. Pass is broken up, but pass interference is called against Team B. Team A takes over the ball at B's 20. Team B is charged with penalty and 30 yards under Yards Lost by Penalty.

Note: In some high school rules, the penalty for pass interference is 15 yards. In this case, Team B would be charged with 15 yards under penalty and Team A would have a first down at Team B's 35. Team A is credited with first down by penalty. There are *no* individual or team passing statistics, as the penalty nullified the play.

Wild Pass from Center

Any loss resulting from an *obvious* wild pass from center is charged to "Center Pass" and not to any individual player. If the opposing team recovers the ball, Team A is charged with the rush and yardage loss. Team A is charged with a fumble lost.

Any gain resulting from a wild pass from center is recorded as though the wild pass had not occurred.

• **Pro Ruling:** On a bad pass from center, the center is charged with a fumble and any yards lost or gained are charged under fumble yardage. (See Pro Ruling on Fumbles.)

DEFENSIVE STATISTICS WORK SHEET

CENTRAL HIGH	TACKLES		FUMBLE REC.		PASS INT.	EAST TECH.	TACKLES		FUMBLE REC.		PASS INT.
	UNASSIST.	ASSIST.	OWN	OPP.			UNASSIST.	ASSIST.	OWN	OPP.	
CRONIN	/	////				BROOKS	///	//			
KNUDSEN	////	卌 ///				ROSE	卌 卌 ///	卌			
ATKINS					///	McCOMB		卌 /		/	
BREWER	卌 /	卌 //				JENSEN	/	/			//
RHODES	//	///	/			BAUER		卌			
SILVA	/	////				FULLER	/	/			
SANDERS	//	卌				HARPER		/			/
MOORE	///	///			/	RODRIGUEZ	//	///	/		
DALEY		//				SWANSON		//			
ANDREWS	/					WALKER		/			
VANCE		/				BLACK		/			
ROLAND		/				ALLAN		//			
SUMMERS	/					VOGEL		/			
DEMPSEY		/				ROBERTS	/				
CRANE	/	//				MEDFORD		卌			
						ALFANO		//			
						STEWART		/			
TOTALS	22	41	1	0	4	TOTALS	21	39	1	1	3

Form 4-A

Defensive Statistics

Although there are no official defensive statistics disseminated for national or conference rankings, many teams record and compile defensive statistics for distribution to interested media or for coaching purposes. They usually include the number of both unassisted Tackles and those on which two players assisted each other, Fumble Recoveries and Interceptions.

A sample work sheet for defensive statistics is shown in Form 4-A.

Qualifications for Individual and Team Leaders

The main purpose of statistics is, of course, to provide comparisons of "how they played the game." Thus, statistical rankings or championships should reflect as much as possible a true comparison. To this end, minimum performances should be required to establish championships.

Qualifications in each category of statistics have been noted previously in the respective sections of this chapter. For handy reference, this material is summarized as a guide.

For purposes of statistics rankings, a player is charged with a game if he is in the game for at least one play. Thus, if a player misses two games in a 10-game season, he is charged with only eight games in the statistics rankings.

Normally, to qualify for the rankings or statistical championships, a player is expected to be in the lineup for a minimum of 75 percent of his team's games. Other "per-game" minimums are stipulated in several categories. Although these are generally accepted minimums, they are arbitrary and conferences or leagues may desire to establish different minimums. The underlying philosophy is that minimums are established to make certain in each category there is a true champion who earned his title by performing under the same comparative conditions as his competitors.

Championships in the following categories are based on the highest Average Per Game, with participation required in at least 75 percent of a team's games:

Rushing (yards)
Passing (completions)
Total Offense (yards)
Pass Receiving (catches)
Interceptions (catches)
Scoring (points)
Kick-Scoring (points)
All-Purpose Running (Yards)

Championships in the following categories are based on the highest

Average Yards Per Return, with average number of 1.5 returns per game as a minimum.

Punt Returns (yards) Kickoff Returns (yards)

Championship in the following category is based on the highest Average Yards Per Punt, with an average number of 2.5 punts per game as a minimum.

Punting (yards)

• **Pro Ruling:** Because all teams play the same number of games, championships are usually determined by actual yardage or number of performances, rather than by average per game.

Rushing: Most net yards. For secondary listing, highest average gain, a minimum of 100 carries is required.

Passing: Must have mininum average of 10 passes attempted for each of team's games to qualify. Rankings based on percentage of completions, percentage of touchdown passes, percentage of pass attempts intercepted and average gain per attempted pass. (For example, see Pro Ruling at end of previous section on Passing.)

Pass Receiving: Most receptions, with a minimum of 35 to qualify. For secondary listing, highest average gain.

Pass Interceptions: Most interceptions.

Punting, Punt Returns and Kickoff Returns: Same as college and high school, except minimum for Punt or Kickoff Returns is average of one return (instead of 1.5) of team's games.

Records

For comparative and historical purposes, all-time records are an integral by-product of statistics. Practical considerations preclude the listing of all possible record entries in this space (the National Collegiate Record Book compiled by Steve Boda of the National Collegiate Sports Service includes nearly 200 pages of records; the NFL Record Manual has more than 400 pages, although some of the latter is devoted to material not exclusively on records).

However, at a minimum, all-time records should be kept in each of the major statistical categories—both for individuals and teams —including, in each category, game records, season records and career records. For teams, they should include both offensive and defensive records.

There is no limit to the number and variety of records which may be compiled and maintained. For instance, in rushing, records may include only the most Rushing yards in a single game by one player. Or, listed under Average Yards Per Carry, there could be various records for the player who carried a minimum of 5 times; another for a minimum of 10 times; for 15, 20 and as far as the record keeper desires.

For a complete listing of record categories, reference to the NCAA or NFL record books is recommended. As a guide, the following categories are suggested.

Rushing: Most rushes (games, season and career), most rushes per game, most yards gained, most yards gained per game, highest average yards per rush, highest average yards per game, most touchdowns by rushing, longest rush. Miscellaneous records could include such items as most consecutive games gaining 100 yards or more, most seasons gaining 1,000 (or 500) yards or more.

Passing: Most passes attempted, completed, had intercepted; highest percentage of completions, most yards gained, most yards gained per game, most touchdown passes, longest play. Miscellaneous records could include—most consecutive passes completed, most passes (consecutive) attempted without interception, most yards gained per attempt, most yards gained per completion.

Total Offense: Most plays, most yards gained, most yards gained per game, most touchdowns responsible for, most points responsible for. Miscellaneous records—highest average gain per play.

Pass Receiving: Most passes caught, most yards, most yards gained per game, most touchdown passes caught, longest play. Miscellaneous records—highest average gain per reception, most consecutive games caught passes.

Punting: Most punts, most yards punted, highest average yards per punt, longest punt.

Interceptions: Most interceptions, most interceptions per game, most yards returned, most touchdowns, longest return. Miscellaneous records—most consecutive games intercepting one or more passes, highest average yards returned per interception.

Punt Returns: Most returns, most return yardage, highest average per return, most touchdowns on returns.

Kickoff Returns: Same categories as Punt Returns.

Total Kick Returns (combined Punt and Kickoff Returns): Same categories as Punt and Kickoff Returns.

All-Purpose Running: Most plays, most yards, highest average yards per play, highest average yards per game.

Scoring: Most points, most touchdowns, most field goals attempted, most points per game, most field goals scored, longest field goal, most point after touchdown attempts by kicking (and by rushing and by passing), most points after touchdown made in each of the three categories. Miscellaneous—most points scored by kicking, most consecutive points after touchdown by kicking.

Work Sheets and Forms

For the most efficient method of recording statistics, one of two methods should be used. Cumulative work sheets enable the statistician to make a quick tally at any point in the game (or at the half or end of the game) to provide a quick summary of individual and team statistics. The other method is a play-by-play report of the game. In any case, a play-by-play should be provided, when possible, as a check to the statistics kept by a work sheet. However, reference to play-by-play requires more time and if a statistical summary is needed immediately after the game, working forms should be used.

The statistician can devise his own work sheets or obtain printed forms, which are available from several sources. Probably the most widely used is the official NCAA Football Statistics Working Chart, providing four forms for each game and bound in a folder to facilitate use in a press box. A 10-game set is available from the National Collegiate Sports Services, Box 757, Grand Central Station, New York, N.Y. 10017. (See Forms 4-B, 4-C, 4-D & 4-E)

OFFICIAL FOOTBALL STATISTICS

WORKING CHART

CENTRAL HIGH — Home Team | OCT. 21, 1972 — (Date) | EAST TECH — Opponents

TIME OF GAME

FIRST HALF: Kickoff 8 P.M.; End of Half 8:56 P.M.; Elapsed Time :56

SECOND HALF: Kickoff 9:14 P.M.; End of Game 10:16 P.M.; Elapsed Time 1:02

Time Outs by Quarters:	1st	2nd	3rd	4th	Total
Home Team					
Opponents					
Officials					

Elapsed Time Between Halves :18

TOTAL ELAPSED TIME 2:16 (Playing time plus intermission)

FIRST DOWNS

Home Team	FP, R, R, FP, Pn, R, R, FP, R, R, R, FP, R, FP, FP, FP	16
Opp.	R, FP, R, FP, R, FP, FP, FP, R, R, FP, Pn, R	13

(R—Rushing. FP—Forward Pass. Pn—Penalty).

FUMBLES

Home Team	+ — − +	2/2
Opp.	— —	0/2

(Own fumbles recovered, plus sign. Own fumbles lost, minus sign).

PENALTIES AGAINST

Home Team	5, 5, 15, 5	4/30
Opp.	15, 5, 5, 5, 15	5/45

SCORING

Home Team Player	Points	Opponents Player	Points
FORD	6	LANE	6
CARTER	1	FORTUNE	1
HOWARD	6	FULLER	6
CARTER	1	FORTUNE	1
MORGAN	6	LANE	6
CARTER	1		
Total	33	Total	28

PUNTING

Home Team Kicker	Yards	Opponents Kicker	Yards
1 JONES	41/41	1 GREEN	46/46
2 "	40/81	2 "	29/75
3 "	32/113	3 "	39/114
4 "	38/151	4	
5 TEAM	0/151	5	
14		14	
15		15	
Total	5/151	Total	3/114

KICKOFF RETURNS

Home Team Player	Yards	Opponents Player	Yards
1 SMITH	32/32	1 LANE	23/23
2 SMITH	30/62	2 FULLER	31/54
3 SMITH	16/78	3 FULLER	12/66
4 HOWARD	21/99	4 LANE	16/82
5 SMITH	12/111	5 LANE	19/101
6		6 LANE	
9		9	
10		10	
Total	5-111	Total	6-113

PUNT RETURNS

Home Team Player	Yards	Opponents Player	Yards
1 SMITH	17/17	1 LANE	12/12
2 SMITH	3/20	2 LANE	9/21
3		3 LANE	11/32
4		4	
5		5	
8		8	
9		9	
10		10	
Total	2-20	Total	3-32

NCAB Form No. 4-A

Form 4-B

OFFICIAL FOOTBALL STATISTICS
WORKING CHART

FORWARD PASSING

	Home Team Passer	Receiver	Yards		Opponents Passer	Receiver	Yards
1	JACKSON	HOWE	14/14	1	FORTUNE	BERG	16/16
2	"	—	X	2	"	—	X
3	"	—	X	3	"	—	X
4	"	HOWE	16/30	4	"	—	(X)
5	"	—	X	5	"	—	(X)
6	"	FORD (T)	67/97	6	"	LANE (T)	88/104
7	"	FORD	(2)/95	7	"	LANE (T)	82/186
8	"	—	(X)	8	"	LANE	14/200
9	"	PHILLIPS	4/99	9	MANN	LANE	21/221
10	"	—	X	10	"	—	X
11	"	—	X	11	"	—	(X)
12	"	—	X	12	FORTUNE	BERG	13/234
13	"	—	X	13			
14	"	HOWE	17/116	14			
15	"	PETERS	32/148	15			
16	HOWE	FORD (T)	47/195	16			
17	JACKSON	MORGAN (T)	18/213	17			
18				18			
19				19			
20				20			
21				21			
22				22			
23				23			
24				24			
25							
				35			
36				36			
37				37			
38				38			
39				39			
	Total No. Att: 17 Compl: 9 Int: 1	Yds:	213		Total No. Att: 12 Compl: 6 Int: 3	Yds:	234

(Show incomplete passes with an X; intercepted passes with (X))

INTERCEPTIONS

	Home Team Player	Yards		Opponents Player	Yards
1	KILLIAN	4/4	1	MURPHY	7/7
2	MORGAN (T)	77/81	2		
3	DANA	13/94	3		
4			4		
5			5		
6			6		
7			7		
8			8		
9			9		
10			10		
	Total	3-94		Total	1-7

FUMBLE RETURNS, MISC.

	Home Team Player	Yards		Opponents Player	Yards
1	CAROLL	7/7	1		
2			2		
3			3		
4			4		
5			5		
6			6		
7			7		
8			8		
9			9		
10			10		
	Total	7/7		Total	

NCAB Form No. 4-B

Form 4-C

OFFICIAL FOOTBALL STATISTICS

WORKING CHART

INDIVIDUAL RUSHING BY HOME TEAM

Player	HOWARD	ROLAND	RUSSELL	MORGAN	JACKSON							TOTALS
1	4/4	(4)/(4)	6/6	82 (7)/82	(6)/(6)							
2	3/7	2/(2)	8/14	4/86	(11)/(17)							
3	29/36	3/1			2/(15)							
4	11-(1)/47	14/15			(4)/(19)							
5	(2)/45											
6	(1)/44											
7	6/50											
8	5/55											
9	16/71											
10												
11												
12												
19												
20												
21												
22												
23												
24												
25												
Times	9	4	2	2	4							21
Gain	74	19	14	86	2							195
Loss	3	4	–	–	21							28
Net	71	15	14	86	(19)							167

NCAB Form No. 4-C ·(Record losses in circled figures) Cop[illegible]

Form 4-D

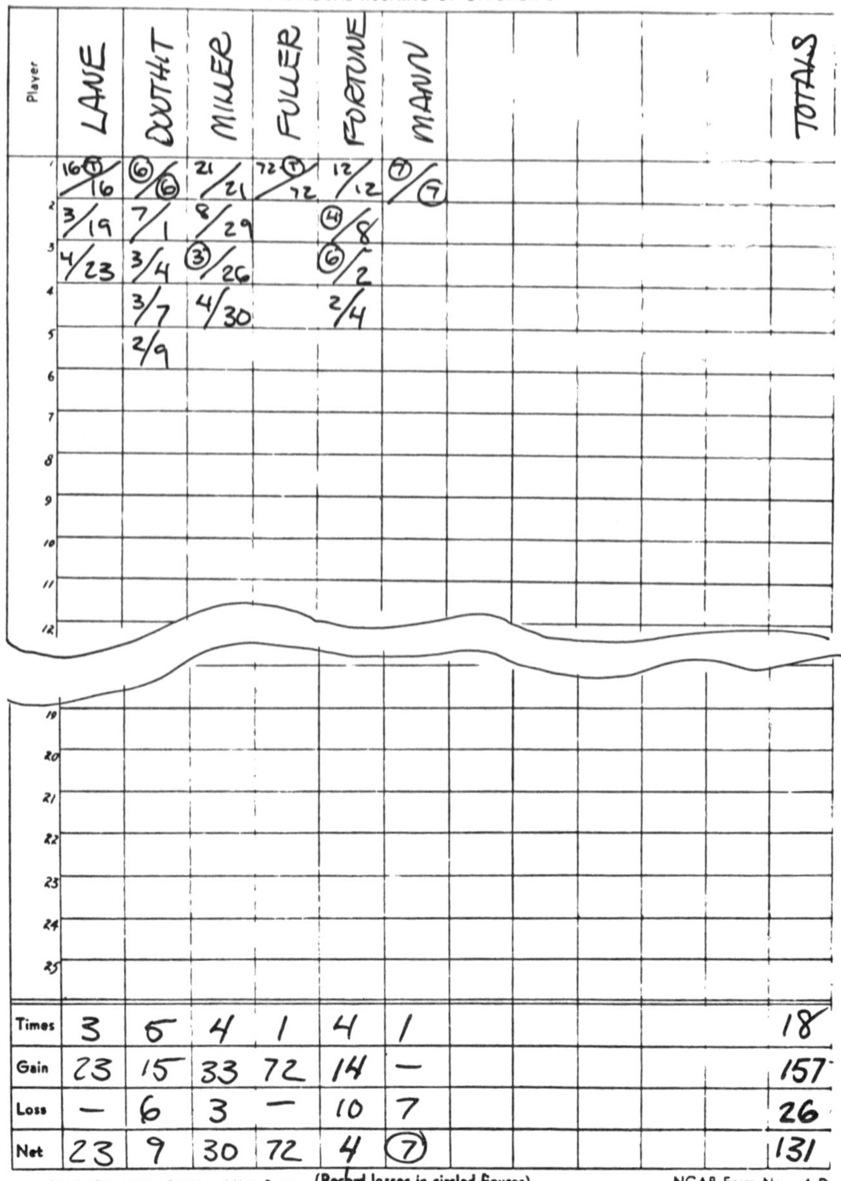

OFFICIAL FOOTBALL STATISTICS

WORKING CHART

INDIVIDUAL RUSHING BY OPPONENTS

Player	LANE	DOUTHIT	MILLER	FULLER	FORTUNE	MANN						TOTALS
1	16(T)/16	(6)/(6)	21/21	72(T)/72	12/12	(7)/(7)						
2	3/19	7/1	8/29		(4)/8							
3	4/23	3/4	(3)/26		(6)/2							
4		3/7	4/30		2/4							
5		2/9										
6												
7												
8												
9												
10												
11												
12												
19												
20												
21												
22												
23												
24												
25												
Times	3	5	4	1	4	1						18
Gain	23	15	33	72	14	—						157
Loss	—	6	3	—	10	7						26
Net	23	9	30	72	4	(7)						131

 (Record losses in circled figures) NCAB Form No. 4-D

Form 4-E

Play-by-play forms and styles can be devised by the statistician, but the information should be complete enough to enable him to compile *all* statistics from it. The play-by-play (see Form 4-F for partial play-by-play report) includes all elements a statistician or record compiler needs.

Form 4-F

SOUTH HIGH BULLDOGS v. EAST TECH TITANS
Municipal Stadium Friday, October 22, 1970

At game time, weather was overcast. Field temperature: 65°. Wind: Gusty to 14 mph out of south.

South High won toss and elected to receive. East Tech will defend north goal.

Time	Down	YTG	YL	Description of Play
15:00	Kickoff		E40	Hart kicks to Walters at goal line who returns 23. 60-yd. kickoff.
14:43	1	10	S23	Nicholas at center for 6. Britt makes tackle.
14:12	2	4	S29	Nicholas up middle for 3. Hale, Britt make tackle.
13:52	3	1	S32	Goodman on keeper around RE for 2 and 1st down. Smith stops.
13:40	1	10	S34	Goodman swing pass to Manning, dropped by Britt for loss of 2.
13:11	2	12	S32	Goodman pass on left flat to Mitchell for 9. Williamson stops.
12:48	3	3	S41	Nicholas at center for no gain. Stopped by center of line.
12:03	4	3	S41	Miller punts into the end zone. 59-yard punt. No return.
SOUTH HIGH				
11:38	1	10	E20	Jackson at rt, dropped for loss of 1 by Hart, Walter, Evans.
10:59	2	11	E19	Ott pass intended for Jackson, intercepted by Harris at E22 and returned for touchdown.
10:31	PAT		E2	Miller kicks the extra point. SOUTH 7 EAST TECH 0
EAST TECH				
10:31	Kickoff		S40	Miller kicks into end zone, taken four deep by Smith. 64-yard kickoff. No return.
10:00	1	10	E20	Jackson at LG for 3. Hart, Peoples tackle.
9:42	2	7	E23	Holland at RE, dropped for loss of 5 by Darien.

9:14	3	12	E18	Ott pass over ctr. to Nixon for 14 & 1st down. Harris made tackle.
8:33	1	10	E32	Jackson over center for 3. Hart, Walter tackle.
8:04	2	7	E35	Ott pass to Nixon on right flat for 6. Harris makes tackle.
7:35	2	1	E41	Jackson up the middle for 2 and first down.
7:00	3	10	E43	Ott pass intended for Summers overthrown at S15.
6:43	2	10	E43	Jackson at center for 1. Stopped by center of line.
6:15	3	9	E44	Ott pass incomplete. No receiver near.
6:00	4	9	E44	Bailey punts, rolls dead at S41. Off side of foot. 15-yard punt.

SOUTH HIGH

5:28	1	10	S41	Nicholas at ctr for 2. Hale & Hart make tackle.
4:49	2	8	S43	Goodman back to pass, dropped by Hale for loss of 5.
4:20	3	13	S38	Goodman's pass to Oldham complete at 50. Runs to E36 where Williamson stops. 26-yard gain.
3:58	1	10	E36	Goodman to Oldham incomplete at 10. Williamson covers.
3:48	1	10	E36	Nicholas at RT for 1. Russell, Davidson, Murphy stop.
3:18	3	9	E35	Goodman swing pass toYoung, overthrown, incomplete.
3:12	4	9	E35	Miller kicks 53-yard field goal out of Goodman's hold.
				SOUTH 10 EAST TECH 0

Some statisticians prefer to keep a chart of action, rather than a play-by-play summary. A chart in printed form is probably quicker, particularly if the play-by-play statistician does not have a typewriter.

One such chart (Form 4-G) is *The Football Score Book*, available from the Athletic Score Book Co., 717 St. James Place, Newport Beach, Calif. 92660.

This chart, included in a 12-game book, provides a column for each series of downs, numbered 1 to 4 at left, and an extra space at the bottom of each column for notes (i.e. clarifying a penalty, identity of player who blocked a kick or recovered a fumble, etc.), or for an extra down in the case of a penalty.

In Form 4-G, the chart shows No. 20 of University kicking off to open the game. No. 24 of State took the ball on his own 10 (50-yd kickoff) and ran it back (R.B.) 14 yards.

Downs		Ball On Yd.Line	S Ball On STATE 24 Yd.Line	U Ball On U 38 Yd.Line	U Ball On S 39 Yd.Line		S Ball On S 12 Yd.Line	S Ball On S 22 Yd.Line	U Ball On S 18 Yd.Line	K Ball On S 5 Yd.Line
1	Ball Carrier	#20-U	# 22	18	37	B. C.	22	78	18	81
	Play	K-OFF	OVER L.T.	PASS-74	OVER C.	Play	FUMBLE	TRAP R.T.	R.E. RUN	REVERSE
	Yds. ±	TO S 10	+ 3	+ 23	+ 2	Yds. ±	− 3	+ 4	+ 9	+ 2
					PEN + 5 O.S.					
2	Ball Carrier	# 24	24		18	B. C.	24	24	37	81
	Play	RUN BACK	TRAP L.T.		PASS - INC	Play	QUICK OPEN	PASS - INTER	OVER L.T.	L.E. RUN
	Yds. ±	+ 16	+ 8		PEN - 15	Yds. ±	+ 7	BY 18	+ 4	+ 2
			PEN. - 5 O.S.		IN. MAN. DB			R.B. 11		
3	Ball Carrier		21		18	B. C.	22			24
	Play		R.E. RUN		QUICK KICK	Play	PITCH OUT			SNEAK
	Yds. ±		+ 3		TO S 12	Yds. ±	+ 6			+ 1 T.D.
					NO R.B.					
4	Ball Carrier		22			B. C.				24
	Play		OVER L.T.			Play				P.A.T.
	Yds. ±		+ 6		+ 5 PEN.	Yds. ±				KICK-GOOD
					- 15 PEN.					
			24							7 PTS.
			PUNT							
			TO U. 31							
			18 R.B. 7							
	T. Y. G.		+ 12	+ 23	+ 2	T. Y. G.	+ 10	+ 4	+ 13	+ 5

Form 4-G

The ball has changed hands and a new series of downs has started, so the scorer goes to the next column. The chart shows it is S's ball on its own 24-yd. line. No. 22 made 3 yards over left tackle. No. 24 made 8 on a trap play at left tackle, but S was offside. The penalty of 5 yards is shown with the letters O.S. to indicate the nature of the penalty. Next, No. 21 made 3 yards running right end. No. 22 and 6 over left tackle, leaving S with fourth down and 3 to go. No. 24 punted to U's 31 where No. 18 of U returned the punt 7 yards.

With a change of possession, the scorer shifts to the next column, showing Team U starting the series from its own 38-yd line. No. 18 passes to No. 74 for 23 yards. This is a first down, so the scorer goes to the next column, where the series starts with Team U in possession on S's 39-yard line. On first down, No. 37 made 2 yards over center and so on.

The T.Y.G. at the bottom of each column shows the total yardage gained or lost in each sequence.

Report Forms

It may be necessary for the statistician to provide a statistical report for news media or for a conference or league.

For news media, a condensed form may be sufficient, or a complete form may be required. Below is the standard "short form" of team statistics which is used by the wire services and most newspapers.

	Central High	East Tech	
First downs	20	19	
Rushing yardage	32-181	42-230	(1)
Passing yardage	289	84	
Return yardage	71	83	(2)
Passes	14-27-3	7-13-4	(3)
Punts	4-38.8	6-40.7	(4)
Fumbles lost	1	0	
Yards penalized	3-35	4-40	(5)

(1) Indicates 42 Rushing Attempts for 230 net Rushing yards.

(2) Combined total of Punt, Intercepted Passes and Fumble returns (not kickoffs).

(3) Indicates 7 Completions, 13 Passes Attempted and 4 had Intercepted.

(4) Indicates 6 Punts for 40.7 average yards per punt.

(5) Indicates 4 Penalties for 40 yards.

Included with this short form usually is a score by quarters and a summary of all scoring.

Example:

Central High	7	7	7	10 – 31
East Tech	0	14	7	6 – 27

Scoring: Weller (C), 83-yard pass from Fortune. Baker PAT; Clancy (ET), 2, run, Burns PAT; Clancy (ET), 32, run, Burns PAT; Smith (C), 6, run, Baker PAT; Williams (ET), 22, pass from Burns, Burns PAT; Weller (C), 35, pass from Fortune, Baker PAT; Dixon (C), run, Baker PAT; Slovak (ET), 18, run, PAT blkd; Baker (C), 32, FG.

Often news media will want an abbreviated report for both individual and team statistics at the end of the first half as well as at the end of the game. Form 4-H, devised by Ned West, Sports Information Director at Georgia Tech, can be used for both halftime and final statistics. It includes both the short-form team statistics and leading individual performers for quick reference.

For detailed and complete football statistics, duplicator master stencils, both team (Form 4-I) and individual (Form 4-J), are available for a very nominal cost from Ned West at 2660 Acorn Ave., N.E., Atlanta, Ga. 30305.

For league purposes, these forms will serve admirably for report forms. Thus, the statistician can avoid duplication of effort by providing the same report form to both the news media and conference. In any event, copies of the complete statistical reports should be maintained in the team's file for permanent records and for historical reference.

Stats Form 102. Order Masters from Ned West, 2660 Acorn Ave., N.E., Atlanta, Ga. 30305

FLASH FOOTBALL STATS

Quick Halftime and After Game Reports of Vital Team Statistics and Individual Leaders
(Approved Wire Services Form)

HALFTIME ← Circle One → **(FINAL)**

TEAM STATISTICS	CENTRAL VISITORS	EAST TECH HOME TEAM
Score	31	27
First Downs	20	19
Rushing Yardage (Net)	181	230
Passing Yardage (Net)	289	84
*Return Yardage (Net)	71	83
Passes (Compl'd - Att'd - Had Intc'd)	27-14-3	13-7-4
Punts (Number - Average)	4 - 38.8	6 - 40.7
Fumbles Lost	1	0
Yards Penalized	3-35	4-40

*Return of Punts, Intercepted Passes and Fumbles (not kickoffs).

INDIVIDUAL LEADERS

CENTRAL (VISITORS)

RUSHING	Att'd	Net Yards	For TD	Long Gain
DIXON	11	94	1	45
RUSSEL	8	67	0	21
SMITH	4	43	1	25

PASSING	Att.-Compl.-H.I.	Yds.	For TD
FORTUNE	17-10-1	229	2
BAKER	10-4-2	60	0

PASS RECEIVING	No.	Yards	For TD
BILLINGS	4	28	0
DIXON	5	120	0
WELLER	3	130	2

PUNTING	No.	Avg.	Long Gain
MERKENS	4	38.8	44

EAST TECH (HOME TEAM)

RUSHING	Att'd	Net Yards	For TD	Long Gain
CLANCY	18	126	2	32
HUGHES	9	40	0	8
SLOVAK	4	33	1	18

PASSING	Att.-Compl.-H.I.	Yds.	For TD
BURNS	13-7-4	84	1
	- -		

PASS RECEIVING	No.	Yards	For TD
WILLIAMS	4	55	1
MILLER	2	21	0
SLOVAK	1	8	0

PUNTING	No.	Avg.	Long Gain
BURNS	6	40.7	48

Form 4-H

Stats Form 100. Order Masters From Ned West, 2660 Acorn Ave., N.E., Atlanta, Ga. 30305

CENTRAL HIGH vs. EAST TECH . OCT 29 , 19 72

FINAL TEAM FOOTBALL STATISTICS

	CENTRAL VISITORS	EAST TECH HOME TEAM
First Downs Rushing	9	13
First Downs Passing	9	6
First Downs by Penalties	2	0
TOTAL FIRST DOWNS	20	19
Number Attempts Rushing	32	42
Yards Gained Rushing	209	243
Yards Lost Rushing	28	13
NET YARDS GAINED RUSHING	181	230
Number Passes Attempted	27	13
Number Passes Completed	14	7
Number Passes Had Intercepted	3	4
NET YARDS GAINED PASSING	289	84
Number Plays Rushing and Passing	59	55
TOTAL OFFENSE YARDAGE	470	314
Number Interceptions	4	3
NET YARDS INTERCEPTIONS RETURNED	45	35
Number Times Punted	4	6
Number Punts Had Blocked	0	0
PUNTING AVERAGE, YARDS	38.8	40.7
Number Punts Returned	4	4
NET YARDS PUNTS RETURNED	21	48
Number Kickoffs Returned	2	5
NET YARDS KICKOFFS RETURNED	50	128
Number Times Penalized	3	4
TOTAL YARDS PENALIZED	35	40
Number Times Fumbled	2	1
NUMBER OWN FUMBLES LOST	1	0

CENTRAL HIGH (Visitors)	7	7	7	10	31
EAST TECH (Home Team)	0	14	7	6	27

Scoring: C- WELLER, 83 yd PASS from FORTUNE, BAKER PAT
ET- CLANCY, 2, RUN, BURNS, PAT
ET- CLANCY, 32, RUN, BURNS, PAT
C - SMITH, 6, RUN, BAKER PAT
ET- WILLIAMS, 22, PASS FROM BURNS, BURNS PAT
C- WELLER, 35, PASS FROM FORTUNE, BAKER PAT
C- DIXON, 45, RUN, BAKER PAT
ET- SLOVAK, 18, RUN, PAT BLOCKED
C- BAKER, 32 FG

Attendance: 3,083 Weather: FAIR

Form 4-I

Stats Form 101. Order Masters from Ned West, 2660 Acorn Ave., N.E., Atlanta, Ga. 30305

FINAL INDIVIDUAL FOOTBALL STATISTICS

CENTRAL HIGH — VISITORS

RUSHING	Att'd	Net Yards	For TD	Long Gain
DIXON	11	94	1	45
SMITH	4	43	1	25
JACKSON	5	2	0	6
MOORE	1	1	0	1
RUSSEL	8	67	0	21
FORTUNE	2	(8)	—	—
BAKER	1	(18)	—	—
TOTALS	32	181	2	—

PASSING	Att.-Compl.-H.I.	Yards	For TD	Long Gain
FORTUNE	17-10-1	229	2	83
BAKER	10-4-2	60	0	41
TOTALS	27-14-3	289	2	—

PASS RECEIVING	No.	Yds.	For TD	Long Gain
WELLER	3	130	2	83
DIXON	4	28	0	16
BILLINGS	5	120	0	41
SMITH	2	11	0	7
TOTALS	14	289	2	—

PUNTING	No.	Yards	Avg.	Long Gain
MERKENS	4	155	38.8	44
TOTALS				

ALL RETURNS	Punts No.	Punts Yds.	Kickoffs No.	Kickoffs Yds.	Intc'ns No.	Intc'ns Yds.
WILLIAMS	1	3				
ATKINS	1	0	2	50	3	28
MOORE					1	17
WILLS	2	18				
TOTALS	4	21	2	50	4	45

EAST TECH — HOME TEAM

RUSHING	Att'd	Net Yards	TD For	Long Gain
CLANCY	18	126	2	32
SLOVAK	4	33	1	18
HUGHES	9	40	0	8
FILLMORE	7	29	0	5
JONES	3	10		4
BURNS	1	(8)	0	—
TOTALS	42	230	3	—

PASSING	Att.-Compl.-H.I.	Yards	For TD	Long Gain
BURNS	13-7-4	84	1	22
TOTALS	13-7-4	84	1	22

PASS RECEIVING	No.	Yds.	For TD	Long Gain
WILLIAMS	4	55	1	22
SLOVAK	1	8	0	8
MILLER	2	21	0	14
TOTALS	7	84	1	22

PUNTING	No.	Yards	Avg.	Long Gain
BURNS	6	244	40.7	48
TOTALS				

ALL RETURNS	Punts No.	Punts Yds.	Kickoffs No.	Kickoffs Yds.	Intc'ns No.	Intc'ns Yds.
SLOVAK	4	48	3	90		
JENSEN			2	38	2	11
HARPER					1	24
TOTALS	4	48	5	128	3	35

Form 4-J

Conference and National Reports

A statistician may be required to serve as league statistician to compile conference statistics for record purposes and for release to news media.

Major college statisticians use the National Collegiate Sports Services reports (Forms 4-K and 4-L) to provide statistics to the NCSS for national rankings, and usually provide copies for both the home and visiting team files. If a conference is involved, a fourth copy of each form is provided for that purpose.

On NCSS Form 4-K, the small letters in each category (''A'' for Rushing, etc.) are for use in identification when the report is filed by Western Union. The space for ''Code'' numbers is inserted at the NCSS prior to processing final rankings by means of a computer.

Regardless of the degree of sophistication in the forms used, the instructions and interpretations in this chapter provide adequate information for a project of this nature.

To review, the order or ranking is included at the end of each category (i.e. Rushing, Passing, etc.) and a list of championship qualifications precedes the earlier section on Records in this chapter.

As a guide for compiling rankings in each category, Forms 4-M and 4-N show a partial report of comparative major-college statistics released by the NCSS. This is the final 1972 report in a series issued weekly by the NCSS, the service bureau of the National Collegiate Athletic Association.

SUMMARY OF FOOTBALL GAME STATISTICS — Home Team

TEAM CODE

Home Team *EAST TECH* First Downs: (Rush) *13* (Pass) *6* (Pen.) *0* Total *19* Penalties Against: (No.) *4* (Yards) *40* Own Fumbles: (No.) *1* (Lost) *0*

IMPORTANT: Most player categories are now ranked on per-game average. Thus, it's vital that you consider every player (on both teams) with any statistics in any game this season (get season player statistics from both SIDs). Then list below the code number and last name of players who have season figures but did NOT play in this game. A game played is one play–whether or not the player touches the ball. All players will be charged with a game unless you tell NCSS otherwise. If a player with first-time statistics has missed games, fill in below–after getting from his SID how many games missed.

DID NOT PLAY IN THIS GAME

Code No. ___ Last Name *JENKINS* Code No. ___ Last Name ___ Code No. ___ Last Name ___ Code No. ___ Last Name ___ Code No. ___ Last Name ___ Code No. ___ Last Name ___ Code No. ___ Last Name ___ Code No. ___ Last Name ___

XXXXXXXX

PLAYERS WITH FIRST-TIME STATISTICS WHO HAVE MISSED GAMES: Code No. ___ Last Name *HARPER* No. Games Missed *2* Code No. ___ Last Name ___ No. Games Missed ___

Player Code	PLAYER	RUSHING					PASSING						TOTAL OFFENSE		RECEIVING			INT RETURNS			PUNTING			PUNT RETURNS			K O RETURNS				X Pt. Kicks		Other X Pts.		Field Goals		
		Rushes	Gain	Loss	Net	TDs	Att	Comp	Int	Yards	TDs	Conv	Plays	Yards	Catches	Yards	TDs	No	Yards	TDs	No	Yards	Blkd	No	Yards	TDs	No	Yards	TDs	TDs	Att	Made	Att	Made	Att	Made	Points
	CLANCY	18	130	4	126	2							18	126																2	0	0	0	0	0	0	12
	SLOVAK	4	34	1	33	1							4	33	1	8	0							4	48	0	3	90	0	1	0	0	0	0	0	0	6
	HUGHES	9	40	0	40	0							9	40																							
	FILLMORE	7	29	0	29	0							7	29																							
	JONES	3	10	0	10	0							3	10																							
	BURNS	1	0	8	(8)	0	13	7	4	84	1	0	14	76							6	244	0							0	4	3	0	0	0	0	3
	WILLIAMS														4	55	1													1	0	0	0	0	0	0	6
	MILLER														2	21	0																				
	JENSEN																	2	11	0							2	38	0								
	HARPER																	1	24	0																	
	TEAM TOTALS	42	243	13	230	3	13	7	4	84	1	0	55	314	7	84	1	3	35	0	6	244	0	4	48	0	5	128	0	4	4	3	0	0	0	0	27

Visiting Team *CENTRAL HIGH* First Downs: (Rush) *9* (Pass) *9* (Pen.) *2* Total *20* Penalties Against: (No.) *3* (Yards) *35* Own Fumbles: (No.) *2* (Lost) *1*

	Rushes	Gain	Loss	Net	TDs	Att	Comp	Int	Yards	TDs	Conv	Plays	Yards	Catches	Yards	TDs	No	Yards	TDs	No	Yards	Blkd	No	Yards	TDs	No	Yards	TDs	TDs	Att	Made	Att	Made	Att	Made	Points
VISITING TEAM TOTALS	32	209	28	181	2	27	14	3	289	2	0	59	470	14	289	2	4	46	0	4	155	0	4	21	0	2	50	0	4	4	4	0	0	1	1	31

Date *10/29/72* Game Site *BOYLE FIELD, ALBANY, N.Y.* Official Attendance *3,083*

Form 4-K

ADDITIONAL STATISTICS

SCORE BY QUARTERS	1st	2nd	3rd	4th	Total
CENTRAL HIGH	7	7	7	10	31
EAST TECH	0	14	7	6	27

Time of Game: Kickoff 8 P.M. End of Game 10:22 P.M. Total Elapsed Time 2:22 (Including intermission)

Weather Conditions FAIR

SCORING SUMMARY

List all scoring plays in sequence. "Time left" means time remaining in the quarter. Under "play," to save you time, please use only: Rush, Pass, INT, PR, KOR, FUM, FG or SAF (instead of writing out interception, punt, kickoff and fumble returns, field goal or safety).

On pass play, list passer first, then receiver and combined yardage of pass and run. All plays are measured from the line of scrimmage except field-goal attempts--from the point of kick to the goal posts (goal line plus 10 yards).

After each touchdown, please continue on the same line and under "FOR EXTRA POINTS ONLY" check (✓) type of PAT (kick, pass or run) and whether good (G) or no good (NG).

Team	Qtr	Time Left	Play	Player(s)	Yards		FOR EXTRA POINTS ONLY Player(s)	K	P	R	G	NG
CENTRAL	1	7:14	PASS	FORTUNE TO WELLER	83	PAT	BAKER	/			/	
EAST TECH	2	6:15	RUN	CLANCY	2	PAT	BURNS	/			/	
EAST TECH	2	5:04	RUN	CLANCY	32	PAT	BURNS	/			/	
CENTRAL	2	0:11	RUN	SMITH	6	PAT	BAKER	/			/	
EAST TECH	3	7:10	PASS	BURNS TO WILLIAMS	22	PAT	BURNS	/			/	
CENTRAL	3	3:46	PASS	FORTUNE TO WELLER	35	PAT	BAKER	/			/	
CENTRAL	4	6:06	RUN	DIXON	45	PAT	BAKER	/			/	
EAST TECH	4	4:28	RUN	SLOVAIK	18	PAT	BURNS	/				/
CENTRAL	4	2:40	FG	BAKER	32	PAT						

NON-SCORING LONG PLAYS
(70 yards or more, including punts)

Team	Play	Player(s)	Yards
	NONE		

Form 4-L

NATIONAL COLLEGIATE SPORTS SERVICES

• BOX 757, GRAND CENTRAL STATION, NEW YORK, N. Y. 10017 • Telephone (212) 685-9622 •

Official Football Statistics

MAILED DEC. 10, 1970—FOR USE ON RECEIPT

FINAL MAJOR-COLLEGE INDIVIDUAL LEADERS

TOTAL OFFENSE

	GAMES	PLAYS	YDS	TDR*	YD.PG
PAT SULLIVAN, AUBURN	10	333	2856	26	285.6
JOE THEISMANN, NOTRE DAME	10	391	2813	20	281.3
JIM PLUNKETT, STANFORD	11	436	2898	21	263.5
BOB PARKER, AIR FORCE	11	442	2783	23	253.0
SONNY SIXKILLER, WASHINGTON	10	420	2268	17	226.8
JOHN REAVES, FLORIDA	11	433	2431	14	221.0
BRIAN SIPE, SAN DIEGO ST.	11	383	2422	23	220.2
JOE SPAGNOLA, ARIZONA ST.	10	325	2164	20	216.4
MARK THOMPSON, DAVIDSON	10	430	2144	15	214.4
DAN FOUTS, OREGON	11	413	2333	20	212.1
BILL CRAIGO, UTEX.EL PASO	10	376	2120	13	212.0
LEO HART, DUKE	11	411	2315	10	210.5
DENNIS DUMMIT, UCLA	11	423	2305	19	209.5
ARCHIE MANNING, MISSISSIPPI	8	315	1594	20	199.3
CHUCK EALEY, TOLEDO	11	398	2111	20	191.9
DARYL WOODRING, VILLANOVA	10	342	1915	18	191.5
WAYNE SMITH, COLO. ST. U.	11	449	2092	14	190.2
STEVE SKIVER, OHIO U.	9	345	1687	11	187.4
CHUCK HIXSON, S.M.U.	9	358	1687	11	187.4
LYNN DICKEY, KANSAS ST.	11	392	2008	9	182.5
JOHN READ, PACIFIC	9	357	1628	14	180.9
CHARLIE RICHARDS, RICHMOND	10	353	1808	15	180.8
TOMMY SUGGS, SO. CARO.	11	315	1948	14	177.1
JIM JONES, SOUTHERN CAL	11	292	1936	15	176.0

* Touchdowns-responsible-for are player's TDs scored and passed for.

RUSHING

	GAMES	PLAYS	YDS	TD	YD.PG
ED MARINARO, CORNELL	9	285	1425	12	158.3
DON MCCAULEY, NO. CARO.	11	324	1720	19	156.4
HANK BJORKLUND, PRINCETON	8	179	1081	7	135.1
GARY KOSINS, DAYTON	9	344	1172	18	130.2
BRIAN BREAM, AIR FORCE	10	294	1276	19	127.6
MIKE ADAMLE, NORTHWESTERN	10	304	1255	8	125.5
ROGER LAWSON, WESTERN MICH.	10	168	1205	13	120.5
BILL GARY, OHIO U.	9	265	1064	11	118.2
PHIL MOSSER, WM. & MARY	11	212	1286	9	116.9
JOHN BROCKINGTON, OHIO STATE	9	240	1041	15	115.7
FRED WILLIS, BOSTON COL.	9	223	1007	11	111.9
STEVE COWAN, CINCINNATI	11	239	1197	9	108.8
DICK JAURON, YALE	9	182	962	9	106.9
TIM FORTNEY, MIAMI, O.	10	265	1063	9	106.3
JOHNNY MUSSO, ALABAMA	11	226	1137	8	103.4
JOHN RIGGINS, KANSAS	11	209	1131	12	102.8
OTIS ARMSTRONG, PURDUE	10	213	1009	2	100.9
DAVE SCHILLING, OREGON ST.	11	254	1084	5	98.5
BOB DUNCAN, CITADEL	9	139	881	10	97.9
DOUG MCCUTCHEN, TEXAS TECH	11	227	1068	3	97.1
SAM SCARBER, NEW MEXICO	10	184	961	13	96.1
BOBBY MOORE, OREGON	10	203	924	6	92.4
MONROE ELEY, ARIZONA ST.	8	141	739	2	92.4
LARRY MCCUTCHEON, COLO. ST.	11	242	1008	6	91.6

Form 4-M

FINAL MAJOR-COLLEGE INDIVIDUAL LEADERS

FORWARD PASSING

	GAMES	ATT	CMP	INT	PCT	YDS	TD	CM.PG
SONNY SIXKILLER, WASHINGTON	10	362	186	22	.514	2303	15	18.6
BOB PARKER, AIR FORCE	11	402	199	15	.495	2789	21	18.1
MARK THOMPSON, DAVIDSON	10	352	179	18	.509	2202	14	17.9
CHUCK HIXSON, S.M.U.	9	285	160	18	.561	1763	10	17.8
BRIAN SIPE, SAN DIEGO ST.	11	337	195	20	.579	2618	23	17.7
JIM PLUNKETT, STANFORD	11	358	191	18	.534	2715	18	17.4
DAN FOUTS, OREGON	11	361	188	24	.521	2390	16	17.1
JOHN REAVES, FLORIDA	11	376	188	19	.500	2549	13	17.1
PAT SULLIVAN, AUBURN	10	281	167	12	.594	2586	17	16.7
JOHN READ, PACIFIC	9	309	149	19	.482	1697	13	16.6
LEO HART, DUKE	11	308	180	12	.584	2236	7	16.4
LYNN DICKEY, KANSAS ST.	11	364	180	26	.495	2163	7	16.4
DENNIS DUMMIT, UCLA	11	344	175	19	.509	2393	14	15.9
JOE THEISMANN, NOTRE DAME	10	268	155	14	.578	2429	16	15.5
ARCHIE MANNING, MISSISSIPPI	8	233	121	14	.519	1481	14	15.1
RICK DONEGAN, SO. MISS.	11	311	165	15	.531	1593	8	15.0
FRANK HARRIS, BOSTON COL.	10	241	138	19	.573	1589	13	13.8
BILL CRAIGO, UTEX.EL PASO	10	309	138	17	.447	2123	10	13.8
CHUCK EALEY, TOLEDO	11	263	149	9	.567	1898	16	13.5
JOE SPAGNOLA, ARIZONA ST.	10	242	133	14	.550	1991	18	13.3
CARYL WOODRING, VILLANOVA	10	263	127	15	.483	1826	16	12.7
JOE REED, MISS. STATE	11	294	138	16	.469	1616	8	12.5
STEVE GOEPEL, COLGATE	11	309	137	19	.443	1802	15	12.5
TOMMY SUGGS, SO. CARO.	11	269	136	18	.506	2030	14	12.4
WAYNE SMITH, COLO. ST. U.	11	321	136	17	.424	1861	8	12.4

PUNTING

(35 OR MORE PUNTS)	NO.	AVG.
MARV BATEMAN, UTAH	65	45.7
RAY GUY, SO. MISS.	69	45.3
JIM MCCANN, ARIZONA ST.	48	42.2
MIKE PARROTT, HOUSTON	64	41.5
PAUL STAROBA, MICHIGAN	54	41.5
RON DAVIS, IDAHO	88	41.4
SCOTT HAMM, AIR FORCE	53	41.2
BOB JACOBS, WYOMING	84	41.0
KEN DUNCAN, TULSA	67	41.0
JACK ANDERSON, CLEMSON	35	41.0
JIM BENIEN, OKLAHOMA ST.	75	40.9
LES FIELDS, PACIFIC	44	40.9
JOHN MCMILLEN, SAN JOSE ST.	54	40.9
FRANK MANN, ALABAMA	46	40.9
BRUCE BARNES, UCLA	70	40.9
TOM WITTUM, NORTHERN ILL	76	40.7
DAN BRENNING, KENT STATE	58	40.6
DAN QUINN, DAYTON	71	40.6
DUANE CARRELL, FLORIDA ST.	63	40.6
MARTY MCGANN, NORTHWESTERN	50	40.6
PAT BARRETT, MIAMI, FLA.	81	40.5
ED MARSH, BAYLOR	88	40.4
KEITH LIEPPMAN, KANSAS	75	40.4
STEVE SMITH, VANDERBILT	66	40.3
JOE LILJENQUIST, BRIG. YOUNG	37	40.2

PASS RECEIVING

	GAMES	CGHT	YDS	TD	CT.PG
MIKE MIKOLAYUNAS, DAVIDSON	10	87	1128	8	8.7
TOM GATEWOOD, NOTRE DAME	10	77	1123	7	7.7
DON FAIR, TOLEDO	11	76	893	4	6.9
MIKE SIANI, VILLANOVA	11	74	1358	12	6.7
ERNIE JENNINGS, AIR FORCE	11	74	1289	17	6.7
WES CHESSON, DUKE	11	74	1080	3	6.7
DAVID SMITH, MISS. STATE	11	74	987	6	6.7
TIM DELANEY, SAN DIEGO ST.	10	62	794	6	6.2
BOB NEWLAND, OREGON	11	67	1123	7	6.1
J.D. HILL, ARIZONA ST.	10	58	908	10	5.8
ED PUISHES, UTEX.EL PASO	10	57	1000	3	5.7
JIM KRIEG, WASHINGTON	10	54	738	2	5.4
OTTO STOWE, IOWA STATE	11	58	772	6	5.3
BOB ALLEN, OHIO U.	9	48	699	4	5.3
TERRY BEASLEY, AUBURN	10	52	1051	11	5.2
DAVE JUENGER, OHIO U.	9	46	540	3	5.1
HONOR JACKSON, PACIFIC	11	55	931	5	5.0
DAVID BAILEY, ALABAMA	11	55	790	6	5.0
RHETT DAWSON, FLORIDA ST.	11	54	946	5	4.9
KEN BURROW, SAN DIEGO ST.	11	54	904	12	4.9
MIKE BOLEN, AIR FORCE	11	53	706	3	4.8
ELMO WRIGHT, HOUSTON	10	47	874	9	4.7
BOB WICKS, UTAH ST.	10	47	642	3	4.7
MIKE MONTGOMERY, KANSAS ST.	11	51	386	1	4.6

SCORING

	GAMES	TD	XPT	FG	PTS	PTPG
BRIAN BREAM, AIR FORCE	10	20	0	0	120	12.0
GARY KOSINS, DAYTON	9	18	0	0	108	12.0
DON MCCAULEY, NO. CARO.	11	21	0	0	126	11.5
FRED WILLIS, BOSTON COL.	9	16	0	0	96	10.7
ERNIE JENNINGS, AIR FORCE	11	19	0	0	114	10.4
JOHN SHORT, DARTMOUTH	9	15	0	0	90	10.0
JOHN BROCKINGTON, OHIO STATE	9	15	0	0	90	10.0
ED MARINARO, CORNELL	9	14	2	0	86	9.6
STEVE WORSTER, TEXAS	10	14	0	0	84	8.4
J.D. HILL, ARIZONA ST.	10	14	0	0	84	8.4

KICK-SCORING

	G	XPA	XP	FGA	FG	PTS	PTPG
BILL MCCLARD, ARKANSAS	11	51	50	15	10	80	7.3
GARDNER JETT, AUBURN	10	44	41	12	10	71	7.1
HAPPY FELLER, TEXAS	10	57	55	14	5	70	7.0
DAVE HANEY, COLORADO	10	36	34	18	12	70	7.0
GEORGE HUNT, TENNESSEE	11	43	42	21	10	72	6.5
TOM DUNCAN, TOLEDO	11	44	36	21	12	72	6.5
DON EKSTRAND, ARIZONA ST.	10	47	38	12	9	65	6.5

PUNT RETURNS

(MIN. 1.5 RETURNS PER GAME)	NO.	YDS	TD	AVG.
STEVE HOLDEN, ARIZONA ST.	17	327	2	19.2
BOB WICKS, UTAH ST.	16	279	2	17.4
RALPH MCGILL, TULSA	27	460	2	17.0
GREG CAMPBELL, LOUISVILLE	16	267	2	16.7
RAYMOND BROWN, W.TEXAS ST.	15	250	0	16.7
DON KELLEY, CLEMSON	24	389	2	16.2
CRAIG BURNS, L.S.U.	21	339	2	16.1
TOM MYERS, SYRACUSE	29	436	0	15.0
MIKE REYNOLDS, UTEX.EL PASO	25	375	2	15.0
GARY WINDY, ILLINOIS	17	252	1	14.8

KICKOFF RETURNS

(MIN. 1.5 RETURNS PER GAME)	NO.	YDS	TD	AVG.
STAN BROWN, PURDUE	19	638	3	33.6
MACON HUGHES, RICE	15	459	2	30.6
JIM KRIEG, WASHINGTON	19	576	2	30.3
DICK HARRIS, SO. CARO.	30	880	1	29.3
JON ROBERTSON, SAN DIEGO ST.	20	557	1	27.9
ROD FOSTER, HARVARD	11	307	0	27.9
HENRY HAWTHORNE, KANSAS ST.	23	632	0	27.5
RON PO JAMES, NEW MEX. ST.	25	680	0	27.2
CLIFF BRANCH, COLORADO	21	564	2	26.9
DICK GRAHAM, OKLAHOMA ST.	17	449	2	26.4

NATIONAL COLLEGIATE SPORTS SERVICES

• BOX 757, GRAND CENTRAL STATION, NEW YORK, N. Y. 10017 • Telephone (212) 685-9622 •

Official Football Statistics

MAILED DEC. 10, 1970—FOR USE ON RECEIPT

INTERCEPTION RETURNS

	GAMES	NO.	YDS	TD	I.PG
MIKE SENSIBAUGH, OHIO STATE	8	8	40	0	1.0
BOBBY MAJORS, TENNESSEE	11	10	177	0	.9
NEOVIA GREYER, WISCONSIN	10	9	116	0	.9
JEFF VARNADOE, CITADEL	11	9	251	3	.8
TIM PRIEST, TENNESSEE	11	9	174	0	.8
PAUL ELLIS, TULANE	11	9	109	0	.8
RAYMOND BROWN, W.TEXAS ST.	10	8	162	1	.8
TOM ELIAS, WESTERN MIC.	10	8	136	1	.8
CRAIG BURNS, L.S.U.	11	8	117	0	.7

ALL-PURPOSE RUNNING

	G	RUSH	REC	RET	YDS	YDPG
DON MCCAULEY, NO. CARO.	11	1720	235	66	2021	183.7
ED MARINARO, CORNELL	9	1425	129	0	1554	172.7
PHIL MOSSER, WM. & MARY	11	1286	139	447	1872	170.2
LARRY MCCUTCHEON, COLO. ST.	11	1008	486	316	1810	164.5
BRIAN BREAM, AIR FORCE	10	1276	237	0	1513	151.3
ERIC ALLEN, MICHIGAN ST.	10	811	125	575	1511	151.1
HENRY HAWTHORNE, KANSAS ST.	11	399	501	748	1648	149.8
CLARENCE DAVIS, SOUTHERN CAL	11	972	203	444	1619	147.2

FINAL MAJOR-COLLEGE TEAM LEADERS

TOTAL OFFENSE

	GAMES	PLAYS	YDS	PERGAME	TD*
ARIZONA ST.	10	870	5145	514.5	42
NOTRE DAME	10	924	5105	510.5	45
AUBURN	10	684	4850	485.0	43
TEXAS	10	840	4681	468.1	56
SO. CALIFORNIA	11	869	4956	450.5	44
DARTMOUTH	9	713	3892	432.4	39
STANFORD	11	866	4687	426.1	39
WEST VIRGINIA	11	823	4677	425.2	42
AIR FORCE	11	902	4660	423.6	46
COLORADO	10	840	4229	422.9	35
NEBRASKA	11	884	4634	421.3	51
OREGON	11	874	4630	420.9	38

Form 4-N

RUSHING OFFENSE

	GAMES	PLAYS	YDS	PERGAME	TD
TEXAS	10	715	3745	374.5	51
NEW MEXICO	10	637	3501	350.1	33
OHIO STATE	9	564	2761	306.8	32
COLORADO	10	625	2998	299.8	29
ARIZONA ST.	10	595	2982	298.2	22
NORTH CAROLINA	11	732	3137	285.2	31
PENN STATE	10	617	2768	276.8	31
CINCINNATI	11	639	3011	273.7	27
DARTMOUTH	9	510	2368	263.1	30
WESTERN MICHIGAN	10	558	2631	263.1	22
MEMPHIS ST.	10	570	2629	262.9	26
OKLAHOMA	11	681	2881	261.9	30

FORWARD PASSING OFFENSE

	GAMES	ATT	CMP	INT	PCT	YDS	PERGAME	TD
AUBURN	10	311	181	12	.582	2885	288.5	17
OREGON	11	441	230	28	.522	3100	281.8	22
SAN DIEGO ST.	11	390	215	24	.551	3029	275.4	28
WASHINGTON	10	415	213	26	.513	2723	272.3	22
STANFORD	11	391	206	21	.527	2950	268.2	18
FLORIDA ST.	11	345	175	16	.507	2837	257.9	17
AIR FORCE	11	404	200	15	.495	2801	254.6	21
NOTRE DAME	10	283	162	15	.572	2527	252.7	16
VILLANOVA	11	385	193	18	.501	2709	246.3	23
FLORIDA	11	396	195	21	.492	2622	238.4	15
UCLA	11	353	181	20	.513	2527	229.7	16
DAVIDSON	10	358	180	19	.503	2253	225.3	15

SCORING

	GAMES	PTS	AVG.
TEXAS	10	412	41.2
NEBRASKA	11	409	37.2
ARKANSAS	11	402	36.5
ARIZONA ST.	10	357	35.7
AUBURN	10	355	35.5
DARTMOUTH	9	311	34.6
WASHINGTON	10	334	33.4
SAN DIEGO ST.	11	364	33.1
NOTRE DAME	10	330	33.0
AIR FORCE	11	353	32.1
NORTH CAROLINA	11	346	31.5
TOLEDO	11	344	31.3

TOTAL DEFENSE

	GAMES	PLAYS	YDS	PERGAME	TD*
TOLEDO	11	727	2044	185.8	8
DARTMOUTH	9	572	1677	186.3	6
MIAMI, O.	10	695	1931	193.1	14
SAN DIEGO ST.	11	742	2263	205.7	16
NOTRE DAME	10	658	2207	220.7	10
TULANE	11	801	2497	227.0	15
ARIZONA ST.	10	729	2378	237.8	15
DAYTON	10	703	2423	242.3	18
LOUISIANA ST.	11	746	2689	244.5	10

* Touchdowns scored by rushing-passing only.

RUSHING DEFENSE

	GAMES	PLAYS	YDS	PERGAME	TD
LOUISIANA ST.	11	356	574	52.2	2
TENNESSEE	11	428	972	88.4	6
DARTMOUTH	9	384	820	91.1	4
NORTH CAROLINA	11	405	1048	95.3	12
NOTRE DAME	10	376	962	96.2	6
PENN STATE	10	442	1008	100.8	12
MIAMI, O.	10	504	1050	105.0	8
MICHIGAN	10	416	1051	105.1	5
YALE	9	407	958	106.4	6

FORWARD PASS DEFENSE

	GAMES	ATT	CMP	INT	PCT	YDS	PERGAME	TD
TOLEDO	11	251	88	24	.351	856	77.8	1
NORTHWESTERN	10	191	61	18	.319	793	79.3	4
MIAMI, O.	10	191	84	14	.440	881	88.1	6
DAYTON	10	221	74	15	.335	928	92.8	3
DARTMOUTH	9	188	76	18	.404	857	95.2	2
SAN DIEGO ST.	11	230	85	12	.370	1062	96.5	6
BOWLING GREEN	9	164	77	12	.470	935	103.9	5
TULANE	11	247	106	28	.429	1184	107.6	1
RICE	10	191	86	19	.450	1087	108.7	5
HARVARD	9	195	82	16	.421	979	108.8	7

P U N T I N G

	GAMES	PUNTS	AVG.
UTAH	10	66	45.0
SO. MISSISSIPPI	11	74	43.9
ARIZONA ST.	10	48	42.2
MICHIGAN	10	54	41.5
TULSA	10	67	41.0
IDAHO	11	92	40.9
HOUSTON	11	65	40.9
UCLA	11	70	40.9
ALABAMA	11	47	40.8
NORTHERN ILLINOIS	10	76	40.7

S C O R I N G   D E F E N S E

	GAMES	TD	XPT	FG	PTS	AVG.
DARTMOUTH	9	6	6	0	42	4.7
TOLEDO	11	9	8	4	76	6.9
LOUISIANA ST.	11	10	9	9	96	8.7
MICHIGAN	10	9	6	10	90	9.0
TENNESSEE	11	13	11	4	103	9.4
NOTRE DAME	10	13	13	2	97	9.7
CINCINNATI	11	14	10	4	108	9.8
OHIO STATE	9	12	9	4	93	10.3
YALE	9	13	16	1	97	10.8
SAN DIEGO ST.	11	16	15	4	123	11.2
MIAMI, O.	10	15	11	3	112	11.2

PASS INTERCEPTION AVOIDANCE--SOUTHERN CALIFORNIA,2.2% HAD INTERCEPTED (6 OF 279 ATTS.);WISCONSIN, 2.5% (5 OF 198); MICHIGAN, 3.0% (6 OF 198); AIR FORCE, 3.7% (15 OF 404); AUBURN, 3.9% (12 OF 311).

PASS INTERCEPTION LEADERS--ARKANSAS, INT. 11.4% (32 OF 280 ATTS. AGST); TULANE,11.3% (28 OF 247); PENN STATE, 10.8% (26 OF 240); OHIO U., 10.8% (17 OF 157). LEADERS IN YARDS--TENNESSEE, 612; NEBRASKA, 532; TULANE, 430; WESTERN MICHIGAN, 423; ARKANSAS, 406; CITADEL, 387.

LEAST PENALIZED TEAMS--WICHITA ST., 28.3 YARDS PER GAME (25 FOR 255); NORTHWESTERN, 29.9 (31 FOR 299); GEORGIA, 32.1 (37 FOR 321); ALABAMA, 31.5 (36 FOR 346).

Chapter 5

Golf

Contrary to most sports, scoring in golf normally is confined to scorecards carried by the individual players or a scorer assigned to the game.

In professional and major amateur tournaments, which attract many spectators, a large master scoreboard usually is placed near the 18th green, showing the hole-by-hole scores of competitors after each has completed his round.

Also, in some major tournaments, a scorer or marker may be assigned to each group (twosome, threesome or foursome), and he carries a board showing the relative position to Par ("2 over" or "1 under," for example) that each player is at the end of each hole.

Nevertheless, even when a scorer or scoreboard is utilized to keep spectators posted on the players' progress, the official scorecards are carried by the individual players or an official scorer. Each player usually is assigned to keep the score of his opponent. However, each player is required to certify his score on each hole and is responsible (and may be disqualified) for any errors made in recording his score.

There are two basic systems of scoring in golf: (1) match play and (2) stroke or medal play.

Match Play

In match play (where players have the same handicap or play at "scratch"—without regard to handicap) each hole is a unit won by the player holing out in the fewest strokes.

The winner is the player who wins the most holes in the match, regardless of his total or gross score for the round. The scoring is cumulative. That is, if a player wins the first hole, he is "1-up" on his opponent. If he wins the second hole, he is then, "2-up." If he loses the second hole, the match is "even." If each player takes an equal number of strokes on the same hole, it is called "halved" and has no bearing on the scoring.

Thus, if a player wins three of the first six holes, two are halved and he loses the other, he is "2-up" at the end of six holes. The score is maintained cumulatively on that basis for the entire 18 or 36 hole match.

It is not necessary to play the entire number of designated holes, if one player takes a lead impossible for his opponent to overcome.

Example: Golfer A leads Golfer B by three units or holes, with only two holes to play. Even if Golfer B wins the remaining two holes, he obviously cannot overcome the deficit in the two remaining holes. Thus, the match is ended with two holes to play and Golfer A is declared the winner, "3-up and 2 to play," or, as it is more commonly expressed, "3 and 2."

If Golfer A's lead is identical to the number of holes left to be played, the status of the match is known as "dormie." That is, Golfer A can win the match by winning or halving any of the remaining holes.

If golfers are tied at the end of the round (usually 18 or 36 holes), the tie is broken by a "sudden-death" playoff, with the match continuing until one player wins a hole, and the match.

Handicap Match Play

In a match played at handicap (see later section on computing handicaps) the lower net score wins the hole. Players match their handicaps at the start of the round and the player with the higher handicap receives a handicap for the match equal to the difference in their assigned handicaps.

Example: Golfer A has a handicap of 8; Golfer B has a handicap of 6. In a match between them, Golfer A receives two strokes (8 minus 6) as a handicap for the round. Thus, on each of the two most difficult holes on the course (a pre-determined rating noted on the scorecard) he receives the benefit of a one-stroke handicap.

On these holes he matches his net score (actual strokes less handicap) against his opponent.

Example: Player A and Player B each take five strokes on the same hole, but it is a handicap hole for Player A. So, he deducts one stroke from his score and has a net score of four. Thus, Player A wins the hole.

Example: Player A has a handicap stroke on a hole on which he scored a six and his opponent, a five. Deduct one stroke from Player A's score, giving him a net score of five, the same as his opponent. The hole is halved.

Should the difference in handicaps be more than 18 (or if a player has a handicap of more than 18 in a tournament), the golfer will receive a two-stroke handicap on the number of holes by which the difference (or his handicap) exceeds 18.

Example: Player A has a handicap of 28, Player B has a handicap of 8, with the difference 20. Player A will receive a two-stroke handicap on each of the No. 1 and No. 2 handicap holes and a one-stroke handicap on the remaining 16 holes.

Example: In a better-ball tournament, Golfer A has a 23 handicap. He'll receive two strokes as handicap on each of the first five handicap holes, one stroke on each of the remaining 13.

A handicap match that ends all even also should be played off, hole-by-hole, until one player or one side wins a hole. The playoff should start on the hole where the match began. Handicap strokes are assigned as in the original round.

Stroke or Medal Play

Stroke or medal play is based on the *total* strokes taken by a player on the predetermined number of holes fixed for the match. The player taking the fewest number of strokes is the winner.

A medal play tournament may range from 9 holes to 72 holes, depending upon the type of tournament. Most major amateur and professional medal play tournaments are played over 72 holes, either four 18-hole rounds over four days, or 18 holes each on two days, with 36 holes played on the final day.

When a medal play tournament is played at handicap, each player's handicap is subtracted from his total strokes (gross score), with the low net score determining the winner.

Example: Player A requires a total of 89 actual strokes in completing 18 holes. His handicap is 18. Subtracting 18 from 89 gives him a net score of 71. All net scores are computed in the same manner for all players, with the winner that player with the lowest net score.

In the event of a tie, the winner is determined either by an 18-hole playoff among those tied for the lead or by a sudden death playoff as in match play.

In a handicap tournament playoff, if a full round of 18 holes is played, the players will use the same handicaps that were assigned in the original round. If it is a sudden-death playoff, players are given handicap strokes on appropriate holes as they would in match play.

Sometimes in medal play, a tie is broken by a playoff over a specified number of holes. That is, instead of a full 18-hole round or sudden-death playoff, the tournament committee specifies a playoff over a fixed number of holes less than 18 (i.e. over 6 holes, or 9 holes). In this case, where the play is at handicap, the percentage of 18 holes to be played shall be applied to the players' handicaps to determine the strokes they receive during the playoff.

Example: Golfer A and Golfer B tie for the lead at the end of a 36-hole medal-play handicap tournament. The playoff is scheduled to be played over 9 holes (50% of 18). Player A's handicap is 8, Player B's is 6. Each receives 50% of his handicap (4 for Player A, 3 for Player B) over the nine-hole playoff.

Bogey or Par Tournaments

Bogey or par competition is a form of play in which each player compares his score for each hole with an arbitrary, imaginary score, fixed by a committee. The player wins, loses, or halves each hole with this "bogey" or "par" exactly as he would with an opponent. The bogey or par score represents the number of strokes in which a good player might reasonably be expected to make each hole. The reckoning for bogey competition is made as in match play. The winner is the competitor who is most successful in the aggregate of holes.

Stableford Competition

Stableford competition is another form of stroke competition. In this form of play, points are awarded in relation to a fixed score at each hole as follows:

1 point . . . Hole completed in one over fixed score
2 points . . . Hole completed in fixed score
3 points . . . Hole completed in one under fixed score
4 points . . . Hole completed in two under fixed score
5 points . . . Hole completed in three under fixed score

The winner is the person who scores the highest number of points.

Matches

Match play between two individuals is called a single.

In a three-ball match, each player simultaneously plays two separate matches (with one ball) against the other two players in his threesome. On each hole, he matches his score against each of the other two players.

In a four-ball match, two players are matched against the other pair. On each hole, the better ball (lowest score) of each two-man team is matched against the better ball of the other.

A scotch foursome matches two players on each side, but each team uses only one ball, with the players alternating strokes.

In team play, such as dual meets between clubs or schools or the Walker or Ryder Cup competitions, a predetermined number of points is assigned to each match, with the team compiling the most total points the winner.

Competition may be in man-to-man singles, match play only, in teams of twosomes, or a combination.

Points are assigned to winners in one of two ways. In the first, the winning golfer or twosome is awarded one point for winning a match (usually 18 holes). If the golfers or teams end up even, each side is given one-half point. The team which has the most aggregate points is the winner. The Walker Cup and the Ryder Cup competitions, matching respectively amateurs and professionals from the United States with their English counterparts, is contested in this manner.

Most high school and colleges use the Nassau system of scoring for dual meets. In Nassau scoring, three points are assigned for each singles and doubles match. One point is awarded to the golfer or team that wins the most holes over the first nine holes; another point is awarded for the second nine, and a third for the 18-hole winner.

Example: Golfer A leads Golfer B, 3-up at the end of nine holes. On the back or second nine holes, Golfer B has a 1-up edge. Thus, for the entire 18 hole round, Golfer A wins, 2-up. Golfer A is awarded one point for winning the first nine and a second point for winning the 18-hole match. Golfer B is credited with one point for winning the most holes on the back nine. Thus, Golfer A defeats Golfer B, 2-1 (See Form 5-A).

If either of the nine-hole segments or the entire 18-hole round ends with the players all even, each is awarded one-half point for each of the segments that end up all even.

Form 5-A

HOLES	1	2	3	4	5	6	7	8	9	OUT	10	11	12	13	14	15	16	17	18	IN	GROSS TOTAL	HANDICAP	NET SCORE
YARDS	311	327	188	431	150	393	140	432	360	2732	189	471	449	439	140	372	527	525	374	3486	6218		
HANDICAP STROKES	14	12	6	4	18	10	16	2	8		13	15	1	5	17	11	7	3	9				
PAR	4	4	3	4	3	4	3	4	4	33	3	5	4	4	3	4	5	5	4	37	70		
GOLFER "A"	4	(4)	4	(5)	3	4	(2)	5	5	36	3	5	5	(4)	3	(4)	6	6	5	41	77		
GOLFER "B"	4	5	4	6	3	4	3	5	5	39	3	(4)	5	5	3	5	6	(5)	(4)	40	79		
	← "A" 3-up →										← "B" 1-up →												
	← "A" 2-up →																						

Circled scores show holes won by each golfer.

Example: Golfer A leads Golfer B, 3-up at the end of nine holes. On the second nine they end up all even. For the 18 holes, Golfer A has a 3-up edge. Thus Golfer A wins the match 2½-½.

Example: Golfer A and Golfer B end up all even on the first nine, end up all even, again, on the second nine, and thus are even for the 18. Each receives one-half point for each segment and the match is tied, 1½-1½.

Team play in high school or college usually is in foursomes, with two singles matches (each player paired against one of the opponents) and one team match (each pair of teammates competing as a team on a better-ball basis against the opponents).

Thus, in each foursome there are nine Nassau points to be contested, three for each singles match and three more for the team competition.

In recording the results of a team match or dual meet, the golfers are listed according to their pairings in singles, with each player's gross score listed following his name. Then the foursome results follow each pair of singles.

Example: In a match between Central High and East Tech, Central defeated East Tech, 14½ to 12½.

Carroll (C), 73, def. Smith (ET), 77, 2-1; Wilson (C), 82, def. Morgan (ET); 88, 3-0. Carroll and Smith def. Wilson and Morgan, 2-1. Russell (ET), 74, def. Droman (C), 81, 3-0; Phillips (C), 79, def. Harvey (ET), 78, 2-1; Russell and Harvey tied Dorman and Phillips, 1½-1½. Dana (C), 83, def. Walters (ET), 84, 2-1; Howard (ET), 84, def. Miller (C), 89, 3-0; Dana and Miller def. Walters and Howard, 2-1. Central, 14½, def. East Tech 12½.

Note: It is the total number of *points,* not the number of individual or foursome winners, that determines the team victor.

Computing Par

Par is the term designated for the score an expert player is expected to make for a given hole. To shoot par on a hole, a player is expected to reach the green in one, two or three strokes, depending upon the distance, then to sink the ball in two putts.

The following yardages usually are the basis for determining par on any given holes.

Par	Men	Women
3	Up to 250 yards	Up to 210 yards
4	251 to 470 yards	211 to 400 yards
5	471 yards and up	401 to 575 yards
6		576 yards and up

There are exceptions to these distances, particularly in the boundary areas, depending upon the degree of difficulty of the hole in relation to others on the course. For instance, on some courses, under certain circumstances, a 460-yard hole might be a par 5, or a 475-yard hole might be a par 4.

On a course where Par is 72 (the normal), it is considered desirable to have two Par-3 holes, two Par-5 holes and five Par-4 holes on each nine. Thus, to achieve the desired balance, Par may be assigned to a hole where the yardage is less or more than the distances prescribed above.

Scorecards

Each golf course or country club has its own scorecard and the basic information is the same. (See Form 5-A)

The card is a chart, with a column for each hole (in the order they are played). Each column lists the number of the hole, the yardage (from tee to hole), the assigned Par for the hole and the assignment of handicap strokes.

Handicap strokes are assigned according to the comparative degree of difficulty (in relation to its par) of each hole on each course (i.e. the most difficult hole is the No. 1 handicap hole, the next most difficult, the No. 2 handicap hole, etc.).

When handicap holes are used, they are applied in the numerical order of the handicap strokes assigned to the particular course.

Example: Golfer A, with a 14 handicap, plays against Golfer B, who has a handicap of 9. Thus, Golfer A receives 5 handicap strokes.

If played on the course using the scorecard in Form 5-A, he would receive the strokes on the five most difficult holes, handicap holes 1 through 5, which in this case are, in order, the 12th, 8th, 17th, 4th and 13th.

Scorecards also usually list the Course Rating (see under Handicaps), provide space for the scorer and competitor signatures, and list any local conditions or rules that apply to that particular course.

Scoring

A scorecard is provided for each competitor, listing his name and the date of the match or tournament. After each hole, the score is inserted by the scorer (whether it is an opponent or an assigned marker or scorekeeper).

When the round is completed, the scorer signs the card and hands it to the competitor. He, in turn, checks his score, hole-by-hole, settles any doubtful points with officials, countersigns the card and submits it to a designated official.

This procedure is important, because golf probably is the only sport where each competitor is completely responsible for tallying his own score. No alteration may be made in the card after it is submitted to an official. If the scorecard, when submitted, includes an incorrect score for any hole, showing less strokes than the player actually took, he is automatically disqualified. Should the card show a score higher than actually played on any hole, the score will stand as submitted.

Handicaps

In order to equalize players of different abilities, a handicap system is utilized in golf to provide even competition.

The normal handicap system is that of the United States Golf Association. Some regional district members of the USGA use a slightly different handicapping formula, but the same principles are followed.

For golfers who are members of a country club or other golf club that is a member of a USGA affiliate, handicaps are computed by the official organization and posted monthly.

There are three basic ingredients in computing a proper handicap. They include the golfer's *adjusted* score, the *Course Rating* and the *differential* between the adjusted score and the Course Rating.

Adjusted Score

In most handicap systems, golfers employ what is known as an

Equitable Stroke Control Procedure (Form 5-B). It places a limit on the number of strokes that may be recorded (regardless of how many are taken) for handicap purposes. The procedure entails a score limit of one over par on any hole for golfers with "plus" or scratch (0) handicap; also, a score limit of 2 over par on as many holes as the handicap is increased over scratch up to an 18 handicap, and one over par on the balance of the holes; also, a score limit of 3 over par on as many holes as the handicap is increased over 18, and 2 over par on the balance of the holes played.

As an example, a golfer with a 16 handicap would be allowed to register a score of 2 over par on each of 16 holes, and one over par on the other two. Thus, 2 over par (a double-bogey) is the most he can record on his official scorecard for handicap purposes.

If the player with a 16 handicap completes his round with 93 strokes, but he scores an 8 on a par 4 hole (and nothing else more than a double-bogey), he would deduct two strokes from that hole, entering a 6 on the scorecard. His adjusted score, then, would be 91 (93 minus 2).

Form 5-B is a chart showing the formula for Equitable Stroke Control.

Course Rating

All courses are rated according to their actual playing difficulty and the rating is assigned by representatives of the authoritative golf organization (USGA or regional association) in the area of the course. The representatives play the course and assign a rating to each hole, according to the degree of difficulty. The sum of the ratings for the 18 holes is called the Course Rating.

Note: Although Par is determined primarily by distance (see earlier section on Computing Par), the Course Rating is determined by degree of difficulty. Thus, for two par-4 holes of the same length, one or the other, for instance, may be rated 3.7 (judged slightly easier than a par-4 for an expert player) or 4.0 (judged to be a reasonable par-4) or a 4.2 (judged to be more difficult than a normal par-4 hole).

Though the normal "par" for a course is 72, the Course Rating can vary greatly. A short, flat course might have a Course Rating as low as, for instance, 64, while a difficult course might have a Course Rating higher than par. As an example, famed Pebble Beach, when played from the championship tees, has a Course Rating of 75, three more than par.

EQUITABLE STROKE CONTROL PROCEDURE

A score limit of one over par on all holes for plus and scratch men.

A score limit of 2 over par on as many holes as the handicap is increased over scratch up to 18 handicap, and one over par on balance of holes.

A score limit of 3 over par on as many holes as the handicap is increased over 18, and 2 over par on balance of holes.

As an example, a 25 handicap man would be allowed a maximum limit of 7—three over par holes in each 18 hole round and eleven two over pars on balance of holes.

EQUITABLE STROKE CONTROL CHART

Handicap	Max. Stroke Limit of	Max. Stroke Limit of	*18 Hole Score Limit
0		1 over par on 18 holes	90
1	2 over par on 1 hole	1 " " " 17 holes	91
2	2 " " " 2 holes	1 " " " the balance	92
3	2 " " " 3 "	1 " " " " "	93
4	2 " " " 4 "	1 " " " " "	94
5	2 " " " 5 "	1 " " " " "	95
6	2 " " " 6 "	1 " " " " "	96
7	2 " " " 7 "	1 " " " " "	97
8	2 " " " 8 "	1 " " " " "	98
9	2 " " " 9 "	1 " " " " "	99
10	2 " " " 10 "	1 " " " " "	100
11	2 " " " 11 "	1 " " " " "	101
12	2 " " " 12 "	1 " " " " "	102
13	2 " " " 13 "	1 " " " " "	103
14	2 " " " 14 "	1 " " " " "	104
15	2 " " " 15 "	1 " " " " "	105
16	2 " " " 16 "	1 " " " " "	106
17	2 " " " 17 "	1 " " " " "	107
18	2 " " " 18 "		108
19	3 " " " 1 hole	2 " " on the balance	109
20	3 " " " 2 holes	2 " " " " "	110
21	3 " " " 3 "	2 " " " " "	111
22	3 " " " 4 "	2 " " " " "	112
23	3 " " " 5 "	2 " " " " "	113
24	3 " " " 6 "	2 " " " " "	114
25	3 " " " 7 "	2 " " " " "	115
26	3 " " " 8 "	2 " " " " "	116
27	3 " " " 9 "	2 " " " " "	117
28	3 " " " 10 "	2 " " " " "	118
29	3 " " " 11 "	2 " " " " "	119
30	3 " " " 12 "	2 " " " " "	120
31	3 " " " 13 "	2 " " " " "	121
32	3 " " " 14 "	2 " " " " "	122
33	3 " " " 15 "	2 " " " " "	123
34	3 " " " 16 "	2 " " " " "	124
35	3 " " " 17 "	2 " " " " "	125
36	3 " " " 18 "		126

*The last column shows 18 hole total scores for a par 72 course if an individual shot his score limit on each hole. While this is most unlikely, it is shown here merely to set forth the equity of this stroke control plan.

Form 5-B

A Course Rating does not have to be an even number. As each hole is rated on the decimal system, the total for 18 holes may well be a 67.9 or a 70.3, or any uneven number that is the sum for 18 holes of that course. For instance, the scorecard shown in Form 5-A is for a country club with a Course Rating of 68.6.

Differential

The differential is the control figure used in handicap computation to equalize the difference in Course Ratings. It is the difference between the adjusted score and the Course Rating.

The differential, because it takes into consideration both the score and difficulty of the course on which it is scored, is considered a more definite measure (than the score itself) of the character of performance by the golfer.

Handicaps, then, are based on the *differential* between the player's *adjusted* score and the *Course Rating* for the course on which he made the score.

Thus, a player who plays regularly on a more rigorous course may have generally higher scores than a golfer with the same handicap who plays on an easier course. If the handicaps are correct, theoretically, if they meet on the same course and both play to their handicaps, they would finish all even.

Computing Handicaps

A current handicap is computed by taking 85 percent of the total of the *differentials* of a golfer's lowest 10 adjusted scores from his most recent 20 rounds or (in some areas) his most recent 15 rounds.

Example: These are the 10 lowest of the most recent adjusted scores of a golfer, with Course Rating and differential shown for each round.

Score	Course Rating	Differential
83	68	15
82	69.2	12.8
83	70	13
86	68	18
86	70.4	15.6
84	68	16
80	71	9
82	69.6	12.4

80	69.6		10.4
84	68		16
		Total	138.2

The average differential for the 10 rounds if 13.82. Multiplying this average by .85 gives 11.8 or, rounded to the nearest figure, a handicap of 12. (See Form 5-C)

However, it isn't necessary to be a mathematician to compute golf handicaps. Once the total differential is determined, it is only necessary to apply it to the chart in Form 5-D, a chart provided by most regional golf associations.

A quick, unofficial form of computing handicaps is to total the five best (lowest) most recent scores and subtract this figure from the total of the pars for the five courses played. When the difference has been determined, the following scale may be applied to establish a handicap.

0-3 = Scratch Handicap	35-40 = 6 Handicap	72-78 = 12 Handicap
4-9 = 1 Handicap	41-46 = 7 Handicap	79-84 = 13 Handicap
10-15 = 2 Handicap	47-53 = 8 Handicap	85-90 = 14 Handicap
16-21 = 3 Handicap	54-59 = 9 Handicap	91-96 = 15 Handicap
22-28 = 4 Handicap	60-65 = 10 Handicap	97-103 = 16 Handicap
29-34 = 5 Handicap	66-71 = 11 Handicap	104-109 = 17 Handicap

Example:

5 best scores	Par
79	71
81	72
85	72
77	72
79	71
401	358

The difference of 43 (401 minus 358) gives the player a handicap of 7.

Normally, full differences in handicaps are utilized in tournaments, both in match and medal play. Sometimes, notably in intra-club tournaments, golfers play at seven-eighths or one-half of their handicap differences.

When a tournament is played at seven-eighths difference, the following table summarizes the adjustments necessary in handicap matches.

When the difference between handicaps is:

1 give 1 stroke	10 give 9 strokes	19 give 17 strokes
2 give 2 strokes	11 give 10 strokes	20 give 18 strokes
3 give 3 strokes	12 give 11 strokes	21 give 18 strokes
4 give 4 strokes	13 give 11 strokes	22 give 19 strokes
5 give 4 strokes	14 give 12 strokes	23 give 20 strokes
6 give 5 strokes	15 give 13 strokes	24 give 21 strokes
7 give 6 strokes	16 give 14 strokes	25 give 22 strokes
8 give 7 strokes	17 give 15 strokes	26 give 23 strokes
9 give 8 strokes	18 give 16 strokes	27 give 24 strokes

Records

Until recent years, there was little public awareness of golf records. When listed, they usually were confined to a list of tournament winners, a fact whose main virtue was in nostalgia.

Primary use of old golf records was in combining the accomplishments of one man, such as the fabled Grand Slam by Bobby Jones, who in 1930 won the four major tournaments of that era, the U.S. Amateur and Open and the British Amateur and Open tourneys.

The mushrooming popularity of golf, evidenced by increased numbers of both participants and spectators, has resulted in compilation of many miscellaneous records, and for those charged with statistics for a major tournament, they can be useful for publicity purposes. Such records are usually available in the office of the regional association of the USGA or from the PGA headquarters in Dunedin, Fla.

For instance, the record in one tourney for the total number of birdies (one under par) or double-bogeys (two over par) on one hole in a tournament may be of some use in publicizing a particularly easy or difficult hole.

However, for general purposes, these records for a golfer, a team or golf course should be sufficient for historical comparison:

Lowest score for a single round—9, 18, 36, 54 and 72 holes.

Lowest average score for a single season or career.

Most rounds and most consecutive rounds under par or under an arbitrary score (such as most rounds under 70).

Most matches and most consecutive matches won (in match and/or team play).

Most tournaments and most consecutive tournaments won.

Most birdies, most pars and most eagles (two under par) in a round or tournament—9, 18, 36, 54 and 72 holes.

DIFFERENTIAL CHART

COVERS ALL COURSE RATINGS

This term is used for handicapping in golf to signify the difference between the 18 hole score and the course rating.

Viz:		
	Adjusted Score	95
	Rating	—72
	Differential	23

Average Differentials			Current Handicap
—5.6	to	—4.4	+3
—4.3	to	—3.2	+2
—3.1	to	—1.9	+1
—1.8	to	— .7	0
— .6	to	+ .6	1
+ .7	to	+1.8	2
1.9	to	3.1	3
3.2	to	4.3	4
4.4	to	5.6	5
5.7	to	6.8	6
6.9	to	8.1	7
8.2	to	9.3	8
9.4	to	10.6	9
10.7	to	11.8	10
11.9	to	13.1	11
13.2	to	14.3	12
14.4	to	15.6	13
15.7	to	16.8	14
16.9	to	18.1	15
18.2	to	19.3	16
19.4	to	20.6	17
20.7	to	21.8	18
21.9	to	23.1	19
23.2	to	24.3	20
24.4	to	25.6	21
25.7	to	26.8	22
26.9	to	28.1	23
28.2	to	29.3	24
29.4	to	30.6	25
30.7	to	31.8	26
31.9	to	33.1	27
33.2	to	34.3	28
34.4	to	35.6	29
35.7	to	36.8	30
36.9	to	38.1	31
38.2	to	39.3	32
39.4	to	40.6	33
40.7	to	41.8	34
41.9	to	43.1	35
43.2	to	44.3	36

Form 5-C

DIFFERENTIAL CHART
Covers All Course Ratings

This term is used for handicapping in golf to signify the difference between the 18 hole score and the course rating.

Viz.		
	Adjusted Score	95
	Rating	–72.4
	Differential	22.6

Total of Lowest 10 of 20 Handicap Differentials			Total of Lowest 10 of 20 Handicap Differentials		
From	To	Handi-cap	From	To	Handi-cap
–41.1	–29.5	+3	76.5	88.2	7
–29.4	17.7	+2	88.3	99.9	8
–17.6	– 5.9	+1	100.0	111.7	9
– 5.8	+ 5.8	0	111.8	123.5	10
+ 5.9	+17.6	1	123.6	135.2	11
17.7	29.4	2	135.4	147.0	12
29.5	41.1	3	147.1	158.8	13
41.2	52.9	4	158.9	170.5	14
53.0	64.7	5	170.6	182.3	15
64.8	76.4	6	182.4	194.1	16

Total of Lowest 10 of 20 Handicap Differentials			Total of Lowest 10 of 20 Handicap Differentials		
From	To	Handi-cap	From	To	Handi-cap
194.2	205.8	17	311.8	323.5	27
205.9	217.6	18	323.6	335.2	28
217.7	229.4	19	335.3	347.0	29
229.5	241.1	20	347.1	358.8	30
241.2	252.9	21	358.9	370.5	31
253.0	264.7	22	370.6	382.3	32
264.8	276.4	23	382.4	394.1	33
276.5	288.2	24	394.2	405.8	34
288.3	299.9	25	405.9	417.6	35
300.0	311.7	26	417.7	and over	36

Form 5-D

Fewer Than 20 Differentials Available.

When at least 5 but fewer than 20 differentials are available, the handicap is computed as follows:

Differentials Available	Differentials To Be Used
5	Lowest 1
6	Lowest 2
7	Lowest 3
8 or 9	Lowest 4
10 or 11	Lowest 5
12 or 13	Lowest 6
14 or 15	Lowest 7
16 or 17	Lowest 8
18 or 19	Lowest 9

Example:
Lowest 3
differentials

12
10
12
34 Average by dividing by 3 = 11.1

Multiply by 10. Use chart to determine handicap. 111.0 = 9 Handicap.

Chapter 6

Ice Hockey

Basic statistics in ice hockey are relatively simple—goals attempted, goals scored, assists, goals allowed, goalie saves and penalties, but they are complicated somewhat by the requirement of scorer's judgment in determining some statistical credits.

The National Hockey League uses a crew (as many as 11 persons) of so-called minor officials for each team, most of them concerned with statistics of some type. And this is even without goalie saves, a category not recognized by the NHL.

Many of the statistical recordings made for the NHL are of little value to the average high school or college statistical program. However, for those who may want in-depth records, all of the NHL statistical categories will be outlined.

Scoring

Although games are won by the team scoring the most goals, in statistical rankings, equal weight is given to goals and assists. One point is given for each goal and one point for each assist. The scoring champion is the player who accumulates the highest number of total points.

Example: Player A scores 25 goals and has no (0) assists. Player B scores 12 goals and is credited with 14 assists. Player B, with 26 points, is the scoring champion.

Goals Attempted

A Goal Attempted or Shot on Goal is charged on any deliberate action by an attacking player to shoot or deflect a puck with his stick into the opposing goal, which actually enters the goal or which, except by intervention of the goalkeeper or any other player, would have entered the goal.

Note: A peculiarity of ice hockey statistics is that Shots on Goal include only those shots which score or would have scored except for action by the goalkeeper (or some other defender). For instance, shots which hit the goal posts and do not go into the net, are not counted as Shots on Goal; nor do shots which completely miss the net, the posts and the goalkeeper.

Statisticians may prefer to record this category in the standard manner of other sports (i.e. charge Goal Attempt on any shot or deflection intended to score a goal, whether it is stopped by the goalkeeper or posts or misses completely); however, all scorers in the same league or conference should use the same standard or comparative statistics will have no meaning.

Goals

The ice hockey scorer or statistician is not required to make a judgment on whether a goal is scored or disallowed when the puck enters the net. This is the responsibility of the referee, as is the designation of the player credited with the goal.

In the case of goals, the scorer merely is a recorder, using the information provided by the referee. However, for his clarification, three special situations should be reviewed:

1. When an attempt on goal is deflected into the net by an offensive player, the goal is credited to the player who deflected the puck.
2. When the puck is put into the goal, in any manner, by a defending player, the goal is credited to the offensive player who last played the puck (however, there can be no assists in this situation).
3. If an offensive player kicks the puck, and it is deflected into the goal by any defensive player (except the goalkeeper), the goal is credited to the player who kicked the puck.

Penalty Shots

Statistically, Penalty Shots are recorded as any other Shot on Goal or Goal Scored. However, some statisticians may prefer to maintain separate entries for these categories as a record of performance by individual players under the special Penalty Shot circumstances.

In cumulative statistics, however, they should be recorded under Shots on Goal and Goals Scored along with those recorded during regular play. Thus, if a player takes 52 Shots on Goal and scores 11 times during regular action, and also attempts 3 Penalty Shots and is successful on one, his cumulative statistics should show 55 shots and 12 goals.

Shooting Percentages

As in other sports, the Shooting Percentage of a player is determined by dividing the total number of Shots on Goal into the total Goals Scored. (Again, separate percentages may be maintained for Penalty Shots, but cumulative statistics should reflect the total performance.)

Example: Using the example under Penalty Shots, above, Player A was charged with 55 Shots on Goal and made 12 Goals. His shooting percentage (12 — 55) is 21.8 percent.

Assists

The scorer is required to make a judgment on awarding Assists and is charged with crediting an Assist to the appropriate player or players on each goal.

The definition for Assists, for both amateur and professional ice hockey, provides a more liberal awarding of Assists than in most other sports.

An Assist is credited to the player or players *taking part* in the play preceding each goal, even though the play may originate in the defensive zone. (Note the definition does not require the assisting player to *set up* a goal by his pass, only that he "take part" in the play that culminates in a goal.)

Although caution is expressed in scoring instructions against awarding Assists too liberally, this definition normally results in an Assist being credited to the last player or last two players who handled the puck preceding a goal.

Scoring of Assists is so liberal, under the definition, that the National Hockey League has found it necessary to provide guidelines to scorers. The NHL recognizes a ratio of 1.55 to 1.65 (that is, an average of 1.55 to 1.65 assists for each goal scored) as an *acceptable* standard.

No more than two Assists may be credited on any one goal. Each Assist counts as one point in the player's scoring record.

Scoring Points

Equal credit is given for Goals and Assists in ice hockey. Thus, each Goal Scored and each Assist counts as one point in a player's scoring record.

Example: Player A scores 14 goals and has 20 assists. Player B scores 24 goals and has 10 assists. Each player is credited with 34 points in the scoring standings.

The scoring champion is that player who accumulates the most total points (Goals plus Assists) during the season.

Saves

The NHL does not recognize this statistical category. However, in college, high school and amateur hockey, a goalkeeper is credited with a "save" whenever he stops a shot, which otherwise would have been a goal (i.e. when his actions prevent the puck from entering the net).

Goals Allowed

A careful record should be maintained to show how many goals are scored while each goalkeeper is on the ice. A standard statistical category is Goals Allowed Per Game. The champion is that goalie who permits the fewest goals per game.

Example: During a season, John Smith plays all or part of 30 games. During the time he is on the ice, opponents score a total of 69 goals. His Goals Per Game average is 2.3 (69 ÷ 30).

Penalties

In the NHL, a separate statistical official, a Penalty Timekeeper, is used to record pertinent penalty statistics and to file a report to the league office following each game. However, in other areas of play, this function probably will be assigned to the scorer. There is no judgment involved. Officials call the penalties; the scorer merely records them.

Included in the overall statistics should be a breakdown of the type of penalty (major, minor, misconduct or match), the time imposed and the starting time of the penalty being served.

For statistical purposes, normally only the total minutes served by each player will be included in cumulative tables.

Miscellaneous

A number of statistical categories are maintained in the NHL to show details of scoring when a team has other than a normal lineup on the ice. These may be useful for coaching purposes and on occasion may serve as a source for feature or publicity material.

These categories include: (a) number of goals scored for and against each team when both teams have the same number of men on the ice, (b) goals scored for and against, when the scoring team has a man advantage, (c) when the scoring team is shorthanded, and (d) goals scored against an empty net (when goalkeeper has been replaced by an extra forward).

Working Forms

Goals

Goals attempted and scored may be recorded either by means of a shot chart or a tally sheet. The latter has the advantage of almost instantaneous summarization, if kept in a simple form. However, a shot chart may be more useful for coaching analysis.

If utilizing a shot chart, it may be in the same form as that used in other sports. The uniform number of the player taking the shot should be inserted (see Form 6-A) on the spot on the chart corresponding to the spot on the playing ice from where the shot was taken. When the goal is made, the number is circled.

The shot chart may be utilized to completely analyze the results of shots. Form 6-A shows a typical shot chart for one period and by underlining or circling the uniform numbers, a record may be made of whether the shot missed the cage, was blocked by the defense, when there was a goalie save or when a goal was scored. The individual totals, then, can be summarized at the end of the period.

A tally sheet may be a simple recording of each shot and each goal (Form 6-B) or may be a pre-printed form such as that used by the NHL (Form 6-C). The latter has numbers pre-printed with space for up to eight attempts by each player in each period. A slanted slash through the number indicates a shot attempt and a circled "x" indicates a successful field goal.

In Form 6-C, Smith had two shot attempts in the first period, one in the second and was successful with his only shot in the third period. Thus, for the game, he has four attempts and one goal. In Form 6-B, this shows simply as a total of four attempts and one goal.

The NHL maintains records of each player on the ice when a goal is scored, either by his team or opponent. Form 6-D shows how this is accomplished. Under "Goals For," it is noted that Smith was on the ice at the time his team scored three of its goals and under "Goals Against," when the opponents scored twice.

The numerals indicate the sequence of scoring by both teams. For instance, the "slash" through the number "2," under "Goals For," shows it was the second goal of the game. The slash indicates a goal scored when both teams have the same number of men on the ice (not necessarily at full strength, but the same number); the circle around

Form 6-A

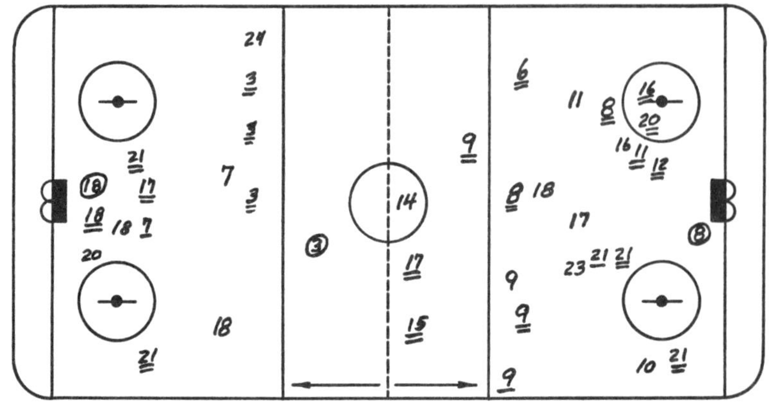

SYMBOLS—Number indicates player shooting. 3—Shot missed cage; 3—Shot blocked by defense; 3—Shot saved by goalie; 3—Goal scored

a number indicates the scoring team had a man advantage; the "x" shows the scoring team was playing shorthanded.

Goalie Saves and Goals Allowed

As noted earlier, the NHL does not recognize this category as a statistical entry, but most other types of ice hockey competition use these statistics. Saves can be recorded on a simple tally sheet and, for corollary interest, might be recorded period-by-period. The same form can be utilized for recording the goals scored against each goalie by inserting an "x" to denote a goal scored.

Form 6-E shows that in one game the team used two goalies, Jones and Walters. In the first period, Jones was credited with 2 saves and allowed 1 goal; in the second period, he had 5 saves; in the third period he allowed 2 goals. Walters was credited with two saves in the third period and allowed one goal. In the overtime period, he had one save. Thus, for the game, Jones was credited with 7 saves and allowed 3 goals; Walters had 3 saves and gave up one goal.

The NHL uses a form similar to its shot tally sheet to indicate Goals Allowed. Form 6-F shows that Jones gave up the 2nd, 4th and 5th goals of the game and the circle indicates goal No. 5 was scored when the opponents had a one-man advantage. Walters permitted the 7th goal of the game to be scored. There is a miscellaneous entry for goals scored when no goalie is on the ice (in the example this did not happen) and space to indicate the time during which the goalie was

PLAYER	NO	attempts	goals
SMITH	3	////	/

Form 6-B

PLAYER	No.	SHOTS 1st	2nd	3rd	OT.	
SMITH	3	1 2 3 4 5 6 7 8	1 2 3 4 5 6 7 8	1 2 3 4 5 6 7 8	1 2 3 4 5 6 7 8	4

Form 6-C

PLAYER	No	SHOTS 1st	2nd	3rd	OT		GOALS FOR		GOALS AGAINST	
SMITH	3	1 2 3 4 5 6 7 8	1 2 3 4 5 6 7 8	1 2 3 4 5 6 7 8	1 2 3 4 5 6 7 8	4	1 2 3 4 5 6 7 8 9 10 11 12	3	1 2 3 4 5 6 7 8 9 10 11 12	2

Form 6-D

PLAYERS	1st	2nd	3rd		totals save	GA
JONES	/X/	~~////~~	XX		7	3
WALTERS			//X	/	3	/

Form 6-E

GOALTENDER	No.	GOALS AGAINST		EMPTY-NET GOALS AGAINST		TIME OF GOALTENDER REMOVAL FOR EXTRA FORWARD ①	②	③	
JONES	27	1 2 3 4 5 6 7 8 9 10 11 12 –	3	1 2 3	Total		19:14 11 SECS		Total 11 SECS
WALTERS	30	1 2 3 4 5 6 7 8 9 10 11 12 –	1	1 2 3				19:35 16 SECS	16 SECS

Form 6-F

removed for an extra forward. In this game, Jones was off the ice for 11 seconds in the second period and Walters for 16 seconds in the third period.

Penalties

There are several types of forms that could be used to record penalties. The NHL uses a separate work sheet for each team, then combines the penalties in one report form (see Form 6-G).

For statistical purposes, either form could be used as a record. Form 6-G shows penalties recorded for both teams on a single sheet that can be used as both a work sheet and form for reporting to the league or conference office. It is self-explanatory, with the name, type of offense and time of penalty indicated. The notation, "Goal at 16:40," indicates Stewart was released from the penalty box before duration of the penalty because a goal was scored.

Box Scores

Ice hockey box scores are relatively standard in all levels of competition. They should show the score by periods, the individual scoring and penalties. The only major difference is in the final entry, where

VISITING TEAM	OFFENSE	TIME	HOME TEAM	PLAYER'S No.	MINORS	MAJORS	MISCONDUCTS	GAME MISCONDUCTS	MATCH
	HOLDING	4:27	E. HICKOX	20	✓				
B. MORGAN	ELBOWING	7:57		7	✓				
	HOLDING	13:09	D. REDMOND	4	✓				
B. MORGAN	INTERFERENCE	13:44		7	✓				
R. SMITH	ELBOWING	18:14		24	✓				
	HOLDING	18:14	F. HARRIS	5	✓				
	HIGH STICKING	19:54	P. SCHALL	3	✓				
B. MORGAN	HIGH STICKING	9:05		7	✓				
B. MORGAN	FIGHTING	14:49		7		✓			
	HIGH STICKING	14:49	S. STEWART	6	✓	GOAL AT 16:40			
	FIGHTING	14:49	S. STEWART	6		✓			
L. MITCHELL	HOLDING	7:16		8	✓				
	ELBOWING	10:12	E. HICKOX	20	✓				
			TOTALS		11	2			

Form 6-G

the NHL uses "Shots on Goal," and some other leagues may show "Goalie Saves."

Form 6-H is a typical box score for a game, won by Central High over East Tech, 4-3. Scores are numbered, in sequence, for each period, followed by the name of the team scoring, the individual scorer, the number of goals he has for the season, the names of the players credited with assists (in parentheses), and the time of the score.

Form 6-H

Central High	1	1	2	–	4
East Tech	1	2	0	–	3

First period—1. Central, Simpson 16 (Watson) 10:16. 2. East Tech, Russell 14 (Smith, Fuller) 14:55. Penalties—Fuller (ET) holding, Heck (CH) elbowing, Redmond (CH) holding, Heck (CH) interference, Smith (ET) elbowing, Rast (CH) holding, Watson (CH) high sticking.

Second period—3. Central, Watson 7 (Simpson, Rast) 2:50. 4. East Tech, Russell 15 (Smith, Johnson) 14:07. 5. East Tech, Fuller 5 (unassisted) 16:40. Penalties—Fuller (ET) high sticking, Fuller (ET) fighting, Moore (CH) fighting.

Third period—6. Central, Wilson 12 (Moore, Lansdale) 10:44. 7. Central, Simpson 17 (Watson) 19:51. Penalties—None.

Shots on Goal

Central High	8	11	14	–	33
East Tech	6	13	8	–	27

If including "Saves by Goalie," it can be a simple numerical total (i.e. Munson (CH) 8, Phillips (ET) 11), or it can be broken down by periods, as the Shots on Goal. Some statisticians also include in the box score the time of each penalty and/or a designation for major penalties.

Cumulative Statistics

For reporting purposes, cumulative statistics need only include games played, scoring statistics and penalties in minutes. Form 6-I is a typical listing of conference leaders at the end of a season.

Form 6-I

Player, School	GP	G	A	Pts	PIM
Ted Simpson, Central High	29	38	48	86	22
Eddie Russell, East Tech	27	22	50	72	31
Mort Simon, Western	31	43	27	70	24

Al Seegar, Southern	18	25	44	69	42
Bill Howell, Poly	29	28	38	66	26

GP—Games Played G—Goals A—Assists Pts—Points PIM—Penalties in Minutes

For goalies, cumulative statistics should include the number of games played, goals allowed, shutouts, total saves and average goals allowed per game. Form 6-J is a typical season's record.

Form 6-J

Player, School	GP	GA	SO	S	Avg.
Larry Higgins, Central High	24	75	3	192	3.1

GP—Games Played GA—Goals Allowed SO—Shutouts S—Saves Avg.—Average goals allowed per game.

The NHL also makes a complete breakdown of what it calls "Important Goals" and "Important Points," most of which are self-explanatory. These include: (1) Game-Winning Goals, (2) Game-Tying Goals, (3) First Goal of Game, (4) Score-Tying Goal, (5) Leading Goal, (6) Insurance Goal (a goal which puts the scorer's team two goals ahead of the opponent) and (7) Proximate Goal. The latter is a goal that brings the scorer's team within one goal of tying the opponent.

The total of these Important Goals scored by each player is divided by the total number of goals scored by him to give a Percentage of Important Goals.

Example: John Smith scores a total of 29 goals, 18 of which are Important Goals. Thus 62.1 percent (18 — 29) of his goals were Important Goals.

There is significance (from a coaching standpoint) and interest (from a news view) in the value of a player as determined by how well he scores when goals are needed.

The Assists made by a player on Important Goals scored by his teammates are added to his own Important Goals to give his Total Important Points. This total, divided by his total points, gives a Percentage of Important Points.

Example: It was noted above tha' Smith had 29 goals, 18 of which were Important Goals. He also had 72 Assists, of which 50 were made on Important Goals by teammates. Thus, he had a total of 101 points

(29 + 72), of which 68 (18 + 50) were important. Therefore, 67.4 (68 ÷ 101) is his Percentage of Important Points.

Records

Records for individuals and teams should be maintained in all the statistical categories reviewed. As a guide, basic record entries are listed below. If desired, each category may be broken down to show the "most" by a center, a right wing, a defenseman, etc.

Most Games Played
Most Consecutive Games Played
Most Goal Attempts (in period, game, season and career)
Most Goals (in period, game, season and career)
Most Penalty Shots (in period, game, season and career)
Most Penalty Goals (in period, game, season and career)
Most Assists (in period, game, season and career)
Most Points (in period, game, season and career)
Most Penalties (in period, game, season and career)
Most Penalty Minutes (in period, game, season and career)
Most Saves by Goalie (in period, game, season and career)
Most Shutouts by Goalie (in season and career)
Most Consecutive Shutouts by Goalie
Most Consecutive Games scoring one or more goals
Most Consecutive Games scoring one or more assists
Most Consecutive Games scoring one or more points
Most 4-Goal Games
Most 3-Goal Games (hat tricks)
Most Game-Winning Goals
Most Important Goals
Most seasons scoring 20 or more goals (or 30, or 40 or 50 goals)
Most consecutive seasons scoring 20 or more goals (or 30, 40 or 50)

Chapter 7

Lacrosse

Lacrosse is one of the few sports where the visiting team scorer is the official scorer, unless otherwise designated by the referee or chief timekeeper.

As official scorer, he has prescribed duties which extend beyond the compilation of statistics. A reasonably competent statistician, however, should be able to manage these added responsibilities along with the recording of statistics.

Duties of the official scorer in lacrosse encompass these functions:

a. Record the name and number of each player making a goal or assist.
b. Maintain a running score and cross-check his totals with the referee at the end of each quarter.
c. Record the name, number and position of each substitute.
d. Keep a record of the number of time-outs taken by each team and notify the nearest official if either team exceeds the number allowed.
e. Record the duration of each penalty, the type of violation and the name and number of the player charged with the infraction.
f. Notify the nearest official should any player incur five personal fouls or if a player enters the game without properly reporting.
g. Notify the timekeeper to blow his horn when the rules prescribe such a signal to notify the officials of a substitution or improper entry on the field of play by a player.

Statistics

The simplest lacrosse statistics are records of the number of goals scored and number of assists by each player on offense and the number of saves by the goalie.

However, a complete statistical report will also include the number of shots at goal attempted by each player, the number of penalties and penalty minutes charged to each player, playing time of each player

First Half

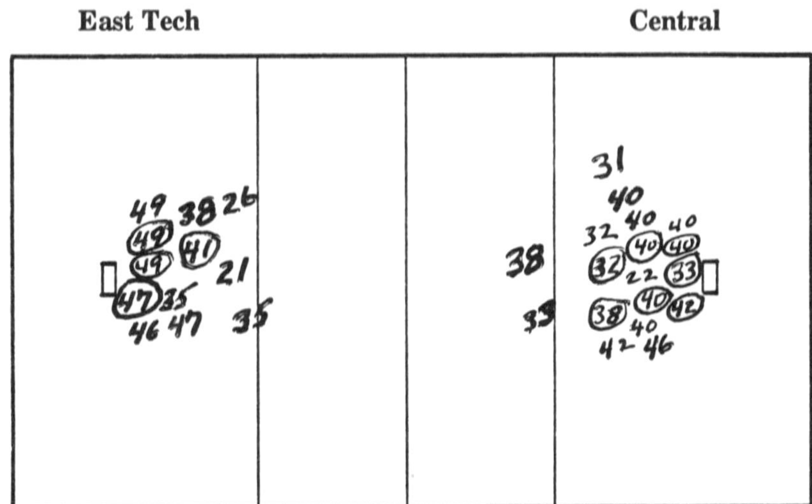

Form 7-A

and, if desired, the number of face-offs attempted by each player and recovered by his team.

Goals

As in most games where an official determination must be made on questionable situations, the scorer's judgment is *not* involved in determining whether or not a goal is scored. The scorer merely makes the appropriate entry in the scorebook or work sheet when an official signals a goal has been scored (by raising both hands in a signal that is the same as that signifying a touchdown in football).

A useful statistic, for both coaching and publicity purposes, is the number of shots attempted by each player.

For coaching analysis, a shot chart (Form 7-A) probably is the most productive work sheet for shooting statistics. This provides the coach with a ready reference on the field position of each player taking shots and how effective he is from various positions.

On the shot chart, the uniform number of a player attempting to score is inserted at the approximate spot on the field where the shot is taken. When the shot is successful, circle the uniform number.

One shot chart can be used for each quarter or each half, so that the shots attempted by each team in one period can be recorded on a single chart. If desired, the statistician can use pencils with different colors to differentiate between the home and visiting team numbers on the chart. However, for most purposes, the position of the attempted shot will clearly indicate which team made the shot.

Some statisticians prefer to combine a shot chart with a work sheet that includes other statistics (see Form 7-I later in the chapter). In this case, the two ends of the shot chart are used to record shots taken in each half by one team.

If a shot chart is utilized, this should be sufficient for shooting statistics, and a quick recap at the end of each half will give individual totals for shots attempted and goals scored.

If a shot chart is not used, a simple tally sheet can be used to note the number of shots attempted and the number of goals made. In Form 7-B, Smith attempted 12 shots and scored four goals.

Form 7-B

CENTRAL	SA	G						
SMITH	~~IIII~~ ~~IIII~~ II	IIII						

SA—Shots Attempted G—Goals Scored

If there is a question about which player scored a goal, consult an official for confirmation of identity.

A shot attempted is charged to a player any time he makes, in the scorer's judgment, a legal attempt to score a goal, or by any action that would result in a goal if the ball is not caught or deflected by an opposing player, or would result in a goal if the ball had not missed the goal.

If a ball is deflected off an offensive player's stick or body into the goal, credit him with both a goal and a shot attempt. However, in such a situation, if the ball misses the goal, do not charge him with a shot attempt.

In the event a player's shot or pass is deflected into the goal by a defensive player, credit the goal (and attempt) to the offensive player making the attempt.

When a player inadvertently throws, kicks or otherwise causes the ball to go into the goal he is defending, credit the goal (and the shot attempt) to the opponent's player nearest the goal.

Assists

A player is credited with an assist whenever he passes, scoops, bounces or bats the ball into the stick of a teammate, who then scores a goal without dodging or evading an opponent.

The intent is to credit a player whose pass is an integral part of the scoring play.

If the dodging or evasive action of a player clearly is responsible for putting him in a position to score, do not credit an assist. However, credit an assist when the scoring player is set up by a pass and then closes in on the goal by *outrunning* an opponent or opponents.

In borderline cases, give the benefit of doubt to the passing player and credit him with an assist.

There can be only one assist credited on any goal scored. When a series of passes leads to a goal, credit the assist only to the player making the final pass to the scoring player.

Assists can be recorded as made on a work sheet along with other individual statistics. Form 7-C shows that Smith was credited with three assists in addition to his scoring statistics.

Form 7-C

CENTRAL	SA	G	A					
SMITH	~~IIII~~ ~~IIII~~ II	IIII	III					

SA—Shots Attempted G—Goals Scored A—Assists

Individual Scoring Points

Although lacrosse games are determined, of course, by the number of goals scored by each team, *individual* statistical rankings traditionally give equal value to goals and assists. Players are credited with one point for each goal and one for each assist. Thus, total points determine the individual scoring championship or rankings.

In the examples given for Smith, he has 4 goals and 3 assists for a total of 7 points, as seen in Form 7-D.

Normally, in a league or conference, or in national rankings such as those issued by the Lacrosse Hall of Fame for the United States Intercollegiate Lacrosse Association and National Collegiate Athletic

Form 7-D

CENTRAL	SA	G	A	PTS				
SMITH	HHT HHT II	IIII	III	7				

SA—Shots Attempted G—Goals Scored A—Assists PTWS—Points

Association, separate listings of leaders are maintained in total scoring, in goals and in assists.

The tables below are examples of scoring leaders for a single season of play. Leaders are ranked on average per game in each category.

SCORING

Player, Team	Games	Goals	Assists	Points	Avg.
Ferguson, St. John's	12	22	49	71	5.9
Mathews, East Tech	14	34	47	81	5.8
Smith, Central	13	43	31	74	5.7
Peach, Poly	14	37	36	73	5.2
Harris, Fremont	14	47	21	68	4.9

GOALS

Player, Team	Games	No.	Avg.
Harris, Fremont	14	47	3.4
Smith, Central	13	43	3.3
Adams, St. John's	12	38	3.2
Collins, Southern	14	39	2.8
Peach, Poly	14	37	2.6

ASSISTS

Player, Team	Games	No.	Avg.
Ferguson, St. John's	12	49	4.1
Mathews, East Tech	14	47	3.4
Roland, Roosevelt	14	45	3.2
Parran, Hoover	13	37	2.8
Peach, Poly	14	36	2.6

Penalties

A record should be maintained of the number of penalties and the time lost by penalties. This holds only nominal interest for statistical purposes, but may provide desirable analytical material for the coach.

In simplest form, a record of penalties can be maintained on the same tally sheet (Form 7-E) with other individual statistics. Note Personal Fouls with a "P," and Technical Fouls with a "T."

In the example, Smith was charged with 2 personals and 3 technical fouls, spending 2 minutes and 1 minute in the penalty box for the personals and 30 seconds for one technical. The ommission of penalty time for

Form 7-E

CENTRAL	SA	G	A	PTS	PEN	MIN		
SMITH	~~////~~ ~~////~~ //	////	///	7	PTP TT	2, 1, ½		

SA—Shots Attempted G—Goals Scored A—Assists
PTS—Points PEN—Penalties MIN—Penalty Minutes

the other two technical fouls indicates the penalty was only loss of the ball.

A record should be maintained of the number of times a player is expelled for committing five personal fouls.

Face-Offs

Coaches may want.a record of the number of face-offs recovered or lost by his team. It also can be useful statistical material for publicity purposes, especially if a particularly adept player enables his team to gain possession of a high percentage of face-offs.

Form 7-F shows that Smith was involved in 9 face-offs and that he or a teammate recovered the ball 6 times.

Form 7-F

CENTRAL	SA	G	A	PTS	PEN	MIN	FO	REC
SMITH	~~////~~ ~~////~~ //	////	///	7	PTP TT	2, 1 ½	~~////~~ ////	~~////~~ /

SA—Shots Attempted G—Goals Scored A—Assists
PTS—Points PEN—Penalties MIN—Penalty Minutes
FO—Face-Offs REC—Recovered

Cumulative Statistics

Statistics from each game should be entered on a cumulative work sheet so that at any time during the season, or at the end of the year, total statistics will be available for each player and the team. The same type of form can be used as for individual games, adding only an entry for the number of games played and for the player's position.

Example: The listing in Form 7-G shows Smith's statistics after 13 games. His position, "c" for center, is added following his name.

Form 7-G

Central High	G.	SA	GOALS	A	PTS	PEN	MIN	FO	REC
Smith, C	13	103	43	31	74	41	38	117	76

G–Games, SA–Shots Attempted, GOALS–Goals Scored, A–Assists, PTS–Total Points, PEN–Number of Penalties, MIN–Number of Penalty Minutes Served, FO–Face-Offs Attempted, REC–Face-Offs Recovered.

Saves

Credit the goalkeeper with a save whenever he stops or deflects, with any part of his body or stick, a ball which, in the scorer's judgment, would have entered the goal had it not been stopped or deflected.

If a goalkeeper stops or deflects a misdirected pass which, in the scorer's judgment, would have entered the goal without the defensive maneuver, credit him with a save.

Shots or passes intercepted by the goalkeeper which would not have entered the goal should not be credited as saves.

Shots or passes which are deflected off the goal posts are not considered saves. However, if the ball first touches the goalkeeper, or his equipment, and then is deflected off a goal post, it should be credited as a save.

A simple work sheet can be devised to compile saves and they should be entered as soon as credited. A combination work sheet (Form 7-H) can be utilized to show the saves of both teams on one sheet. The same sheet can be used to record the goals scored against each goalie, a practical entry when a team uses more than one goalkeeper in a game.

Form 7-H

EAST TECH	S	GA	CENTRAL	S	GA
CANTRELL	卌 卌 卌 II	卌 卌 I	FOSTER	卌 卌 卌 III	III
			MORGAN	II	II

S—Saves GA—Goals Against

Complete statistics for a goalkeeper should show the number of games played, the number of goals allowed, the average number of goals allowed per game, the number of saves, the average number of saves per game and the number of shutouts.

Example:

Player, Team	G.	Goals	Avg. Goals	Saves	Avg. Saves	ShO
Cantrell, Central	12	51	4.3	204	17.0	2
Jacobs, Western	14	71	5.1	227	16.2	0
Foster, East Tech	15	93	6.2	248	16.5	1

Combination Work Sheets

Some statisticians prefer to combine all statistical recording for one team on a single work sheet, providing space for all the entries on Forms 7-A to 7-H.

This can be done with ruler and pencil as shown in Form 7-I. In this case, the two sides or ends of the shot chart would represent the first and second half for one team. A similar form would be used for opponents' statistics.

Saves by the goalkeeper should be recorded on this form in the columns at each end of the field. Goals scored against each goalie should be noted in the same space, with an "x" inserted for each goal scored. At the top of this column, insert the uniform number of the goalie. If more than one goalkeeper is used, record saves and goals scored against the substitute goalie or goalies in the lower portion of the column. Form 7-I shows that a goalie with uniform number 4 played the entire first half and part of the second and that his substitute, number 8, played part of the second half.

Scorebook

If time permits, the statistician may prefer to record all statistics in the official scorebook, then tally the cumulative figures at the end of the game.

Probably the best scorebook for this purpose is the *Official Lacrosse Scorebook,* published by Bachrach-Raisin Co., Towson Industrial Park, Towson, Md. 21204. This book provides a separate page for each team in each game (see Form 7-J for partial reproduction), with space to record all pertinent statistics except shots attempted and face-offs.

Form 7-I

CENTRAL HIGH

S-G 2nd HALF 1st HALF S-G

PLAYER	SA	G	A	PTS	PEN	MIN	FO	REC
SMITH,C	~~||||~~ ~~||||~~ ||	||||	|||	~~||||~~ ||	PTP TT	2, 1, ½	~~||||~~ ||||	~~||||~~ |

S-G—Saves-Goals SA—Shots Attempted G—Goals A—Assists PTS—Points PEN—Penalties MIN—Penalty Minutes FO—Face-Offs REC—Recoveries

However, the Bachrach-Raisin scorebook can be used for recording these statistics by utilizing the space provided at center, bottom, for "Scoring Summary." Insert "Shots Attempted," "Face-Offs" and "Recoveries" in the spaces marked "Name," "Goals" and "Assists." The scoring should be summarized, but it can be done on the team's cumulative statistics (Form 7-G).

If using this scorebook, insert the names and uniform numbers in proper positions for each player on the starting teams, with both first and last names, *before* the game starts. It is imperative that each coach confirm the identity of the player listed at In-Home position, for this man will be designated to serve any penalties charged against the team as a unit.

Space is provided to indicate the quarters played in by each player, a statistic primarily of use in determining team awards for playing time at the end of the season.

Substitutes should be entered in the book as they report to enter

	1	2	3	4	Overtime		Total
CENTRAL	1	2	2	4	0	2	11
EASTTECH	2	2	3	2	1	0	10

OPPONENT EAST TECH
Coach JACK GREEN
OPPONENT'S RECORD TO DATE 3 Wins 2 Losses

TIME OUTS

1	2	3	4	1 ov.	2 ov.
			X		X

BACHARACH - RASIN COMPANY
WORLD'S LARGEST WORLD'S FINEST LACROSSE SUPPLIERS
Towson Industrial Park
Towson, Maryland, 21204
Telephone: A/C 301 825-6747

Score	Goal By	Assist	Per.	Time
1	40	34		
2	49	46		
3	34			
4	49	46		
5	34			
6	35	46		
7	40	46		
8	34			
9	35			
10	40	46		
11				
12				
13				
14				
15				
16				
17				
18				

P-T	No.	Infraction	Per.	Time
P	14	From behind	1	8:00
P	16	ON THE head	2	6:00
P	16	From behind	2	9:10
P	15	cross check	3	3:18
P	29	Tripping	11	:50
[illegible]	[illegible]	[illegible]	4	[illegible]
P	18	From behind	4	10:20

1st	SAVES	2nd half		Overtime	
𝍸 𝍸 11	12	𝍸 𝍸 𝍸 111	18	𝍸 1111	9

SCORING SUMMARY

No.	Name	Goals	Assists
46	PAUL MOORE	0	5
34	PETE KING	3	1
40	MARV OWEN	3	0
35	AL REAMS	2	0
49	LARRY BROWN	2	[illegible]

Quarters Played 1	2	3	4	Name	No.	Position	
✓	✓	✓	✓	PAUL MOORE	46	I.H.	ATTACK
✓	✓	✓	✓	LARRY BROWN	49	O.H.	ATTACK
✓	✓	✓	✓	MARV OWEN	40	I.A.	ATTACK
✓	✓	✓	✓	LEE MICHAELS	33	R.W.	MIDFIELD
✓	✓	✓	✓	PETE KING	34	C	MIDFIELD
✓	✓	✓	✓	AL REAMS	35	L.W.	MIDFIELD
✓	✓	✓	✓	DUNCAN BUCK	12	I.D.	DEFENSE
✓	✓	✓	✓	NORM MINETA	15	P	DEFENSE
✓	✓	✓	✓	BOB CROSS	16	C.P.	DEFENSE
✓	✓	✓	✓	JESS ANTLER	9	Goal	
	✓	✓		STEVE O'NEIL	31	R.W.	2nd MIDFIELD
	✓	✓		BRUCE MARTIN	39	C	2nd MIDFIELD
	✓	✓		CHARLIE BROWN	37	L.W.	2nd MIDFIELD
✓			✓	ANDY HAMILTON	14	C.P.	SUBS
			✓	FRED FORTUNE	18	P.	SUBS

Form 7-J

the game, checking off the appropriate box under "Quarters Played," to indicate when he entered the game.

To save time, in all other scorebook columns enter only the numbers of players involved.

There is space in this book to record the time-outs charged to each team and a box to insert the score by quarters. All other scorebook entries can be made with the instructions provided earlier in this chapter.

Records

Records should be maintained in all lacrosse statistical categories for both historical reference and for publicity purposes. At a minimum, these records should be kept up-to-date for both individuals and team.

Shots Attempted—Most, in one quarter, half, game, season and career.
Goals—Most, in one quarter, half, game, season and career.
Goals—Highest average goals scored per game, in one season and career.
Assists—Most, in one quarter, half, game, season and career.
Assists—Highest average number per game in one season and career.
Points—Most total goals and assists in one quarter, half, game, season and career.
Points—Highest average total goals and assists per game, in one season and career.
Penalties—Most penalties charged with, in one season and career.
Penalties—Most penalty minutes served, in one season and career.
Face-Offs—Most successful face-offs (recovered by own team) in game, season and career.
Saves—Most, by goalkeeper, in one quarter, half, game, season and career.
Saves—Highest average number per game, in one season and career.
Goals Allowed—Fewest by goalkeeper, in one game, season and career.
Goals Allowed—Lowest average per game, in one season and career.
Shutouts—Most, by goalkeeper, in season and career.

Chapter 8

Rugby

Rugby is a delightful game for statisticians, as well as for spectators and players, because the traditional laws of rugby have maintained the sport as a single-minded game—get the ball over the goal line.

Although the accent is emphatically on team play, individual scoring statistics may be maintained to provide records of individual excellence.

Ways of Scoring

There are five ways to score in rugby: (1) Penalty Goal, (2) Goal from Free Kick, (3) Dropped Goal, (4) a Grounding Goal or "Try," and (5) a Conversion. Scoring by any of the first four methods results in three points, and the Conversion, which is awarded following a Try, is worth two points if successful.

Penalty Goal

When a penalty try is awarded by the referee, the kick may be taken by any member of the team awarded the kick and may be taken from any place between the goal posts, on or behind the "mark" (spot of foul). If successfully place-kicked or drop-kicked over the goal posts, between the uprights, it is a penalty goal worth three points.

Free Kick

Three points can be scored by either a place-kick or a drop-kick by a player who is awarded a free kick after making a fair catch. The player must kick at or behind the mark where he called for the fair catch.

The primary difference between a penalty kick and a free kick (both of which are worth three points if kicked successfully) is in the activity of the defensive team during the kicks.

On a penalty try, the defensive team must stay 10 yards away from the spot of the foul (mark) and may not move until the ball is kicked. On a free kick, the defensive team may stand right up to the mark and may charge as soon as the ball touches the ground on a place-kick or as soon as the player "offers" to kick on a drop-kick or punt.

Note: A player cannot score by punting. A successful penalty or free kick or dropped goal must be made by a place-kick or drop-kick.

Dropped Goal

This is a drop-kick, which may be taken by any player from any spot on the playing field at any time during play, except from a kick-off or a 25-yard drop-out. It is worth three points if successfully clearing the cross bar of the goal, between the uprights.

Try and Conversion

A try and conversion are similar to a touchdown and point-after-touchdown in American football. When a player scores a try (three points) in rugby, the team is offered the opportunity to gain an additional two points by a conversion kick.

There is one striking difference between American football and rugby conversions. In rugby, the conversion kick must be taken from exactly in front of where the try was scored, on a line parallel to the sidelines. Anyone can take the conversion kick, and it can be taken from as far out from the goal line as desired, but it must be taken in line with the spot where the ball went over the goal line to score the try.

A try, worth three points, is made when a player "grounds" the ball in the opponents' in-goal, or end zone as it would be called in American football.

Note: The American Rugby Union has been experimenting with a scoring system that provides four points, instead of three, for a try.

To score a try, the ball must be grounded in-goal by a player holding the ball in his hand and bringing it in contact with the ground or, if the ball is on the ground already, by pressing down on it by hand(s) or arm(s) or by falling on it so that the ball is anywhere beneath the player from neck to waist.

The impetus which caused the ball to go over the goal line is immaterial. The only thing that counts is which team grounds the ball in-goal. If it's the team attacking that in-goal, it's a try and three points.

When the defensive team grounds the ball it is given a 25-yard drop-out, if the offensive team had been responsible for the ball crossing the goal line; or a five-yard scrum, if the defenders had provided the impetus which sent the ball over the goal line.

Scoring Statistics

The determined emphasis on team play in rugby has made individual statistics of little consequence to those involved in the conduct of the game. In rugby circles, the feeling prevails that "all 15 men" are responsible for a try, for instance, not the player who actually grounds the ball.

Nevertheless, rugby writers tend to report individual statistics as an added fillip for readers and because it does provide them with material to use in advance stories or in reporting results of games. Thus, it would be well to maintain individual scoring statistics in rugby for both publicity and historical purposes.

Work Sheets

The recording of rugby statistics is a simple maintenance chore with a tally sheet, showing the number of trys scored and the number of scoring kicks.

Additional interest may be derived from a recording of the number of scoring kicks attempted and made in each kicking category.

Thus Form 8-A shows partial scoring statistics for a team from Central High.

Form 8-A

		Penalty Kicks		Free Kicks		Dropped Goals		Conversions		TOTAL
Central High	TRYS	ATT	MADE	ATT	MADE	ATT	MADE	ATT	MADE	POINTS
Smith	0	8	5	1	0	6	2	8	7	35
Langsley	11	0	0	0	0	0	0	0	0	33
Horn	3	0	0	1	0	9	5	0	0	24
Keith	0	3	2	2	1	1	0	7	5	19

Records

Again, the stress on team achievement has relegated rugby records to a minor and, in some cases, a nonexistent role. However, there should be interest in records when available, and a statistician could initiate that interest by a record compilation.

These categories could provide material for records and permanent reference:

Trys—Most in game, season and career.
Penalty Kicks—Most attempted and most made in game, season and career.
Free Kicks—Most attempted and most made in game, season and career.
Dropped Goals—Most attempted and made in game, season and career.
Conversions—Most attempted and made in game, season and career.
Points—Most scored in game, season and career.
Longest—Penalty Kick, Free Kick and Dropped Goal attempted and made.

Chapter 9

Soccer

Basic soccer statistics, except for those categories peculiar to the play of the game itself, are similar to ice hockey and lacrosse.

Like the other two sports, there are four fundamental statistics commonly used for both publicity and record purposes: (1) shots attempted, (2) goals scored, (3) assists on goals, and (4) saves by goalkeepers.

Other statistics may be maintained for coaching purposes, but in most cases the team totals provide the necessary information, and individual statistics in these areas (such as throw-ins) are primarily accidental. However, these areas will be covered because a soccer statistician normally will be expected to record them if they are useful to the coach.

Goals Attempted and Made

A player is charged with a Shot at Goal any time he attempts to score a goal by legally kicking, heading or shouldering the ball at the opponent's goal.

It is not necessary for the scorer to determine if the shot at goal was legal. The referee will note this by awarding a free kick to the opponents if the shot attempt was improper.

If the infraction occurs at the time of the shot at goal, one which would nullify a successful attempt, do not charge the player with an attempt.

Credit a player with scoring a goal whenever he has propelled the ball across the goal line, between the goal posts, and the goal scored is signified by the referee.

When a player propels the ball toward the goal and it is deflected into the goal by a teammate, do not charge the original shooter with a goal attempt. Credit him with an assist, and charge the teammate who scored with a shot at goal, as well as a goal scored.

If a goal is awarded to a team because a defensive player inadvertently (or deliberately) deflects or kicks the ball into his own goal, credit the goal and the attempt to the player who made the shot if, in the scorer's opinion, the ball would have gone into the goal had it not been touched by the defensive player.

In the same situation, in the scorer's judgment, if the ball would not have gone into the goal (without being touched by the defensive player), traditionally the goal and the attempt are credited to the goalkeeper of the offensive team. Occasionally, in some areas, the goal may be credited to the offensive player nearest the ball. Be sure to charge a shot attempt to the player who originally propelled the ball toward the goal.

Penalty Kicks

From a scoring standpoint, Penalty Kick attempts and goals are scored like any other goal attempted or scored. However, for statistical purposes, it may be of additional news value to provide separate categories for the Penalty Kicks attempted and scored.

Thus, the total goals attempted and scored by a player or team will be the sum of the attempts and goals from the field plus the attempts and goals from Penalty Kicks.

Example: During a season, John Smith of Central High attempted 28 goals from the field and was successful on 6. In addition, he was called upon to attempt 7 Penalty Kicks and converted 3. His scoring is summarized below:

	Goals		Penalty Kicks		Total Goals	
Player, Team	ATT	MADE	ATT	MADE	ATT	MADE
Smith, Central	28	6	7	3	35	9

Shot Charts

A useful coaching tool is a shot chart, showing the position of the shooter on each goal attempt. This can be done by reproducing a diagram of the goal area for each quarter and inserting the uniform number of the players at the approximate spot on the field from which they attempted shots at the goal.

As in basketball or other sports where a shot chart is used, circle the number when a shot is successful. On penalty kicks, insert the letter "P" following the uniform number.

If the time of scoring is desired, a series of boxes can be inserted beneath the shot chart to indicate time of goals. Insert "P" following the time on penalty kicks.

Form 9-A shows that in the first quarter, Team A took 7 shots from the field, 2 of them penalty kicks. Two were successful, including one penalty kick.

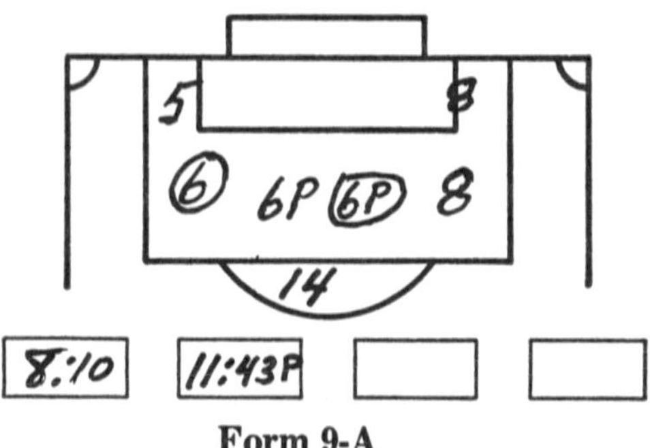

Form 9-A

Assists

Credit an assist to a player any time he makes a direct pass to a player who then immediately attempts and makes a goal.

The intent of the assist is to credit a player whose pass was instrumental in setting up a successful shot. Thus, if Player A passes to Player B, who then dribbles the ball to maneuver into position for a shot, the pass did not "set up" the shot. It was set up by Player B's actions, not by the pass, and no assist is credited.

Individual Scoring

A compilation of scoring statistics should show at a glance the complete performance in scoring areas for each individual and team. A cross-check should be made to be certain that the sum of all individuals equals the team totals.

Corner kicks have no real statistical significance because the choice of players making corner kicks usually is incidental. However, because of the importance of corner kicks in resolving tie games, many teams include this category in both individual and team statistics.

Thus, the complete statistical rankings for Smith would be shown as follows:

	Goals		Penalty Kicks		Total Goals			CORNER
Player, Team	ATT	MADE	ATT	MADE	ATT	MADE	ASSISTS	KICKS
Smith, Central	28	6	7	3	35	9	7	23

For publicity purposes, a shorter statistical report form may be more practical, showing only games played, goals, assists and total points.

Player, Team	GAMES	GOALS	ASSISTS	POINTS
Smith, Central	12	9	7	16

• **Pro Ruling:** At least one professional league has experimented with a statistical system that bases individual rankings on a point system, with two points for each goal and one point for each assist. Thus, for Conrad of Atlanta, who made 11 goals from the field, 2 penalty kicks and 5 assists, rankings would show him with 26 points on 13 goals plus 5 for assists and a total of 31 points.

	Goals		Penalty Kicks		Total Goals			TOTAL
Player, Team	ATT	MADE	ATT	MADE	ATT	MADE	ASSISTS	POINTS
Conrad, Atlanta	51	11	5	2	56	13	5	31

In the short form, Conrad's statistics would appear as follows:

Player, Team	GAMES	GOALS	ASSISTS	POINTS
Conrad, Atlanta	11	13	5	31

Saves

A goalkeeper is credited with a "save" whenever he prevents a goal by stopping, in any legal manner, an attempted shot at goal by an opponent. He is credited with a save whether he kicks away, blocks or catches the shot at goal.

Statistical records should show the total saves made by a goalie and the goals scored against him. Additional statistical interest and probable publicity material may be obtained by recording the number of shutouts registered by a goalkeeper and the average number of goals allowed per game.

Example: Harris of Central High played in 10 games, during which he was credited with 58 saves and opponents scored 12 goals. In three games, Central's opponent was held scoreless. Thus, with 12 goals in 10 games, Harris allowed an average of 1.2 goals per game.

Player, Team	GAMES	SAVES	GOALS	SHUTOUTS	AVERAGE PER GAME
Harris, Central	10	58	12	3	1.2

Turnovers

There are several statistical entries in soccer which are of value to the coach, but have little significance for statistics, because they do not reflect specific individual accomplishment.

The selection of the player to execute corner kicks, goal kicks, throw-ins and free kicks normally is incidental and does not reflect a statistical performance. Moreover, the results of these actions have little significance, statistically, other than ball possession.

The only turnover category which must be maintained is the number of corner kicks by each team, because in many leagues and tournaments, the winner of a tie game is that team which had the most corner kicks in the game.

Otherwise, turnover statistics are of value primarily to the coach, and then generally on a negative basis. That is, the coach is interested in errors made by his players in making a throw-in or corner kick.

For instance, if a player continually boots corner-kicks over the goal line, thus losing ball possession, the coach will use this compilation to choose another player to kick from the corner. Likewise, a coach is interested in statistics that show repeated errors by a player or players on throw-ins.

For turnover statistics, a simple tally sheet is sufficient in each case. If individual statistics in these categories are not required by a coach, totals should be maintained only for each team.

If individual statistics are recorded, a score sheet should be utilized that includes column entries for turnovers as well as scoring and goalkeeping statistics.

Example: Smith of Central High in one game is called upon to make three corner kicks. On one, he boots it over the defensive goal, with a resultant goal kick by the defensive team. An "E" or "X" should be used to note the error, as seen in Form 9-B.

Example: In one game, Smith is called upon to make 6 throw-ins. He successfully throws to a teammate on four occasions, but on two of them an opponent recovers the ball. Thus, indicate the throw-in errors with an "E" or "X" on Form 9-C.

Fouls

Although primarily of coaching interest, a record should be kept of fouls committed by each player. Because a coach is interested in knowing if an individual player is repeatedly offside, a separate tally should be recorded for this infraction. (See Form 9-D).

Players	Corner Kicks
SMITH	/E/

Form 9-B

Players	Throw-ins
SMITH	/X///X

Form 9-C

Players	Fouls	Offside
SMITH	//	/

Form 9-D

Work Sheets

A homemade work sheet can be devised easily to maintain a simple tally of all soccer statistics (Form 9-E), though there are some published scorebooks available in sporting goods stores. If devising your own work sheet, you should prepare one for the home team and another for the visiting team for each game.

In preparing a homemade score sheet, be sure to include basic information about the game, including date, site, etc. Some coaches may also want a record maintained for the number of minutes played by each player.

The same type of form can be used for cumulative statistics, so that at any time during the season or at the end of the season, a permanent record is available with the totals for each player and the team. When used for this purpose, Form 9-E should have an additional line added at the bottom to insert the totals in each category for all opponents.

In Form 9-E, the abbreviations include Position (POS), Minutes Played (MIN), Shots Attempted (SA), Goals Scored (G), Penalty Kicks Attempted (PKA), Penalty Kicks Made (PK), Assists (A), Saves by

Home Team CENTRAL HIGH Date OCT. 15, 1972 Site HOOVER FIELD

Players	POS	MIN	SA	G	PKA	PK	A	S	CK	TI	GK	FK	F	O
SANTOS	G	88						////						
FARRELL	RB	88									//			
SMITH	LB	88									///	/		
JONES	RH	69	/							//E		//		
RODRIGUES	CH	88	/				/						/	
BOGART	LH	88	///							//		/		
PARKER	OR	88	卌	/			/		//E/	E/		//		/
BALDWIN	IR	88	//											/
EDWARDS	CF	88	////	/	//	/								
PHILLIPS	IL	76	////				/							
CRUZ	OL	88	///	/					//E				/	
STEVENS (sub)	RH	19												
MORRISSEY (sub)	IL	12	/	/									/	
Totals			24	4	2	1	3	4	7	7	5	6	3	2

Form 9-E

Goalkeeper (S), Corner Kicks (CK), Throw-Ins (TI), Goal Kicks (GK), Free Kicks (FK), Fouls (F) and Offside (O). The letter "E" inserted in the sample Form 9-E indicates errors when making corner kicks or throw-ins.

Team Standings

In a league where the champion is that team which compiles the highest won-lost percentage, ties usually are counted as a one-half win and one-half loss for percentage purposes.

In other leagues, where the champion is that team which compiles the highest number of points, it is based on a formula which provides two points for each victory, one point for each tie and no points for a loss.

It is, of course, important that a championship formula be adopted in advance of the season, because in some cases a different formula will produce a different champion.

Example: During a season, Central High plays 11 league games, winning 7, losing 3 and tying 1. East Tech plays 12 league games, winning 7, losing 3 and tying 2. The extra tie game played by East Tech would result in a championship for Central High if the title is decided by won-lost percentage, but East Tech would be the champion if the title is determined on the basis of points. In league standings, entries also should be made for goals scored by and against each team.

Team	W	L	T	PCT.	PTS	GOALS	OPP
Central	7	3	1	.682	15	27	13
East Tech	7	3	2	.667	16	32	17

The percentage is computed by giving a one-half win and one-half loss for each tie. Thus Central, for percentage purposes, has 7½ wins and 3½ losses. Dividing 7½ (or 7.5) by the total games, 11, gives a percentage of .682. Giving Central two points for each win and one for a tie, 7 times 2 plus 1 gives a total of 15 points.

• **Pro Ruling:** In at least one professional league (North American), the champion has been determined on a point system that awards 6 points for each win and 3 points for each tie.

In addition, bonus points are awarded in each game for goals scored. Each team receives one point in the standings for each goal it scores, up to and including three. The bonus points are awarded to each scoring team, whether it is the winning or losing team.

Example: In a game between Atlanta and New York, Atlanta won, 2-1. Atlanta is credited with 6 points in the standings for the win and an additional 2 points for scoring 2 goals. New York receives 1 point only, the bonus point for scoring its goal.

Example: In another game, Dallas defeats Toronto, 6-4. Dallas receives 6 points for the win and 3 bonus points for its *first three* goals. In the team standings, then, Dallas is credited with a total of 9 points for the game. Toronto receives 3 bonus points for its *first three* goals.

Team standings should also show total goals scored and total goals allowed. Below is a sample of partial season standings for a four-team division of the North American Soccer League.

Team	W	L	T	GOALS FOR	GOALS AGAINST	BONUS POINTS	TOTAL POINTS
Atlanta	9	2	2	26	13	24	84
Dallas	4	3	5	14	12	14	53
Washington	3	4	5	15	16	14	47
St. Louis	1	7	2	13	25	13	25

Records

For record-keeping purposes, historic statistics in each scoring category should be compiled. At a minimum, the following records should be maintained for both individuals and teams. Separate records may be maintained for league games and for overall schedules.

Shots Attempted—Most, for one period, one game, one season and career.
Goals Scored—Most, for one period, one game, one season and career.
Penalty Kicks Attempted—Most, for one period, one game, one season and career.
Penalty Kicks Made—Most, for one period, one game, one season and career.
Assists—Most, for one period, one game, one season and career.
Saves by goalkeeper—Most, for one period, one game, one season and career.
Shutouts (by Goalkeeper and team)—Most, for one season and career.
Average Goals Allowed (by goalkeeper and team)—Fewest per game, for season and career.

Chapter 10

Swimming and Diving

The scorer or statistician in swimming meets, whether dual or tournament, is not required to make judgments in either time or place of competitors, or in the official scoring. These determinations are the responsibility of meet officials.

Order of finish and times of each race, whether heat or finals, are obtained by the scorer from the head judge or timer. At the conclusion of the last event, the meet referee is required to audit and certify the scorer's tabulation of results and scoring.

If a scoreboard is in operation at the meet, this information may be taken directly from the scoreboard. The home team statistician may be assigned to operate the scoreboard and instructions on its operation will be provided by the coach or athletic administrator.

Where there is no official scoreboard, results of the race may be obtained directly from the official. Form 10-A shows a report form that may be used by the judges. This form may be used for either a heat or finals. It can be used as an entry blank and report form, with names and lane assignments recorded prior to the start of the race, and order of finish and times inserted at the conclusion of the race. This same form may be used as a model for an event report form to be distributed to media.

Form 10-A includes all the information necessary for the statistician to compile an accurate record of each event in the entire meet. A slight modification may be needed in the form for relay events. A similar form may be utilized for diving, but normally a separate scorecard is used for each diver, as noted in the diving section (Form 10-H).

100-YD FREESTYLE 5/12

Lane	Competitor (School)	Place	Time
1	JOHN HAWKS (ET)	6	52.0
3	BEN BRIGGS (ET)	1	50.3
5	CHARLES LYONS (ET)	4	51.3
2	JOE HICKS (CH)	3	50.5
4	BILL HART (CH)	2	50.4
6	HOMER COLE (CH)	5	51.7

Form 10-A

Basic statistics to be maintained for permanent records and for publicity purposes include the order of finish of each event, the time of the winner or place-winner and team scoring.

For simplification, media reports and permanent records should be maintained in the same style. If the area media do not use all the information included in the report form, it is a simple matter for them to delete the unwanted information.

Because there is a difference in points awarded for the order of finish, there are minor differences in the final reports for dual meets, triangular meets and tournament or championship results.

Dual Meets

For permanent records, the statistician may want to include the names of all competitors finishing each event. However, for media purposes, only the names of the point-winners usually are included in the results.

Depending upon the traditional style of area media, dual meet results may list the first four finishers or may include only the first three, because points in dual meets are awarded only to the first three places. Again, depending upon media preference, times may be included for all place-winners or for the winner only.

Normally, results are listed in chronological order of the events. If permanent records are to be maintained with each event started on a new line (see Form 10-B), then a revised style (Form 10-C) should be used for media purposes. Form 10-C is the style most likely to be used in the area newspapers.

200-yard medley relay—Central High (Clark, Turner, Nielsen, Steele) * 1:48.3; East Tech (Wade, Robinson, Hughes, Edmonds) * 1:48.6.

200-yard freestyle—Wright (ET) 1:59.2; Reed (CH) 2:01.6; Bryant (ET) 2:02.

(Start a new paragraph for each event following, with final team scores entered as the last line.)

Central High 52 East Tech 43

Form 10-B

200-yard medley relay—Central High (Clark, Turner, Nielsen, Steele) * 1:48.3; East Tech (Wade, Robinson, Hughes, Edmonds) * 1:48.6. 200-yard freestyle—Wright (ET) 1:59.2; Smith (CH) 1:59.4; Reed (CH) 2:01.6; Bryant (ET) 2:02. 200-yard Individual Medley (IM)—Perkins (ET) 2:12.1; Hall (ET) 2:13; Miller (CH) 2:13.7; Kelly (CH) 2:13.8. . . . List all subsequent events in chronological order, all in the same paragraph, followed by final team scores. . . . Central High 52 East Tech 43.

Form 10-C

***Note:** Some media prefer to list the complete team only of the winning team in relay events.

Triangular Meets

Points are awarded for five places in individual races and two places in relays in triangular meets. Therefore, reports of triangular meets should be expanded to include the first five finishers in individual events and at least the first two in relays.

Form 10-D shows the results of the first two events in a triangular meet, as the report should be prepared for media. Following the results of all events, the team scores should be added.

200-yard medley relay—Central High (Clark, Turner, Nielsen, Steele) 1:48.3; East Tech 1:48.6; Lincoln High 1:51.4. 200-yard free-style—Wright (ET) 1:59.2; Smith (CH) 1:59.4; Harris (L) 1:59.5; Jones (L) 1.59.8; Reed (CH) 2:06.6. . . .

Central High 68, East Tech 54, Lincoln 46.

Form 10-D

Championship Meets

Reports for records and media for championship, conference and invitational meets will vary, according to tradition and media preference.

In some areas complete results of all trials will be required, as well as the final results. This may be done in the same style as for dual or triangular meets, merely expanding the results to include as many swimmers and divers as there are point-winning places in the meet (usually six).

In some areas, chronological results may be preferred, and it certainly will be desired by media on a meet that extends over two or three days. In this style, results of trials and of finals will be intermixed, exactly in order of the competition.

However, for permanent records (and media usually will want a copy as a summary for each event), the trials and finals of each event should be listed together, as in Form 10-E.

50-yard freestyle—*First Heat:* John Steele (L) 23.4; Paul Edmonds (P) 23.5; Lloyd Taylor (ET) 23.8; Tony Herbert (MH) 23.9; Hal Palmer (P) 24.0; Norm Ferris (CH) 24.7. *Second Heat:* Dan Wilson (CH) 23.5; Merv Phillips (R) 23.7; Morris Graves (L) 23.9; Dave Wright (F) 24.0; Bob Rolin (B) 24.1; Fred Hughes (S) 24.9. *Finals:* Wilson 23.3; Phillips 23.4; Taylor 23.5; Graves 23.8; Edmonds 23.9; Steele 23.9.

Form 10-E

Team scores, in descending numerical order, should be entered at the end of all results.

Scoring

Scoring values in swimming vary according to the number of teams entered in the meet and the number of places to be awarded in the competition.

In dual meets, it is customary to score three places in individual events and one place in the relays; in triangular meets, five places in individual events and two in the relays; in championship meets, six places in both individual and relay events. However, scoring values differ for individual and relay events.

When the size of the pool limits the number of swimmers in the finals, championship meets may be scored with five or four places, instead of six. Form 10-F is a table of point scoring to cover each type of meet.

Number of Places In Meet	Points For Individual Events					
	1st	2nd	3rd	4th	5th	6th
3	5	3	1			
4	5	3	2	1		
5	6	4	3	2	1	
6	7	5	4	3	2	1

Number of Places In Meet	Points for Relay Events					
	1st	2nd	3rd	4th	5th	6th
1 (dual meet)	7	0				
2 (triangular)	8	4	0			
4 (championship)	10	6	4	2	0	
5 (championship)	12	8	6	4	2	0
6 (championship)	14	10	8	6	4	2

Form 10-F

In dual meets, only the first two finishers from one team are awarded points. In the event of ties in finals, points involved are divided equally among those swimmers involved in the tie.

In some larger meets, such as the National Collegiate championships, points are awarded for 12 places on a scale of 16-13-12-11-10-9-7-5-4-3-2-1 for individual events and double points, 32-26-24-22-20-18-14-10-8-6-4-2 for relays.

Points for the first six places are awarded solely on the basis of the Championship Final of each event; points for the other six places are awarded on the basis of the Consolation Final.

Note: The six fastest qualifiers in each event qualify for the Championship Final; the next six fastest swimmers qualify for the Consolation Final. A swimmer in a Consolation Final cannot advance higher than seventh place, either by time or by disqualification in the Championship Final. In the case of a disqualification in either the Championship or Consolation Finals, those behind the disqualified competitor advance one place each. However, the point or points involved in the "open" place are not assigned to any team.

Example: In the 100-yard freestyle, Swimmer A finishes fourth in the Championship Final, but is disqualified. His team receives no points for his performance. The swimmers finishing fifth and sixth are advanced to fourth and fifth, respectively, and their teams receive the points (11 for fourth, 10 for fifth) for those places. This leaves sixth place open and the 9 points for sixth place in this event are not awarded to any team. Note that *no* swimmer from the Consolation Final is advanced to fill the open sixth place in the Championship Final.

Diving

Scoring in diving is a little more complicated because one point scale is used to determine the order of finish and another point scale is used to credit results in points to the team scoring.

When the final places have been determined in diving, the respective teams of the divers are credited with points just as in any other individual event, in accordance with the point values in Form 10-F.

In determining the order of finish, each dive is assigned a certain score and the diver with the highest accumulated number of points at the end of the competition is the winner. The diver with the next highest total number of points is second, and so on.

In compiling points for the competition, divers earn points both for the degree of difficulty of each dive and the excellence of execution of each dive.

The degree of difficulty of each dive is predetermined. A complete table of the degree of difficulty of each dive can be found in the *National Collegiate Scholastic Swimming Guide,* available at the NCAA Publishing Service, Box 1906, Shawnee Mission, Kan., 66222.

However, if using a swimming scorebook, such as the *Official Swimming Score Book* by James Smith, available through Swimming World Publications, P.O. Box 3667, Stanford, Ca. 94305, a page is provided that combines on one page both a record of degree of difficulty for each dive attempted plus a scoring form.

Form 10-G shows the Diving Entry and Announcers form from this book. It shows the type of dive and degree of difficulty for each of John Smith's six dives in three-meter competition. This form provides information for the judges and for the public address announcer.

His first attempt is a forward dive, layout position, which has a degree of difficulty of 1.6. He next attempts a forward two-and-a-half somersault, pike position, which has a degree of difficulty of 2.3, and so on.

The degree of difficulty is then entered on the Scoring Form (Form 10-H) in the proper column, preparatory to entering the judges' scores for the excellence of his dives.

DIVERS' ENTRY & ANNOUNCERS FORM-NCAA & AAU

1 METER | 3 METER (circled) | DIVING ORDER: 1ST

NAME: JOHN SMITH

AFFILIATION: CENTRAL

1 Meter Dives: Lay Out	Pike	Tuck	Dive No.	Order 1 M	Order 3 M	Description	3 Meter Dives: Lay Out	Pike	Tuck
1. FORWARD DIVES									
1.4	1.2	1.2	101		1	Fwd Dive	1.6	1.3	1.3
1.7	1.5	1.4	102			Fwd Som	1.8	1.7	1.7
—	1.7	1.6	103			Fwd 1½ Som	2.1	1.6	1.6
—	2.2	2.0	104			Fwd Dble Som	—	2.2	2.1
—	2.6	2.3	105		2	Fwd 2½ Som	—	2.3	2.1
—	—	2.6	106			Fwd Trple Som	—	2.7	2.5
—	—	3.0	107			Fwd 3½ Som	—	3.0	2.7
—	1.7	1.5	112			Fwd Fly Som	—	1.7	1.6
—	1.9	1.8	113			Fwd Fly 1½ Som	—	1.8	1.7
2. BACK DIVES									
1.6	1.6	1.6	201			Back Dive	1.7	1.7	1.7
1.7	1.6	1.5	202			Back Som	1.6	1.7	1.5
2.4	2.3	2.2	203		3	Back 1½ Som	2.2	2.2	2.0
—	2.3	2.2	204			Back Dble Som	2.4	2.2	2.0
—	—	—	205			Back 2½ Som	—	3.0	2.8
—	1.8	1.7	212			Back Fly Som	—	—	1.6
—	—	—	213			Back Fly 1½ Som	—	—	2.1
3. REVERSE DIVES									
1.7	1.7	1.7	301			Rev Dive	1.9	1.9	1.7
2.0	1.8	1.6	302			Rev Som	1.9	1.7	1.5
2.8	2.5	2.3	303			Rev 1½ Som	2.6	2.4	2.2
—	—	2.2	304			Rev Dble Som	—	2.4	2.2
—	—	—	305		4	Rev 2½ Som	—	3.0	2.8
—	1.8	1.7	312			Rev Fly Som	—	—	1.6
—	—	—	313			Rev Fly 1½ Som	—	—	2.4
4. INWARD DIVES									
1.7	1.3	1.2	401			Inw Dive	1.6	1.3	1.2
—	1.9	1.7	402			Inw Som	—	1.7	1.5
—	2.4	2.2	403			Inw 1½ Som	—	2.2	2.0
—	—	2.3	404			Inw Dble Som	—	2.4	2.3
—	—	—	405		5	Inw 2½ Som	—	2.9	2.6
—	—	—	412			Inw Fly Som	—	—	1.8
—	—	—	413			Inw Fly 1½ Som	—	—	2.3

1 Meter Dives: Lay Out	Pike	Tuck	Free	Dive No.	Order 1 M	Order 3 M	Description	3 Meter Dives: Lay Out	Pike	Tuck	Free
5. TWIST DIVES											
1.8	1.7	—	—	5111			Fwd Dive, ½ Tw	1.9	1.8	—	—
2.0	2.1	—	—	5112			Fwd Dive, 1 Tw	2.0	2.1	—	—
—	—	—	1.7	5121			Fwd Som, ½ Tw	1.9	1.7	—	—
—	—	—	2.0	5122			Fwd Som, 1 Tw	—	—	—	2.0
—	—	—	2.2	5124			Fwd Som, 2 Tws	—	—	—	—
—	2.1	2.0	—	5131			Fwd 1½ Som, ½ Tw	—	2.0	1.9	—
—	—	—	2.2	5132			Fwd 1½ Som, 1 Tw	—	—	—	2.1
—	—	—	2.7	5134		6	Fwd 1½ Som, 2 Tws	—	—	—	2.4
—	—	—	—	5136			Fwd 1½ Som, 3 Tws	—	—	—	2.9
—	—	—	—	5152			Fwd 2½ Som, 1 Tw	—	—	—	2.8
1.6	2.0	—	—	5211			Back Dive, ½ Tw	1.6	1.9	—	—
2.1	—	—	—	5212			Back Dive, 1 Tw	2.0	—	—	—
—	—	—	1.7	5221			Back Som, ½ Tw	1.8	1.8	—	—
—	—	—	1.9	5222			Back Som, 1 Tw	—	—	—	2.0
—	—	—	2.1	5223			Back Som, 1½ Tw	—	—	—	2.1
—	—	—	2.1	5231			Back 1½ Som, ½ Tw	—	—	—	2.1
—	—	—	2.6	5233			Back 1½ Som, 1½ Tw	—	—	—	2.4
—	—	—	2.8	5235			Back 1½ Som, 2½ Tws	—	—	—	2.7
1.8	2.2	—	—	5311			Rev Dive, ½ Tw	2.0	2.2	—	—
2.2	—	—	—	5312			Rev Dive, 1 Tw	2.2	—	—	—
—	—	—	1.8	5321			Rev Som, ½ Tw	—	—	—	2.0
—	—	—	2.0	5322			Rev Som, 1 Tw	—	—	—	2.2
—	—	—	2.2	5323			Rev Som, 1½ Tw	—	—	—	2.2
—	—	—	2.2	5331			Rev 1½ Som, ½ Tw	—	—	—	2.2
—	—	—	2.7	5333			Rev 1½ Som, 1½ Tw	—	—	—	2.5
—	—	—	2.9	5335			Rev 1½ Som, 2½ Tws	—	—	—	2.8
2.0	1.7	—	—	5411			Inw Dive, ½ Tw	2.0	1.8	—	—
—	—	—	—	5412			Inw Dive, 1 Tw	2.2	2.2	—	—
—	1.9	1.9	—	5421			Inw Som, ½ Tw	—	2.0	2.0	—
—	—	—	2.2	5422			Inw Som, 1 Tw	—	—	—	—
—	—	—	—	5432			Inw 1½ Som, 1 Tw	—	—	—	2.6

NOTE: 1. Circle Degree of Difficulty.
2. Enter Dive Order.
3. Enter Degree of Difficulty on Scoring Form.

Form 10-G

NAME JOHN SMITH								AFFILIATION CENTRAL			
DIVE	JUDGES' AWARD							TOTAL AWARD	DEGREE OF DIFFICULTY	FINAL POINTS	
	1	2	3	4	5	6	7				
1	~~8~~	7	6.5	7.5	~~6~~			21	1.6	33	60
2	8	~~8.5~~	8	7.5	~~6~~			23.5	2.3	54 87	05 65
3	~~6~~	5.5	5	~~5~~	5.5			16	2.2	35 122	20 85
4	~~9~~	8	8.5	8	~~7.5~~			24.5	2.8	68 191	60 45
5	~~7.5~~	~~6~~	7	6.5	7			20.5	2.9	59 250	45 90
6	7.5	7	6	8	7			21.5	2.4	51 302	60 50

Form 10-H

After each dive, judges independently score the excellence of the dive, on a scale ranging from 0 (zero), for an attempt on which the diver fails completely, to 10, for a perfect dive. Then the sum of their scores is multiplied by the arbitrary value assigned to that dive as the degree of difficulty (Form 10-G). The total is the competitor's score for that dive. At the end of the competition, points for each dive are added to give the diver his final point tally. That diver with the highest point total is the winner.

When more than three judges are used, the highest and the lowest scores for each dive are cancelled and the score is determined on the basis of the remaining judges' scores.

Example: In the example of Smith's dive, above, there actually were five judges, who score his dive, respectively, 8.0, 7.0, 6.5, 7.5 and 6.0. The highest score (8.0) and the lowest (6.0) are cancelled, leaving the three middle scores cited in the example.

A separate score or tally sheet is maintained for each diver, showing all the scores of the judges and the calculation of his point total. Form 10-H is an example of the performance of one diver in a dual meet.

In Smith's first dive (Form 10-H), the highest and lowest scores (8.0 and 6.0) were cancelled, leaving him with scores of 7.0, 6.5 and 7.5. The total for these three dives was 21. Multiplying by the degree of difficulty (1.6), Smith had a score of 33.60 for that dive. In the second dive, his total score was 54.05, for a two-dive total of 87.65. Scores for all dives are accumulated, so his final score for six dives is 302.5.

Keeping Score

Several types of swimming scorebooks are available for use both as work sheets and permanent records.

As in all scorebooks, space usually is allotted for identifying the competing schools or teams, the date, place and site of the meet, and the pqol size (the latter for record purposes). In the main body of the scorebook, forms are provided for quick recording of the results of each event.

The scorebook used in examples here is the aforementioned *Official Swimming Score Book* by James R. Smith. So that it may be used as a permanent record, the front section of this scorebook has space to list the team roster, scores of all dual meets and conference or other championship meet results, plus a summary of the season's record.

Dual Meets

In this book, scoring summary sheets are included for both dual meets and championship meets. Form 10-I shows a dual meet form completed for the first two events of a meet between Central High and East Tech.

EVENT		HOME TEAM				SCORE			OPPONENT TEAM			
		LANE	ENTRIES	TIME	PLACE	CENTRAL		EAST TECH	PLACE	TIME	ENTRIES	LANE
1	200-YD MEDLEY RELAY	3	DARIEN RUSSELL HILL ROLIN	1:41.4	1	7		0	2	1:41.7	LOGUE FORTUNE BATES CHRISTOPHER	4
2	200-YD FREESTYLE					3		6				
		2	BUCKLEY	1:49.1	4				3	1:47.8	WALL	5
		3	HONIG	1:47.5	2	10		6	1	1:46.6	JOHNSON	4

Form 10-I

In the first event, the 200-yard medley relay, the home team, Central High, is assigned Lane No. 3 and wins the event in 1:41.4. The opponent, East Tech, starting in Lane 4, is second in 1:41.7. Under the scoring (Form 10-F), Central High receives 7 points and East Tech none (0).

In the second event, the 200-yard freestyle, the Central High swimmers, Buckley and Honig, are assigned Lanes 2 and 3; the East Tech competitors, Johnson and Wall, Lanes 4 and 5.

As noted by the time and place designations, Johnson won the event, followed by Honig and Wall. This gives East Tech 6 points (5 for 1st, 1 for 3rd) for the event and a two-event total of 6 points. Central earns 3 points for Honig's second-place finish. Added to the 7 points for the first event, Central has a total of 10 points after the first two events.

This scorebook has space for a total of 14 events, enough for any high school or college dual meet.

Championship Meets

For championship meets a different style summary is used, as noted on Form 10-J. This form provides space for scoring 12 places in each event and is divided into two blocks, one for Championship Finals and one for Consolation Finals, as noted in the 200-yard medley relay on this form. The top six names (three on each side) are for the Consolation Finals; the bottom six, for the Championship Finals.

If only six places are to be awarded points, use either the top or bottom blocks, as shown in the example of the 200-yard freestyle event on Form 10-J.

EVENT		LANE	QUAL TIME	NAME & TEAM	FINAL TIME	PLACE	PLACE	FINAL TIME	NAME & TEAM	QUAL TIME	LANE
1	200-YD MEDLEY RELAY	1	1:45	SOUTHERN	1:44.1	10	8	1:43.5	HARRISON	1:43.7	6
		2	1:43.3	MANNING	1:43.3	7	11	1:44.6	GEORGE PREP	1:43.7	5
		3	1:44	CITY HIGH	1:45	12	9	1:43.9	WASHINGTON	1:44.2	4
	MOORE HASTINGS BROOKS O'TOOLE	1	1:42.4	NORTHERN	1:40.8	2	3	1:41.2	WESTERN	1:42.6	6
		2	1:42.6	POLY	1:40.2*	1	5	1:41.7	EAST TECH	1:42	5
		3	1:43.1	CENTRAL	1:41.4	4	6	1:41.9	KINGSTON	1:42.3	4
2	200-YD FREE-STYLE	1									6
		2									5
		3									4
		1	1:45.3*	O'TOOLE, POLY	1:46.0	1	5	1:47.3	WAKEFIELD, NORTHERN	1:48.4	6
		2	1:45.9	ARCHER, MANNING	1:46.7	3	2	1:46.6	JOHNSON, EAST TECH	1:46.6	5
		3	1:47.7	HONIG, CENTRAL	1:47.5	6	4	1:47.1	CURTIS, CITY HIGH	1:48.2	4

Form 10-J

When using this form, or a similar one, the names of the finalists should be inserted, with qualifying times, in the appropriate lane at the conclusion of preliminary heats.

When records are set, this can be noted with an asterisk (see after the time for Poly in the 200 medley). This provides quick reference for noting the record in the media report and in permanent records at the end of the meet.

In relay events, the names of the winning team can be inserted at the left of the form, beneath the listing of the event, such as in the 200 medley in Form 10-J.

There is a separate space provided in this book for entering team point totals in championship meets.

Split Times

Most scorebooks provide space for split or partial times for each event. Insert the time for each segment in the appropriate space. Form 10-K shows the split times for a Central High swimmer in the 200-yard freestyle, noting the time for each segment of the race.

		A	B	C
200	JOE SMITH	1:59.4	31.2	60.9
150		1:28.2	29.7	
100		58.5	30.4	58.5
50		28.1		

Form 10-K

Column A shows the cumulative times at the end of each 50-yard segment of the race. Column B is the time for each individual 50-yard segment (58.5 less 28.1 leaves 30.4 for the second leg). Column C shows times for each 100-yard segment of the race. Each race can be broken down into appropriate segments for this purpose.

Times should be inserted in Column A during the race as times are provided by the split-time timer; then the simple arithmetic necessary to ascertain entries for Columns B & C may be completed at the statistician's convenience.

Split times are of use primarily for coaching purposes, but they are of interest to media in important races and those in which records are set.

Records

Swimming records are standardized and maintained for each event in which there is competition in either amateur (AAU) or college (NCAA or NAIA) meets. There are two sets of records compiled for high schools, depending upon the length of the pool in which the record was set.

College Records

To be recognized in college competition, records must be set in bonafide competition and must be made in a Short-Course pool, one not less than 25 yards in length, but less than 50 yards long. Records are recognized for the following 17 events by the National Collegiate Athletic Association.

50-Yard Freestyle	100-Yard Backstroke	200-Yard Individual Medley
100-Yard Freestyle	200-Yard Backstroke	400-Yard Individual Medley
200-Yard Freestyle	100-Yard Breaststroke	400-Yard Freestyle Relay
500-Yard Freestyle	200-Yard Breaststroke	800-Yard Freestyle Relay
1000-Yard Freestyle	100-Yard Butterfly	400-Yard Medley Relay
1650-Yard Freestyle	200-Yard Butterfly	

Note: Intermediate times are not accepted as records. That is, the time for a 100-yard segment of a 200-yard race is not recognized as a 100-yard record (even if it surpasses the listed record).

Amateur Records

The Amateur Athletic Union, through the International Amateur Swimming Federation, officially certifies American and world records made in this country. In addition to the 17 Short-Course records maintained in college swimming, the AAU lists records in the metric equivalent distance for each of the 17 races, plus the 400-meter freestyle and the 200-yard and 200-meter freestyle relay.

In addition, the AAU maintains records for Long-Course Swimming, in Olympic-size pools 50 meters or 55 yards long. These include all the 19 metric distances listed previously, plus comparable records in yards, in multiples of 55.

That is, instead of 100 yards and 200 yards, records are listed for 110 yards (2 x 55) and 220 yards (4 x 55).

Note: Intermediate times are not accepted as records. That is, the time for a 100-yard segment of a 200-yard race is not recognized as a 100-yard record (even if it surpasses the listed record).

Interscholastic Records

National records are maintained separately for high schools and for prep schools, in two groups each. Twenty-yard course records are recognized in pools not less than 20 yards in length, but not more than 25 yards long. Short-Course records are recognized in pools not less than 25 yards long, but less than 50 yards in length.

Short-Course records are maintained for the following 12 events.

SHORT-COURSE

* 50-yard Freestyle	100-Yard Butterfly
100-Yard Freestyle	*200-Yard Individual Medley
200-Yard Freestyle	*200-Yard Freestyle Relay
400-Yard Freestyle	400-Yard Freestyle Relay
100-Yard Backstroke	*200-Yard Medley Relay
100-Yard Breaststroke	400-Yard Medley Relay

Twenty-yard course records also are maintained in 12 events, but different distances are substituted in the four events marked above with asterisks (*). The reason is obvious. In a 20-yard pool, a 50-yard freestyle would end in the middle of the pool. Thus, in pools of this size, a 60-yard freestyle is used, requiring three full laps, ending at one end of the pool. Similarly, 160-yard races are substituted for 200-yard events.

The four events involved are listed below:

20-YD. COURSE

60-Yard Freestyle	160-Yard Individual Medley
160-Yard Freestyle Relay	160-Yard Medley Relay

Note: Intermediate times are not accepted as records. That is, the time for a 100-yard segment of a 200-yard race is not recognized as a 100-yard record (even if the time surpasses the existing record).

Chapter 11

Tennis

Unless otherwise designated, an Umpire is the official scorer in a tennis match. Thus, a statistician or record-keeper need only collect official scoresheets from the Umpire to compile whatever statistics are desired.

At many major tournaments, various types of scoreboards are utilized to show details of important matches and the results of all matches. Again, these results (though they should be checked to make certain they are official) provide all the information statisticians need for most purposes.

To completely understand the results, the statistician should be thoroughly knowledgeable about the tennis scoring process.

The winner in a tennis match, whether singles or doubles, is the competitor who wins the most number of odd-numbered sets, normally two out of three or three out of five. A single set is used to determine a winner only in rare instances, usually in special exhibitions.

A set is won by the player (or doubles team) who first wins six games, with the provision that he must have at least a two-game margin over his opponent, unless a tie-breaker is in force.

A game is won by the player (or doubles team) who gains at least a two-point advantage over his opponent after a minimum of four points have been played.

Games

Points won in a tennis game are labeled to designate the status of the game at any stage.

The first point won by a player or side is designated "15," the second "30," and the third "40." The fourth point is "game" point, provided the player with four points has an advantage of at least two points over his opponent.

If the players or sides each have one point, or each two, it is called "15-all" or "30-all." After each side has two points, when they are even in points, the status is called "deuce."

When a side has a one-point lead or advantage (after each side has won at least two points), it is called "advantage." If the side with advantage wins the next point, that side is the winner of the game. If it loses the point, the score reverts to deuce. This procedure continues until one side has won two consecutive points after deuce.

When a player has not won a point, his score is designated as "love."

The score of the player serving is always given first, such as "15-love" or "15-40." In each case, the server has one point.

The progression of proper scoring for a single game is shown below. Player A is the server.

Point Won By	Score
Player A	15-love
Player B	15-all
Player B	15-30
Player B	15-40
Player A	Advantage B
Player A	Deuce
Player A	Advantage A
Player A	Game for A

The player or side winning the first six games is the winner of the set, provided the player or team has a two-game margin over the opponent(s).

If there is not a two-game margin, the players or teams continue play until one side does have a two-game margin, except when the tie-breaker is utilized.

Example: When Player A wins his sixth game, he leads his opponent, 6-5. Play must continue until he leads by two games (8-6, for instance) or his opponent rallies to gain a two-game margin (7-9, for instance).

Increasingly, now, a tie-breaker formula is used to prevent long matches (the longest set in tournament history went to 49-47 before a winner was determined).

The tie-breaker goes into effect after a set score reaches 6-6. The basic tie-breaker is a nine-point formula, with the winner the side that first wins five points. Other tie-breaker formulas (such as the best 4 out of 7 points) may be used, and should be announced at the start of the match.

In a nine-point tie-breaker, the sides alternate in serving for two consecutive points each, except in the ninth point, where the serve is made by the side which did not have the advantage of the first two serves in the tie-breaker. Following is the proper nine-point tie-breaker procedure.

Singles

At 6-all, Player A, who normally would serve the next game, serves for two points; Player B then serves two points, the players change courts and serve in the same order, Player A two, then B two. If the score stands at 4-4 at this point, Player B serves the final point. In each case, the player starts serving from the right-hand court and serves his second from the left, until the ninth point, when Player B may serve the final point from either side. As soon as one player has scored five points in the tie-breaker series, that player is declared the set winner at 7-6.

Doubles

At 6-all, Player A, who normally would serve the next game, serves two points, then his opponent, Player X, who has just served the last game, serves two points. The teams change sides and Player B (Player A's partner) serves two points and Player Y (Player X's partner), serves two. If the score has reached 4-4, Player Y serves the final point. Again the serves are alternated from the right to left-hand court, except on the ninth point, where the server has the option of using either side. The side that first wins five points wins the set, 7-6.

If another tie-breaker procedure is used and the scorer is not familiar with the method, he should obtain from an official a copy of the tie-breaker rule in effect.

Scoring

Printed scorecards usually are provided by tennis ball manufacturers with each box of balls. If not available, the scorer can easily draw up his own scoring sheet in a similar style (see Form 11-A).

In this scorecard, there is space for scoring three sets. At top right in the space for each set, there is a diagonal space to insert the names of the players. The names head columns in which a progressive game score is recorded.

In the column at left, the numbers refer to the game being played. The next column is headed "server." In this column is placed the initials of the player who is the server in the game.

PLAYERS CHANGE SIDES AFTER EACH ODD GAME OF SET
X BALL CHANGE AT "CB"

Set No. 1

Game	Server	DH	JR
1	DH	1	0
2	JR	1	1
3	DH	2	1
4	JR	3	1
5	DH	4	1
6	JR	4	2
7	DH	5	2
8	JR	6	2
9	DH		
10	JR		
11	DH		
12	JR		
13	DH		
14	JR		
15	DH		
16	JR		
17	DH		
18	JR		

PLAYERS CHANGE SIDES AFTER EACH ODD GAME OF SET
X BALL CHANGE AT "CB"

Set No. 2

Game	Server	DH	JR
1	JR	0	1
2	DH	1	1
3	JR	1	2
4	DH	2	2
5	JR	2	3
6	DH	3	3
7	JR	3	4
8	DH	4	4
9	JR	4	5
10	DH	5	5
11	JR	6	5
12	DH	7	5
13	JR		
14	DH		
15	JR		
16	DH		
17	JR		
18	DH		

PLAYERS CHANGE SIDES AFTER EACH ODD GAME OF SET
X BALL CHANGE AT "CB"

Set No. 3

Game	Server	DH	JR
1	DH		
2	JR		
3	DH		
4	JR		
5	DH		
6	JR		
7	DH		
8	JR		
9	DH		
10	JR		
11	DH		
12	JR		
13	DH		
14	JR		
15	DH		
16	JR		
17	DH		
18	JR		

Form 11-A

Since the service is alternated, after the toss of a coin to determine who is to serve first, the scorer should insert the initials of the players in the appropriate boxes down to the bottom of the column.

This should be done prior to each game, because during rapid play the scorer may not have time to insert initials and enter scoring notations. If he does attempt it, the haste may lead to error.

For each succeeding set, the server's initials for each game should be inserted after the proper game, again, before the set begins. In doubles, the initials of the four servers should be inserted in alternating order.

The tally marks in the small squares on the body of the card indicate the winner of each point. The marks in the top row of squares are the scores for the server, and the marks in the lower squares indicate the points scored by his opponent.

Example: In Form 11-B, DH was the server in the first game; he scored first (15-love), his opponent scored second (15-all) and third (15-30); DH scored next (30-30); DH scored again, with an ace (40-30); his opponent tied the game by scoring next (deuce); DH scored next (advantage DH) and then won the game by scoring again (game DH).

Form 11-B

C B		SERVER	POINTS Set No. 1
	1	DH	

Circled entries indicate an "ace," a point-winning serve that is hit beyond the reach of (untouched by) the receiver.

In Form 11-C, the column at the right of the card bearing DH's initials shows that he won the first game because it has the number 1 in it. His opponent's score at this stage is "love" and is shown by a zero. JR won the second game, making it "1-1." DH won the third game, giving him a 2 to 1 advantage in games, and so on. DH was the winner of the set by a margin of 6-2. In the next set DH won 7 games to 5 (Form 11-D), thus giving him the match.

It is advisable that the scorer have the Umpire sign the card when the match is completed. If a subsequent question about a score is raised, it can be referred to the signing official.

Dual Meets

In dual meets between teams, normally 6 singles and 3 doubles

PLAYERS CHANGE SIDES AFTER EACH ODD GAME OF SET
X BALL CHANGE AT "CB"

Set No. 2

C B	Game	Server	POINTS	JR	DH
	1	JR		1	0
	2	DH		1	1
	3	JR		2	1
	4	DH		2	2
	5	JR		3	2
	6	DH		3	3
	7	JR		4	3
	8	DH		4	4
	9	JR		5	4
	10	DH		5	5
	11	JR		5	6
	12	DH		5	7
	13	JR			

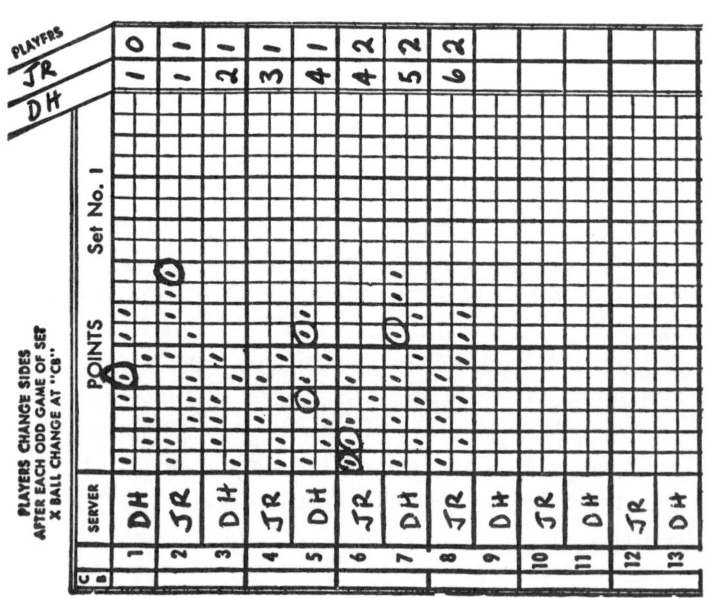

PLAYERS CHANGE SIDES AFTER EACH ODD GAME OF SET
X BALL CHANGE AT "CB"

Set No. 1

C B	Game	Server	POINTS	JR	DH
	1	DH		0	1
	2	JR		1	1
	3	DH		1	2
	4	JR		1	3
	5	DH		1	4
	6	JR		2	4
	7	DH		2	5
	8	JR		2	6
	9	DH			
	10	JR			
	11	DH			
	12	JR			
	13	DH			

Form 11-C

matches are played. Sometimes it is 3 and 2 or 4 and 1, but in any case, it always must be in odd numbers of matches. The team that wins the most total matches (singles and doubles) wins the dual meet.

Example: Following is the result of a team dual meet in which Team A won three singles and two doubles, to win the match, 5-4.

> John Brown (A) def. Bill Anderson 6-2, 5-7, 6-3; Joe Smith (B) def. Tom Connor 6-3, 6-4; Bill Bowman (A) def. Tom Gorman 6-1, 6-2; John Botan (A) def. Jack Sears 6-4, 3-6, 6-2; Harry Hickey (B) def. Jim Davis, 6-1, 6-4; Sam Ewing (B) def. Walt Crest 6-4, 3-6, 6-2. Brown and Connor (A) def. Anderson and Gorman 6-4, 4-6, 6-4; Fred Co and Les Fieldler (B) def. Frank Volpe and Botan 6-2, 6-3; Tom Fisher and Bowman (A) def. Bob Hughes and Stan Lindgren 6-0, 6-1.

This form is suitable for reporting results to news media, though often when reproduced first names are omitted.

Tournaments

In tournaments it is normal to have single eliminations—one loss and the player or team is eliminated. A "ladder" chart may be used to show results, similar to the sample reproduced in Form 11-D.

Tournament Scoring

When teams are entered in tournament play, such as in a conference or National Collegiate championship, one point is awarded to the team of each player for each "advancement."

If the player advances by winning a match played or wins by default, he is awarded one point. If he advances because of a bye, he must win his next match for his team to receive a point for the bye round.

Example: John Smith of Central High draws a bye in the first round and defeats Jay Kingsley of East Tech in the second round. Smith earns one point for his team for the bye and one for defeating Kingsley for a total of two points.

Example: Smith draws a bye in the first round and is defeated by Kingsley in the second round. Smith's team does not receive a point for the bye round. East Tech earns one point for Kingsley's win.

The team earning the highest total of points is the tournament winner.

Form 11-D

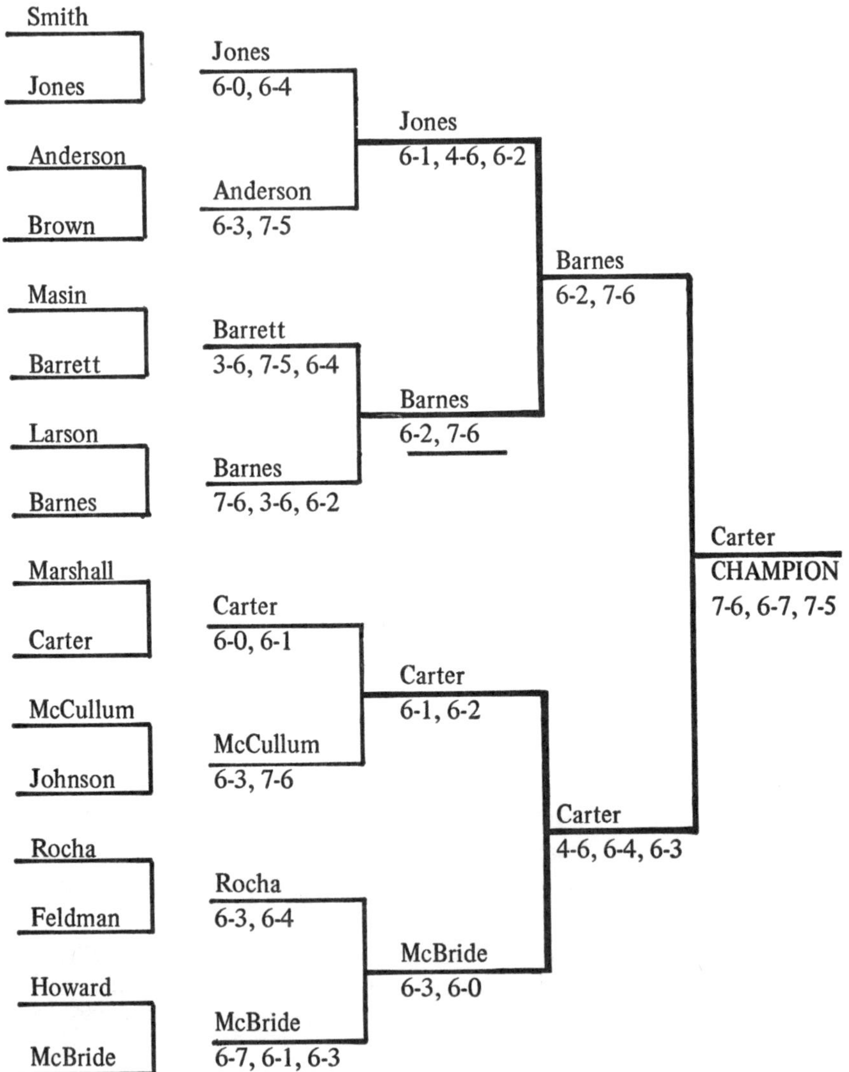
Smith
Jones
Anderson
Brown
Masin
Barrett
Larson
Barnes
Marshall
Carter
McCullum
Johnson
Rocha
Feldman
Howard
McBride
Jones
6-0, 6-4
Anderson
6-3, 7-5
Barrett
3-6, 7-5, 6-4
Barnes
7-6, 3-6, 6-2
Carter
6-0, 6-1
McCullum
6-3, 7-6
Rocha
6-3, 6-4
McBride
6-7, 6-1, 6-3
Jones
6-1, 4-6, 6-2
Barnes
6-2, 7-6
Carter
6-1, 6-2
McBride
6-3, 6-0
Barnes
6-2, 7-6
Carter
4-6, 6-4, 6-3
Carter
CHAMPION
7-6, 6-7, 7-5

VASSS Scoring

Another system of scoring in tennis, although rarely used, should be detailed because it has been employed in tournaments and may be adopted on a broader scale in the future.

It is the Van Alen System of Simplified Scoring (VASSS), devised by James Van Alen, a longtime advocate of changes in basic tennis play and scoring. Van Alen was one of those instrumental in the introduction of the tie-breaker, now in general use.

In Van Alen's system, scoring is similar to table tennis, with the winner of each serve credited with a single point (1, 2, 3, 4, etc., as opposed to 15, 30, 40, Advantage, etc.). The player or doubles team first scoring 31 points is the winner, provided the margin over the opponent is two points or more. If tied at 31-31, the nine-point tie-breaker formula is used to determine the winner.

The 31-point round serves as both a game and set. Matches may be the regular 2 out of 3 or 3 out of 5 or the match may be either 2 or 4 sets, with the nine-point tie-breaker utilized to decide the winner if sets are divided.

In VASSS play, the players serve five consecutive times before changing serve, the same as in table tennis.

The VASSS system was first used in a professional tournament at Newport in 1958. Occasionally, in a pro round-robin tourney, the winner has been that player who compiled the most total points in all of his matches.

Points, in a round-robin tourney, may be earned by an arbitrary assignment of points for each win (usually a multiple of 20—20, 40, 60 or 80). Another formula calls for the winner of each match to receive 31 points for the number of points won by him in the round, plus a five-point bonus for winning, plus the unplayed points in the set.

Example: John Smith wins his match, 31-10. He receives 31 points for the number of points he won in the round, a five-point bonus, plus 19 points for the unplayed points (difference between 31-10 and 31-29). Thus, for the round, Smith earns 55 points.

In other VASSS round-robin tourney scoring, each player receives one point for each point he earned in his round. Thus, if John Smith defeats Jay Kingsley, 31-10, Smith earns 31 points and Kingsley, 10.

Peculiarly, the tourney winner could be a player who did not win a single match, but the sum of his losing points was the highest total during the tournament (i.e. a player could score 28 or 29 points in each of several losing matches, but compile more points than a player who won most of his matches but scored only a few points in losing one or two).

Records

Available categories for tennis records are relatively few. A permanent record should be maintained for all tournament results, not only to show a historical listing of champions, but to use as a reference for the performance over the years of any single player or doubles team in a particular tourney.

For the individual player, a few records may be of use to the statistician or publicist. These can be maintained by use of the scorecard or by permanent listing of scoring records.

Most Aces in a single game, set, match, season or career.
Most consecutive points, games, sets and matches won.
Most tournaments won.
Most consecutive tournaments won.
Most matches won in dual competition, in tourneys and career.

Chapter 12

Track and Field

Statistics in track and field are complex only because of the great variety of events for which there is competition: running and field events, indoor and outdoor, cross country, decathlon and, on occasion, the pentathlon.

For instance, standard outdoor sprint and middle distance race competition includes the 100, 220, 440, 880 and mile run, or their metric equivalent.

Indoors, depending upon the facility and tradition of the meets, comparable races have been run at 50, 60, 70, 75, 80, 100, 220, 300, 440, 500, 600, 660, 880, 1,000, 1320 and one mile.

In the hurdles, standard events currently are the 120-yard high hurdles, 440-yard intermediate hurdles and, sometimes, the 220-yard low hurdles (180 yards in high schools). Indoors, hurdlers may compete at 40, 45, 50, 60, 65, 70 or 75 yards in either the highs or lows.

At one time, interest in track statistics was only in the winning time, height or distance of each event. No more. Now, the statistician is expected to provide complete performance charts for at least each place winner, with partial times (i.e. time of each 220-yard segment of an 880-yard run, for instance) for the winners. In noteworthy events or close finishes, often there is demand for split or partial times for all contenders.

Track and field statisticians are indefatigable. The hard-core figure filberts, known affectionately as track nuts, can reel off records and outstanding performances in the multitude of events, will eagerly and indelibly memorize and memorialize not only winning times and distances, but the partial times for all competitors—or at least the place-winners. In the field events, the winning distance or height is barely sufficient.

Throw-by-throw or jump-by-jump statistics are necessary for these avid trackophiles.

There are enough intense track fans to support one periodic publication, *Track & Field News,* published in Los Altos, California, by Bert and Cordner Nelson. Edited with such dedication that it has become accepted as the track and field "bible," this publication provides detailed split times and individual field performances for every competitor in important meets throughout the world.

Such avid interest, which has seeped through in lesser degrees to even the more casual track fan, means that the statistician's primary chore is to establish a routine which insures the rapid gathering and dissemination of all the statistical material needed for a particular meet.

A single statistician cannot be expected to record performances in such depth, unless he himself is a real track nut. But he can determine with his coach a satisfactory compromise that will satisfy the needs of the coach, the fans and the media.

On the happy side, the track and field statistician is not responsible for timing runners or measuring height or distance. These are functions of meet officials, though on occasion it may be necessary for the statistician to help coordinate the activities of timers and judges.

For statistical purposes, he obtains the official times, distances and places from designated officials and then processes them for dissemination to the public address system and records them for historical purposes.

It is not the normal function of the statistician to organize a track meet. A well-planned and executed track meet is a near-science in itself and usually is the responsibility of the coach, athletic administrator and the games committee.

We will be concerned here only with the statistical and record facets of track and field, and the best methods of utilizing the results. However, fulfilling this capacity in a competent manner is a challenge. Because of the numbers of competitors and events, good organization is essential for the statistician.

He must be prepared well in advance of the meet with all work sheets and reference material. The latter includes a listing of current world, American, conference, school, meet and track records for all events scheduled.

Prior to the meet, a routine should be established for the statistician to obtain official results of each event as quickly as possible from the chief judge for each event. This information should be relayed to the public address announcer and any media representatives on hand and should be expedited in the most practical way, whether by written form or by voice. The latter method is least desirable because of the inherent hazard of errors in verbal communication. Even when this is the most practical way (for instance, a walkie-talkie report would be the quickest in a large stadium where the press box is a long distance from the finish line of a race), a written report of the results should follow the verbal transmission as a check against inaccuracies.

Work Sheets

Forms to be used in track meets come in all varieties, depending upon the preference of the statistician, the nature of the meet and the requirements to adequately provide information to spectators and media.

In a dual meet between small schools, a simple scorebook is the only work sheet needed. For a large meet that attracts spectators and media in large numbers, the amount of material used would tax the inventory of the corner stationery store.

Basic forms include entry blanks for use in advance of each event, report forms from the judges, report forms for the public address announcer and media, summary forms and a scorebook.

Entry Blanks

Prior to a meet, the statistician should have a supply of entry blanks for each event. Form 12-A shows a simple entry blank for the 100-yard dash. If the meet is well-organized, it should be possible to prepare these in advance. In the limited time available, it is much simpler to cross out an entry than to fill out a complete entry form just as the event begins.

The entry blank for each event should include the first and last name of each competitor and his uniform number, if any. When possible, insert after each competitor's name his previous best performance (time, distance or height) in that event. If his best career performance was achieved in a previous year, insert that performance as well as his best during the current season. (See Form 12-A)

If this same form is to be used for a report sheet, pertinent records in the event should be inserted at the bottom. Records can be extensive, with complete details included on current records, or they can be limited only to records that may be useful for the particular meet. For instance, in the 100-yard dash, where the best previous time for any competitor may be only 10.1, the listing of the world record of 9.1 is not likely

Event 100-YD DASH Date 5/12/

	Competitor School (No.) Best Time		
	JOHN HAWKS, ET (241) 9.6-1971, 9.7-1972		
	BEN BRIGGS, ET (242) 9.8		
	CHARLES LYONS, ET (243) 10.0		
	JOE HICKS, CH (318) 9.5		
	BILL HART, CH (319) 9.6		
	HOMER COLE, CH (321) 10.1		

Form 12-A

World record: 9.1, Bob Hayes, 1963, Jim Hines, 1967, Charlie Green, 1967, John Carlos, 1969. American Record: Same. National High School record: 9.3, William Gaines, 1967. Track record: 9.5, Joe Hicks, 1971. Central High record: 9.5, Joe Hicks, 1971. East Tech Record: 9.4, Alvin Horn, 1970.

to have any significance. However, many statisticians prefer to list all records on the report sheet for each event.

The entry blank can serve a quadruple purpose, if desired. It can be (a) an entry blank, (b) a lane assignment sheet, (c) a judge's report form, and (d) a press report form.

Form 12-B shows Form 12-A, with the lane assignments added in front of each competitor's name. Note that one pre-meet entry was scratched and an additional entry made at the start of the event.

Judge's Report Form

At the conclusion of each event, the judges should enter, on a prepared form, the order of finish of the event and the exact time, distance or height of the scoring competitors. In the case of field events, the

Event 100-YD DASH Date 5/12/

Lane	Competitor School (No.) Best Time		
5	JOHN HAWKS, ET (241) 9.6-1971, 9.7-1972		
~~—~~	~~BEN BRIGGS, ET (242) 9.8~~		
1	CHARLES LYONS, ET (243) 10.0		
4	JOE HICKS, CH (318) 9.5		
2	Bill HART, CH (319) 9.6		
6	HOMER COLE, CH (321) 10.1		
3	GEORGE CONN, ET (251) 10.0		

Form 12-B

judge should enter the performance of each competitor for each throw or jump attempted.

The extent of the information to be included depends upon the requirements of the meet. At a minimum, the time, distance or height of the winner should be entered, but in modern day meets this information is included for at least all placewinners.

A special form may be utilized for this purpose, or the original entry blank form can serve. Form 12-C shows Form 12-A, with lane placements added on the left (as in Form 12-B) and, on the right, the order of finish and time of each runner.

For field events, the judge's report form, showing each attempt by each competitor, may be used for record or media purposes. Form 12-D shows a typical judge's report form for the long jump.

Press Report Forms

Copies of Forms 12-C & 12-D can be used to provide official results to the public address announcer and the press. But, where practical, a special summary of results should be provided (Forms 12-E-1 and 12-E-2) in the style normally used by the media in the area. The com-

Event 100-YD DASH Date 5/12/

Lane	Competitor School (No.) Best Time	Place	Time
5	JOHN HAWKS, ET (241) 9.6-1971, 9.7-1972	3	9.8
~~—~~	~~BEN BRIGGS, ET (242) 9.8~~		
1	CHARLES LYONS, ET (243) 10.0	4	9.8
4	JOE HICKS, CH (318) 9.5	2	9.7
2	BILL HART, CH (319) 9.6	1	9.5
6	HOMER COLE, CH (321) 10.1	6	10.2
3	GEORGE CONN, ET (251) 10.0	5	10.0

Form 12-C

Event LONG JUMP Date 5/12/

Name, School (No.)	Best Jump	Trials			Finals		
MERV HOLLINS, ET (281)	24-4¼	22-6	23-7	22-10	F	22-9	(23-2½)
CLAUDE WILLIAMS, ET (283)	21-6	20-4	F	19-5	19-11	(20-6)	20-5¼
MIKE MOORE, ET (284)	21-5½	20-2	19-1½	F	—		—
CARROLL COLE, CH (375)	22-6	20-7	20-6	20-6	(20-7)	19-11	20-6
HAL ARDEN, CH (376)	21-5½	F	F	20-1	—		—
DANNY FRANKLIN, CH (311)	20-5	19-1¼	F	20.2	F	20-5	20-4

Form 12-D

World record: 29-2¼, Bob Beamon, 1968. American record; Same. National High School record: 25-7, Jerry Proctor, 1967. Track record: 24-10, Joe Darby, Lincoln High, 1971. Central High record: 24-3, Mike Sanders, 1969. East Tech record: 23-4½, Ernie Kingman, 1970.

Note: For type of report sheet to be used for high jump or pole vault, see Form 12-G under "Scoring" in a later section.

petitors should be listed in order of finish, with notations made of any records tied or broken. In races where the wind is a factor in recognition of records, wind velocity should be noted.

> 100-yd dash—1. Bill Hart (C) 9.5 (ties old track and school record set by Joe Hicks, May 15, 1971); 2. Joe Hicks (C) 9.7; 3. John Hawks (ET) 9.8; 4. Charles Lyons (ET) 9.8; 5. George Conn (ET) 10.0; 6. Homer Cole (C) 10.1.

Form 12-E-1

To conserve space, some media prefer not to use the numerals denoting order of finish, but list the competitors only in order of finish (Hart (C) 9.5, Hicks (C) 9.7, etc.). For dual meets, it is likely the media will want only the point winners (first three places) and some prefer only the time of the winner. Local traditions determine which style should be used.

> Long jump—1. Merv Hollins (ET) 23-2½; 2. Carroll Cole (C) 20-7; 3. Claude Williams (ET) 20-6; 4. Danny Franklin (C) 20.5; 5. Mike Moore (ET) 20-2; 6. Hal Arden (C) 20-1.

Form 12-E-2

Again, media may prefer listing only the first three place and point winners, and they may want only the winning distance. However, if all the material is included, it is easy for a writer to cross out information not wanted. It is better to provide more material than necessary than not enough.

For a complete meet summary at the end of competition, merely put together the results of each event (such as Forms 12-E-1 and 12-E-2) on one report.

If this material is to be typed and distributed to media at the end of the meet, do not wait until the final event to prepare the entire summary. Results of each event should be typed on a master form as it is concluded, so that at the end of the last event the summary will be concluded. This is highly important to media representatives who have deadlines to meet.

Scoring

Points are awarded to each team competing in a meet proportionately to the finishing position of individuals and relay teams in each event.

It is recommended by the official college and high school track and field rules committee, as published in the National Collegiate Athletic Association's *Official Track & Field Guide,* that in dual meets three places be awarded points in individual events and the winning team, only, receives points in relays.

In triangular and quadrangular meets, it is recommended that points be awarded for the first four places.

The official rules provide formulas for assigning points in both individual and relay events, according to the number of places to be picked in the meet. These are shown in Form 12-F.

SCORING

Number of Places In Meet	*Scoring (Individual Events)*				
	1st	*2nd*	*3rd*	*4th*	*5th*
2	5	3			
3	5	3	1		
4	5	3	2	1	
5	6	4	3	2	1

Number of Teams In Meet	*Scoring (Relays)*				
	1st	*2nd*	*3rd*	*4th*	*5th*
2	5	0			
3	5	3	0		
4	5	3	2	0	
5	6	4	3	2	0

NOTE—***In conference meets, points for relays should be the same as for individual events.***

Form 12-F

In conference or national championships or in special meets where many teams compete, it is normal to provide points for the first six places. To accommodate so many places and still provide the proper weight in points to the winner, the points awarded are doubled, so that scoring is done on a 10-8-6-4-2-1 basis in both individual and relay events.

When two or more competitors tie for a place, the points for the places involved are divided equally between them.

Example: In a meet awarding points for three places, two men tie for second in one event. The 3 points for second and 1 point for third are divided, with each competitor earning two points. The competitor finishing fourth receives no points.

Example: In a meet awarding points for four places, two men tie for second in one event. The 3 points for second and 2 points for third are divided, with each competitor awarded 2½ points. The competitor finishing fourth is awarded one (1) point.

In field events, tie-breaking procedures are administered by the event judges, and the statistician is required only to process the results. However, he should know the procedures as background intelligence to provide this information to the media and to the public adddress announcer.

In the events that are decided by measuring distances (throwing events, long jump and triple jump), ties are broken by using the second-best performance of the competitors; if these are the same, by using the third-best performance of each, and so on.

In the high jump and pole vault, ties are broken by awarding the place and points to the competitor with the fewest jumps attempted at the height last cleared by each tied competitor. If these are the same, the place and points are awarded to the competitor with the fewest misses at all heights, up to and including the last height cleared; and if still tied, to the competitor with the fewest total jumps attempted (whether successful or not) throughout the competition, up to and including the last height cleared.

If a tie still remains, the points involved are divided among the tying competitors, unless the tie is for first place. In that event, officials will conduct a jump-off to resolve the tie.

In the jump-off, competitors tying shall each have one more jump at the height at which they failed and, if no decision is reached, the bar is lowered or raised, as determined by meet officials, and competitors each take one jump at each height until the tie is resolved.

Example: Form 12-G shows the performance of four competitors who each cleared 6-ft. 4-in. and failed at 6-5 in the high jump.

PERFORMANCE RECORD–HIGH JUMP

	5′10″	6′0″	6′1″	6′2″	6′3″	6′4″	6′5″	Total Failures	Total Jumps	Pos.
A	–	X√	√	X √	–	XX√	XXX	4	8	2
B	√	√	√	X	X √	XX√	XXX	4	9	3
C	√	√	X	√	XX√	XX√	XXX	5	10	4
D	√	–	–	XX√	XX√	X √	XXX	5	9	1

(Key: – Did Not Jump; √ Cleared; X Failed)

Form 12-G

The four-way tie is broken in the following manner:

a. Since D cleared 6 feet 4 inches on his second attempt, while the others cleared on their third attempts, he is declared the winner.
b. Since C has more failures than either A or B, he is given fourth place.
c. Since the total number of jumps made by A is less than that made by B, he is given second place, and B, third place.

Scorebooks

A permanent record of each track meet should be maintained in some type of scorebook. If summary reports of each event are not required for media or public address announcer during a meet, a good scorebook is sufficient to record all information needed for a track meet.

Such a scorebook is the *All-American Track & Field Score Sheet,* published by Barkham Garner at 717 St. James Place, Newport Beach, Ca. 92660. This scorebook comes in two styles. One is for dual meets or other competition where no more than five places are scored, and is adequate for cumulative team scoring for seven or eight teams. The other All-American book is designed for larger meets and provides space for scoring six places, and for the cumulative scoring of 35 to 37 teams.

In either book, results should be recorded chronologically, as each event is finished and the official results are obtained from the event judge or meet referee.

Form 12-H shows a reduced reproduction of the scorebook for eight events of a dual meet between Central High and East Tech.

In this meet, Central High won the first event, the 440-yd. relay, and its time (42.4) is entered in the appropriate space. Time for the second-place team (42.8) may be entered in the space provided for third place in other events.

In regular events, the time or distance of the second and third-place finishers may be entered above their names.

You will note at the right-hand side that team scoring is shown on each line, with the slanted line separating the scores for that individual event and for the teams' cumulative scores.

In this meet, for the first event, Central High is credited with five points for winning the event and a cumulative total (after one event) of five points. The second place team in relays receives no points, so zeroes are entered for East Tech.

In the second event, the mile run, the winning time was 4:18.2, with Gomez of East Tech winning, followed by Harris of East Tech (4:19) and Morgan of Central (4:26). In team scoring, East Tech receives

CENTRAL HIGH vs EAST TECH 5/12/72 CENTRAL Running Score

	Time or Distance	First Place	School	Second Place	School	Third Place		Fourth Place		Fifth Place		CH		ET
440-YD RELAY	42.4	HICKS, COLE SMITH, HART	C	BRIGGS, CONN ABLE, HAWKS	ET	(42.8)						5/5		0/0
MILE	4:18.2	GOMEZ	ET	4:19 HARRIS	ET	4:26 MORGAN	C					1/6		8/8
120-YD H.H.	14.9	CREW	C	LEWIS LOGUE	ET C	} tie, 15.2						7/13		
SP	58-1½	STOCK	ET	57-4 MILLER	C	53-1½ BRADY	C					4/17		5/15
440	48.4	SMITH	C	49.6 CONN	ET	50.6 MITCHELL	C					6/23		3/18
LJ	23-2½	Hollins	ET	20-7 COLE	C	20-6 Williams	ET					3/26		6/24
100	9.5	HART	C	9.7 HICKS	C	9.8 HAWKS	ET					8/34		1/25
880	1:52.7	BROWN	C	1:54.4 BAXTER	ET	1:58.1 GRANT	ET					5/39		4/29

Form 12-H

five for first place and three for second, for a total of eight. For two events, now, East Tech has a cumulative total of eight. Central receives one point for a third-place finish in the mile. Added to the five points for the first event, Central, after two events, has a cumulative total of six points.

In the 120-yd. high hurdles, Central's Crew won in 14.9 seconds. There was a tie for second (as noted by inserting both names in the space for second place) between Lewis of East Tech and Logue of Central, both timed in 15.2.

They split the three points for second and one point for third, giving each team two points. With Crew's five points for winning, Central has seven points in this event and three-event cumulative total of 13. East Tech adds Lewis' two points to its previous eight for a three-event total of 10.

This event-by-event tally is continued, so that by the time the final event of the meet is entered, the scorebook contains not only the order of finish and times, heights and distances for each place-winner, but shows immediately the total points for each team in the meet.

The larger All-American scorebook is identical in style to that shown in Form 12-H. The only difference is in the additional space provided for six places and for the larger number of teams in scoring.

Records

Track and Field is one of the few sports where international records are recognized. This added emphasis makes it important to keep up-to-date records, and it also provides standards so that the statistician knows what records to maintain. Track records are maintained and published in every area of competition.

The number of records in track and field is literally unlimited. There are world records, American records, records for universities and colleges, for junior colleges, for high schools and for U.S. Track & Field Federation and AAU competition, etc.

In addition, there are records for competition at each individual relay meet, at each championship meet, at each individual track site and for each school.

Records in all these categories are maintained for both outdoor and indoor competition (though there are no official world records in indoor track). As pointed out earlier, within each category (i.e. sprints, hurdles, etc.) there are as many records as there are different distances at which competition is held.

The number of records to be maintained by a statistician will be determined by tradition at the individual school and by those which will be most useful to the coach and the media.

At a minimum, records should be maintained for each school and for each track in these categories (distances are given in yards, but when there is competition at comparable metric distances, these, too, should be compiled):

Outdoor Records

100-yards & 100 meters	120-yard & 110-meter high hurdles
220-yards & 200 meters (straightaway)	*220-yard & 200-meter low hurdles (straightaway)
220-yards & 200 meters (full turn)	*220-yard & 200-meter low hurdles (full turn)
440-yards & 400 meters	440-yard & 400-meter intermediate hurdles
880 yards & 800 meters	High jump
One-mile & 1500 meters	Pole vault
Two-miles	Long jump
Three-miles & 5,000 meters	Triple jump
Six miles & 10,000 meters	**Shot put
3,000 meter steeplechase	***Discus throw
440-yard & 400-meter relay	**Hammer throw
880-yard relay	Javelin throw
One-mile & 1600-meter relay	Sprint medley relay
Two-mile relay	480-yard shuttle hurdle relay
Four-mile relay	Marathon
Distance medley relay	Decathlon

*—180-yard low hurdles in high schools. **—12 pounds in high school.
***—3 pounds, 9 ounces in high schools.

Indoor Records

60 yards	70-yard high hurdles
440 yards	High jump
500 yards	Pole vault
600 yards	Long jump
880 yards	Shot put
1,000 yards	35-pound weight
One-mile	Triple jump
Two-miles	One-mile relay
Three-miles	Two-mile relay
60-yard high hurdles	Distance medley relay

Decathlon

Competition in the decathlon is not a standard event in most meets. Except for infrequent and isolated special scheduling, decathlon competition is staged only on a national or international scale.

Scoring in the decathlon is individual only, and points are awarded on an arbitrary scale in proportion to each competitor's performance in each of 10 events.

PTS	Running events			Hurdles	Jumping events			Throwing events		
	100 m	400 m	1.500 m	110 m						
	sec.	sec.	min.	sec.	cm	cm	cm	m	m	m
800	-	-	4.02,0	-	-	690	-	15,19	45,99	63,17
799	-	-	4.02,1	-	-	-	397	15,17	45,93	63,09
798	-	-	4.02,2	-	-	689	-	15,15	45,88	63,00
797	-	50,2	4.02,3	15,5	-	-	-	15,14	45,82	62,92
796	-	-	4.02,4	-	193	688	396	15,12	45,77	62,84
795	-	-	4.02,5	-	-	-	-	15,10	45,72	62,75
794	-	-	4.02,7	-	-	687	395	15,09	45,67	62,67
793	-	-	4.02,8	-	-	-	-	15,07	45,61	62,59
792	-	50,3	4.02,9	-	-	-	-	15,05	45,56	62,51
791	-	-	4.03,0	-	-	686	394	15,04	45,50	62,42
790	-	-	4.03,1	-	-	-	-	15,02	45,45	62,34
789	-	-	4.03,3	-	-	685	-	15,00	45,39	62,26
788	-	50,4	4.03,4	-	192	-	393	14,99	45,34	62,17
787	-	-	4.03,5	15,6	-	684	-	14,97	45,28	62,09
786	-	-	4.03,6	-	-	-	-	14,95	45,23	62,01
785	-	-	4.03,7	-	-	683	392	14,94	45,18	61,92
784	-	50,5	4.03,9	-	-	-	-	14,92	45,13	61,84
783	-	-	4.04,0	-	-	-	391	14,90	45,07	61,76
782	-	-	4.04,1	-	-	682	-	14,88	45,02	61,68
781	-	-	4.04,3	-	-	-	-	14,87	44,96	61,59
780	11,1	-	4.04,4	-	-	681	390	14,85	44,91	61,51
779	-	50,6	4.04,5	-	191	-	-	14,84	44,85	61,43
778	-	-	4.04,7	-	-	680	-	14,82	44,80	61,35
777	-	-	4.04,8	15,7	-	-	389	14,80	44,74	61,26
776	-	-	4.04,9	-	-	679	-	14,79	44,69	61,18
775	-	50,7	4.05,0	-	-	-	388	14,77	44,64	61,10
774	-	-	4.05,2	-	-	678	-	14,75	44,59	61,02
773	-	-	4.05,3	-	-	-	-	14,74	44,53	60,94
772	-	-	4.05,4	-	-	677	387	14,72	44,48	60,85
771	-	-	4.05,5	-	-	-	-	14,70	44,42	60,77

Form 12-I

The tables of points for the decathlon are adopted and approved by the International Amateur Athletic Federation. In this grueling event, individuals compete against other men, but only incidentally. The real competition is between the individual and the graduated table of points.

The decathlon encompasses competition in the 100 meters, 400 meters, 110-meter high hurdles and 1500 meters on the track and six field events, the long jump, shot put, high jump, discus, pole vault and javelin.

The winner in decathlon competition is the individual who accumulates the highest total points for all 10 events. See Form 12-I for a partial reproduction of the decathlon point tables, showing the gradation of points awarded for varying performances in events.

The maximum number of points in each event is 1200.

It is possible for a man to win the decathlon without posting the best time or distance in any single event. Thus, the statistical focus is on the final accumulation of points. Therefore, statistical report forms should be devised to enable the statistician to make a quick summary of points earned.

Form 12-J shows a work sheet for an individual event, the 400-meter run. Because competitors perform in heats, a form may be used for each heat or (because the relative finish of each man in each heat is unimportant), one work sheet can be utilized for each event.

Decathlon 400-METERS **Date** 6/24/

Competitor Team (No.) Best Time		
BRUCE DAVIES, ST. John's (84) 50.6	50.3	792
EARLE Fuller, SOUTH Ky. (106) 50.4	51.3	749
RANDY HURST, CENTRAL ST. (86) 49.9	50.2	797
LANNY KING, MILLER U. (111) 52.0	54.3	629
LAWRENCE MANN, NATIONAL (91) 53.6	55.0	603
GEORGE MOE, CARTER TECH (108) 51.7	53.4	663
DON OWENS, HARRISON (102) 49.4	50.7	775
CHUCK STEVENS, STATE U. (99) 55.2	50.2	792
Russell THORPE, NORTHERN (94) 51.8	52.4	703

Form 12-J

Form 12-K

DECATHLON SUMMARY SITE Hometown, Ga. DATE 5/24/72

Name, Team (No.) Best Previous	100	LJ	SP	HJ	400	HH	DISC	PV	JAV	1500	Total
Bruce Davies, St. John's (84)	756	717	542	695	782	707	578	592	630	689	6,688
Earle Fuller, South Ky. (106)	703	680	622	660	749	710	530	527	625	574	6,380
Randy Hurst, Central State (86)	746	725	530	650	797	727	524	555	546	712	6,512
Lanny King, Miller U. (111)	639	642	741	651	629	637	710	599	559	563	6,370
Lawrence Mann, National (91)	598	666	810	623	603	541	801	610	740	613	6,605
George Moe, Carter Tech (108)	624	666	602	679	663	635	604	671	612	656	6,412
Don Owens, Harrison (112)	665	621	882	642	775	646	850	790	730	668	7,269
Chuck Stevens, State U. (99)	776	647	541	648	792	678	542	612	504	635	6,375
Russell Thorpe, Northern (94)	692	633	610	640	703	678	652	653	604	669	6,534

World Record: 8,417, Bill Toomey (So. Calif. Striders), 1969. American Record: Same. Collegiate Record: 7,406, Rich Wanamaker (Drake), 1970. Field Record: 7,307, Norman Smith (Central State), 1969.

Enter the names either alphabetically or in order of appearance. A place is provided for the time or distance of each competitor and the total points allotted by the standard scoring tables (see Form 12-I) for each performance.

For instance, in Form 12-J, it is noted that Hurst was timed in 50.2 for the 400-meter run. The table (Form 12-I) allots 797 points for a time of 50.2.

For the total competition, a work sheet and report form (Form 12-K) can be identical, providing a place for each name and the points earned by each competitor in each event, and the total points earned in 10 events by each competitor.

For a complete summary of the decathlon, a report such as Form 12-L should be prepared, listing four entries (three in running events) for each competitor—(1) time or distance in feet and inches, (2) metric equivalent in distance for field events (because the Decathlon Scoring Table is tabulated in centimeters and meters), (3) points credited for each event, and (4) cumulative points at the end of each event.

Form 12-L shows a partial summary form of this type, with Davies timed in 11.2 seconds in the 100 meters for 756 points (and a one-event total of 756 points). In the second event, he long-jumped 21-ft. 4-in. or 651 centimeters for 717 points and a two-event total of 1473 points.

DECATHALON SUMMARY

Competitor Team (No.)	100	Points Total	LJ CM	Points Total	SP M
BRUCE DAVIES	11.2	756	21-4	717	3
ST. JOHN'S (84)		756	651	1473	1

LJ—Long Jump CM—Centimeters SP—Shotput M—Meters

Form 12-L

Either Form 12-K or Form 12-L will serve adequately as a permanent record of decathlon competition. However, if summary reports are desired by media for reproduction, they should be prepared in the traditional style used by media in the area.

At a minimum, the names and 10-event point totals for each competitor should be included, as shown in Form 12-M.

Don Owens, Harrison, 7,269 points; Bruce Davies, St. John's, 6,688; Lawrence Mann, National, 6,605; Russell Thorpe, Northern, 6,534; Randy Hurst, Central State, 6,512; George Moe, Carter Tech, 6,412; Earle Fuller, South Kentucky, 6,380; Chuck Stevens, State U., 6,375; Lanny King, Miller U., 6,370.

Form 12-M

If desired, the comparative results of each event can be reproduced, showing times or distances and points earned by each competitor. Form M shows results of the 400-meter competition.

400-meters: Randy Hurst, Central State, 50.1, 797 points; Bruce Davies, St. John's, 50.2, 792; Chuck Stevens, State U., 50.2, 792; Don Owens, Harrison, 50.7, 775; Earle Fuller, South Kentucky, 51.3, 749; Russell Thorpe, Northern, 52.4, 703; George Moe, Carter Tech, 53.4, 663; Lanny King, Miller U., 54.3, 629; Lawrence Mann, National, 55.0, 603.

Form 12-N

A similar listing for each event should be included, followed by the final summary (Form 12-M).

Pentathlon

Infrequently, competition is held in the pentathlon, an event similar to the decathlon, but with only five events—a sprint (either 100, 200 or 400 meters), the 1500-meter run, the long jump, javelin and discus. Points are assigned from the same tables as the decathlon (see Form 12-I) and the winner is the competitor who compiles the highest total of points for the five events.

Cross-Country

Statistics in cross-country are limited to three categories—order of finish, individual times and team scoring. Ordinarily, the statistician obtains this information from meet officials, but on occasion he may be required to perform double-duty, acting as a finish judge or timer as well as recording results.

In either situation, the statistician can record the necessary information quickly and accurately with adequate working forms. *The Cross-Country Scorebook,* published by the Athletic Score Book Co., 717 St.

Meet **Dual** V's **East Tech** Team **Central High** Course **Forest Park**

Weather & Course Condition **Good** Course Record **7:37**

Date **11/3/72** Your School Record on Course **7:42**

TIME:

Min.	Min.	Min.	Min.	Min.	Min.	Min.	Min
8	9	10	11				
00	00	00	00	00	00	00	00
1	1	1	1	1	1	1	1
2	2	2	2	2	2	2	2
3	3	3	3	3	3	3	3
4	4	4	4	4	4	4	4
5	5	5	5	5	5	5	5
6	6	6	6	6	6	6	6
7	7	7	7	7	7	7	7
8	8	8	8	8	8	8	8
9	9	9	9	9	9	9	9
10	10	10	10	10	10	10	10
11	11	11	11	11	11	11	11
12	12	12	12	12	12	12	12
13	13	13	13	13	13	13	13
14	14	14	14	14	14	14	14
15	15	15	15	15	15	15	15
16	16	16	16	16	16	16	16
17	17	17	17	17	17	17	17
18	18	18	18	18	18	18	18

Place	Time	Name	School
1	8:04	John Brown	C
2	8:07	Joe Escobar	ET
3	8:09	Wally Akers	C
4	9:02	Mort Levin	C
5	9:05	Bruce O'Brien	ET
6	10:00	Al Reich	ET
7	10:07	Frank Shue	C
8	10:08	Manny Hofman	ET
9	10:15	George Roberti	ET
10	11:04	Tom Sigler	C

Score Box

	CH	ET
1	C	
2		ET
3	C	
4	C	
5		ET

Form 12-O

James Pl., Newport Beach, Ca. 92660, can be used both for a working form and for permanent records of each meet.

Form 12-O shows a partial reproduction of one page of this scorebook, which is adequate for all but the largest meets. There is room on each page for 36 finishers and if the entry list is longer, a second page can be utilized for this purpose.

At the top of this form, space is provided for pertinent information about the meet. For ready reference, when applicable, the course records may be inserted in the space indicated.

At the left, the numerals are printed to provide for a wide variance between the finishing times of the winner and the last-place runner. These should be circled or marked with a slanted line as the individual runners finish.

For instance, in the example shown in Form 12-O, 8 minutes had elapsed in the race as the lead runners approached the finish line. The scorer inserted the figure "8" at the top of the left-hand column. Then, as the timer reports the finish times, a slash of the pencil (or a circle) records the exact time of each finisher.

In the example, under the first column, there is a slash through the numerals 4, 7 and 9. This indicates the winner was timed in 8:04, the second place finisher 8:07, and the third 8:09 minutes.

No other runner crossed the finish line until after the 9-minute mark and, in the example, the first finisher thereafter was timed in 9:02, followed by the fifth-place finisher, 9:05. This procedure is followed until all runners have crossed the finish line.

After the race, the scorer collects the place tickets from officials in numerical order and records the time, name and school for each runner in order of finish (as noted in the center of the scorebook).

The score box at the right of Form 12-O is used as an easy reckoner for dual meet scoring. Initials of the teams are inserted at the top of the columns, then repeated in the proper column for each competitor who finishes the race. Sometimes dual meets are determined by the order of finish of the first four or first six finishers from each team. The procedure to be followed is the same in each case.

Note: Under the official rules, the first *seven* finishers actually enter into scoring calculations, although points are counted only for the first five. Each of the first five finishers for each team is credited with points corresponding to the *place* he finished in the race (i.e. 5 for 5th, 8 for 8th, etc.). Although the sixth and seventh runners of a team to finish do not score points toward their team's total, their places, if better than those of any of the first five of an opposing team, serve to increase the team score of the opponents.

Example: In a cross-country dual meet, runners for Team A finish 1st, 3rd, 6th, 7th, 12th, 13th and 14th, while runners for Team B finish 2nd, 4th, 5th, 8th, 9th, 10th and 11th. Team A is credited points for its first five finishers, 1, 3, 6, 7 & 12 for a total of 29, while Team B's runners earn 2, 4, 5, 8 & 9 for a winning low total of 28.

Form 12-O, however, depicts a meet in which there were only five competitors for each team.

In Form 12-P, the score box from Form 12-O is reproduced for the entire Central High-East Tech meet. It is noted that the Central High runners finished 1st, 3rd, 4th, 7th and 10th, for a total of 25 points. East Tech harriers finished 2nd, 5th, 6th, 8th and 9th for a total of 30 points. Thus Central won the meet, 25 to 30.

For larger meets, this box can be extended with ruler and pencil, *in advance* of the meet, to cover the 36 places for finishers provided on each page. In this instance, the left-hand column would be used for places 1 through 18; the right-hand column for places 19 through 36. Form 12-Q is a partial reproduction of the score box used for this purpose.

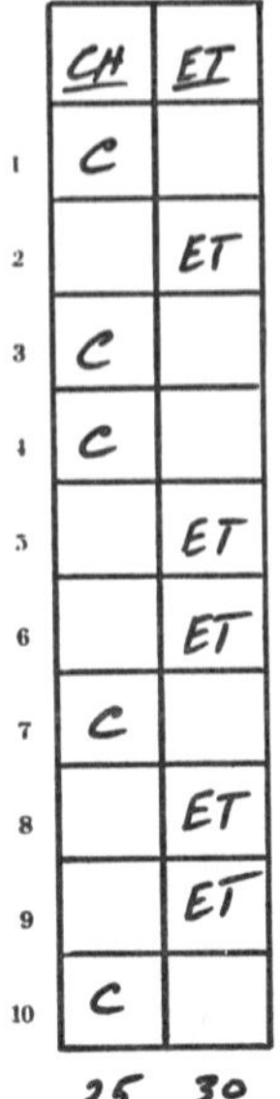

Form 12-P

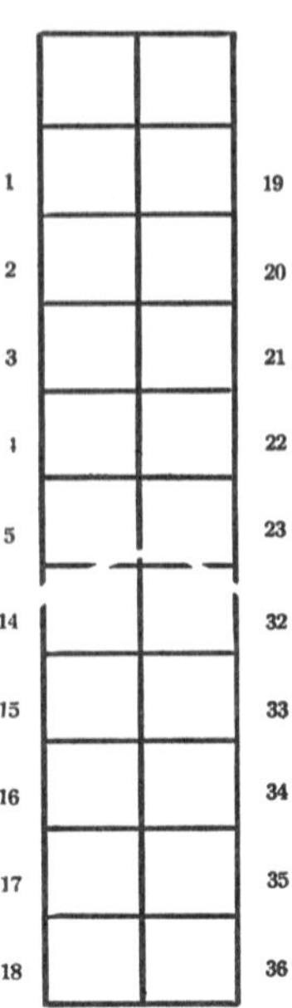

Form 12-Q

The pages of this scorebook can be filed as permanent records and may be used to provide a report to interested media. However, it is suggested that a summary form, in the style normally used by newspapers in the area, be prepared for this purpose.

Form 12-R shows a news summary form that is standard for dual meets, such as the Central High-East Tech meet detailed on Form O. Form S shows the type of report carried by news media for a larger meet, in this instance, the 1971 National Collegiate (NCAA) championship meet.

1. John Brown (C) 8:04; 2. Joe Escobar (ET) 8:07; 3. Wally Akers (C) 8:09; Mort Levin (C) 9:02; 5. Bruce O'Brien (ET) 9:05; 6. Al Reich (ET) 10:00; 7. Frank Shue (C) 10:07; 8. Manny Hofman (ET) 10:08; 9. George Roberti (ET) 10:15; 10. Tom Sigler (C) 11:04.

Central High 25 East Tech 30.

Form 12-R

1. Steve Prefontaine, Oregon 29:14.9; 2. Gary Bjorklund, Minnesota 29:21; 3. Mike Slack, N. Dakota St. 29:26; 4. Dan Murphy, Wash. St. 29:37; 5. Richard Reid, Brigham Young 29:30.

6. Richard Sliney, N. Ariz. 29:47; 7. Cornelius Cusack, E. Tenn. St. 29:51; 8. Edward Leddy, E. Tenn. St. 29:51; 9 Richard Cross, Illinois 29:55; 10. Jerome Howe, Kansas St. 29:59.

11. Hector Ortiz, Western Kentucky 30:02; 12. Davis Wottle, Bowling Green 30:06 . . . (continue listing, five to a paragraph, through first 25 finishers).

Team scoring: Oregon 83, Washington State 122, Pennsylvania 158, Villanova 161, East Tennessee State 193, Kansas State 215, Bowling Green 226, Penn State 269 . . . (continue listing scores of all teams).

Form 12-S

Note: Depending upon media preference, Forms 12-R or 12-S may include only last names, may include time only for the winner, and the numerals designating place of finish may be omitted.

Records in cross-country are usually confined to record times—records for each course and school records for runners at various distances, as competition is held over courses ranging in distance from one-and-a-half miles to seven miles.

Of additional interest might be consecutive records for both individuals and teams—most consecutive victories, etc.

Chapter 13

Water Polo

The duties of the water polo statistician are comparable to those for basketball, ice hockey, soccer and lacrosse. Similar information is recorded and the pace of the game is very rapid.

Since the Official Scorer is technically a member of the officiating team, it is recommended that he concentrate only on his duties as scorer and be free from the responsibilities of the statistician.

The Official Scorer shall:

1. Record the goals scored for each player.
2. Record the personal and major fouls for each player.
3. Record the team fouls.
4. Record the time-outs charged to each team.
5. Keep a record of the names, numbers and positions of all players in the starting lineup and all substitutes who enter the game.
6. Identify the contest (date, place of game, name of officials).
7. Summarize the game totals.

In addition to these official recordings, he must also:

1. Blow the desk horn to announce a player's 5th personal foul and each 10th team foul.
2. Inform the coach and referee of the ineligibility of a team to receive additional time-outs when the maximum number permitted has been taken.
3. Announce the entry of a substitute by blowing the desk horn.

Statistics

Each coach will instruct the statistician in the types of statistical information, forms and summaries he wants. The instructions in this chapter should enable the statistician to record statistics and prepare any of the report forms commonly used as coaching aids.

These basic statistics should be maintained in all categories for news media and for purposes of keeping records:

1. Field Goals Attempted
2. Field Goals Made
3. Field Goal Percentage
4. Goalkeeper Saves
5. Goalkeeper Saves Percentage
6. Assists
7. Turnovers (usually broken down into types, i.e. bad passes, technical fouls, offensive fouls, etc.)

Worksheets

There are many types of worksheets for use in water polo statistics. A good scorebook can be used as a worksheet, as well as providing space for a complete summary of the game.

Form 13-A

Central High	FGA	FG	PTA	PT	PTS	A	T
O'Connor	///	/			/	/	/
McGrew	///	/			/	/	/
Powell	~~////~~ ///	///	//	//	~~////~~	/	~~////~~
Beechan	~~////~~	/			/	///	/
Simmons	////	/			/		/
Bowman	/						
Monger	//						
TOTALS	26	7	2	2	9	6	9

FGA—Field Goal Attempts; FG—Field Goals Made; PTA—Penalty Throw Attempts; PT—Penalty Throws Made; PTS—Total Points; A—Assists; T—Turnovers

If only numerical totals are wanted for individual statistics, a simple homemade chart (Form 13-A) can be prepared easily. When using this type of form, merely tally each FGA, FG or other statistic as it occurs.

Field Goals

Charge a player with a Field Goal Attempt (FGA) whenever he shoots, throws, or taps the ball at the goal in an attempt to score. Credit him with a Field Goal (FG) and one point if the referee signifies a score.

It is the scorer's judgment whether a player is "attempting to score," and thus is charged with a FGA.

On a Field Goal Attempt, when the ball rebounds off the goal posts or off the goalkeeper, if a player taps or bats the ball back toward the goal, or otherwise attempts to score, charge a FGA for each attempted score.

When a player shoots and then fouls a player from the opposing team by following through into him, he is charged with a FGA (and credited with a FG if the goal is made). If the foul is called before the ball leaves the shooter's hands, the ball is dead before the shot and there is no FGA, and no FG.

If a defensive player inadvertently tips the ball into his own goal, credit the FGA and FG to the captain of the offensive team.

Form 13-B shows that Brad Powell of Central High had 8 Field Goal Attempts and was successful on three of them.

Central High	FGA	FG					
POWELL	~~IIII~~ III	III					

Form 13-B

Field Goal Percentage

To compute a player or team's Field Goal Percentage, divide the number of Field Goals made by the number of Field Goals Attempted.

Example: Player A is charged with 8 FGA and is credited with making 3 FG. His Field Goal Percentage is .375 (3 divided by 8).

Minimum standards to qualify for the FG Percentage championship are not rigid, but they should be established in a manner designed to insure a true champion. For instance, it would not be equitable to compare the performance of a player who takes only three shots in three games with a player who has 40 FGA in 10 games.

A study of the cumulative statistics will usually show a clear-cut pattern that will enable the statistician to establish a minimum. Depending upon the type of play and level of competition, the minimum probably will be in the range of two to four shots per game for individual qualification.

The primary principal is that players should be ranked on performance as nearly comparable as possible.

In Field Goal Percentages, individuals and teams are ranked in descending order of percentages.

Shot Chart

Another type of worksheet is a shot chart, which can be devised to include any information desired, both for statistical and coaching purposes.

When using a shot chart (Form 13-C), each time a player attempts a Field Goal, write his cap number at the approximate spot in the pool from which he attempted the shot. When the shot is successful, circle the number.

If the shot is a Penalty Throw, add a letter "P" after the uniform number. An entry for a player wearing a cap, numbered 28, when taking a Penalty Throw, would be 28P or 28-P. If successful, circle the entry. Form 13-C shows a shot chart for Central High in the game tallied on Form 13-A. Some coaches may prefer the shot chart to be maintained separately for each period or each half, though Form 13-C shows shots for an entire game for one team.

Penalty Throws

Although a Field Goal and Penalty Throw each count as one point, most coaches prefer a notation to indicate when a shot attempt or goal was on a Penalty Throw. As noted earlier, when using a shot chart, merely add the letter "P" to indicate a Penalty Throw.

If using a tally sheet, a column for Penalty Throws should be included. Extending Form 13-B to include Penalty Throws, Form 13-D shows that in addition to 8 FGA and 3 FG, Powell attempted 2 Penalty Throws and was successful on each.

If the coach or statistician wants Penalty Throw Percentages, they are computed the same as Field Goal Percentages. Divide the number of Penalty Goals by the number of attempts.

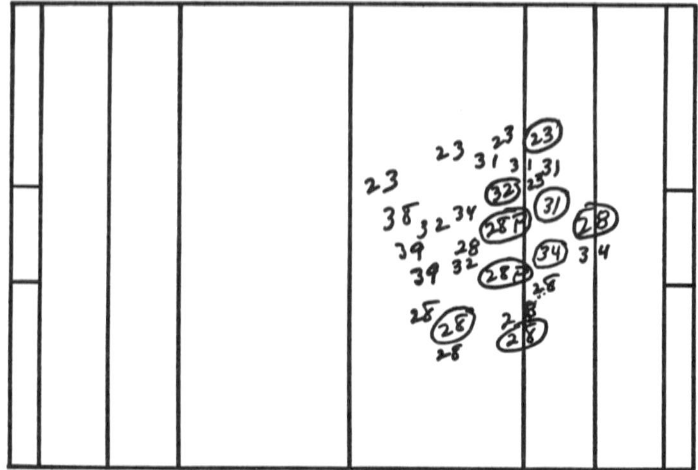

Form 13-C

Central High	FGA	FG	PTA	PT			
POWELL	HHH ///	///	//	//			

Form 13-D

Example: Central High attempted 30 Penalty Throws during the season and made 26. The team Penalty Throw Percentage is .877 (26 divided by 30).

Scoring

Scoring statistics can be added on the tally sheet or can be taken directly from the scorebook. A player is credited with one point for each Field Goal and one point for each successful Penalty Throw.

Form 13-E shows Powell made 3 FG and 2 PT for a total of 5 Points.

Scoring championship is determined by the highest number of points or goals scored during the season.

Assists

A player is credited with an assist whenever he makes a pass that directly *contributes* to a Field Goal.

The scorer must make a judgment on whether a pass "directly contributes" to the scoring of a Field Goal. It is *not* the intent to credit

Central High	FGA		PTA	PT	PTS		
POWELL	卌 |||	|||	||	||	卌		

Form 13-E

an assist on *every* pass that precedes a scoring play, but to provide credit only on those passes which by their execution make the scoring play possible.

Only one assist may be credited for any single Field Goal scored, regardless of how many times the ball was handled prior to the score.

Recording of assists usually is a simple cumulative numerical procedure and the tally worksheet used for other statistics can be utilized for this purpose. Form 13-F shows that Powell also was credited with one assist.

Central High	FGA	FG	PTA	PT	PTS	A	
POWELL	卌 |||	|||	||	||	卌	|	

Form 13-F

Turnovers

Turnovers may be defined as the loss of the ball to the opponent before an attempt at the basket is made. This may occur in several ways:

a. Bad pass (P)
b. Offensive foul (OF)
c. Excessive time in offensive ball control (T)
d. Man in two-yard area not preceded by the ball (2)
e. Technical violations (TV)

Space is sometimes provided on shot charts (Form 13-C) for turnovers, or they may be recorded on a separate worksheet (Form 13-G), which provides space to enter the uniform numbers of the players called for violations, with the type of violation noted by the symbols described above.

If using a tally sheet, Form 13-H shows Powell's complete game statistics, including turnovers.

	Team A	TURNOVERS	Team B	
P	8	1	46	TV
TV	10	2	33	2
P	8	3	48	P
P	15	4	46	P
OF	6	5	40	TV
T	20	6	46	P

Form 13-G

Central High	FGA	FG	PTA	PT	PTSS	A	T
POWELL	𝍸 III	III	II	II	𝍸	I	𝍸

Form 13-H

Sprints

Because of the importance of gaining control of the ball at the start of the game (in effect, it means an extra 45 seconds with the ball), some coaches like to maintain a record of their players' performance in the "sprint" that opens the game.

This can be done with a simple tally sheet, indicating the name(s) of the player(s), how many times they were assigned to the sprint and how many times they were successful in gaining possession of the ball.

How to Keep Score

There are several types of water polo scorebooks, but the same basic procedures can be used with each. A good scorebook provides a more detailed account of a game than the simple tally sheet showed earlier.

Perhaps the most complete is the *Official Water Polo Score Book*, by James R. Smith, available at P.O. Box 3667, Stanford, Ca. 94305 (see Form 13-I). This book, as do others, provides space for individual

SCORING FORM																PERFORMANCE RECORD						
DATE 1/19/73					PLACE CENTRAL HIGH											SEASON (CUMULATIVE)						
TEAM CENTRAL HIGH					GOAL SCORERS		1 JOE HUGHES / 2 MILT RUFFINS										GOALS				FOULS	
					GOALS SCORED							FOULS										
					QUARTERS				OVERTIME													
NAME	POSITION	NUMBER	GOAL ASSISTS	GOAL ATTEMPTS	1st	2nd	3rd	4th	1st	2nd	3rd	1	2	3	4	5	QUARTERS PLAYED	ASSISTS	ATTEMPTS	SCORED	PERCENT	PERSONAL	MAJOR
STAN HINSON	G	22															53						
LOU BEECHAM	LG	23	2,3,4	2,3,3,3,4			1					1	1	2	2		56	8	67	29	43.3	42	
HAL BOWMAN	RG	38		3								1	2	3	4		58	2	48	18	37.1	45	
PAUL McGREW	CG	32	1	1,2,4				1				1	1	2	4	4	55	2	42	16	33.2	41	1
DAN O'CONNOR	CF	34	3	1,2,3	1							1	2	3	4	4	62	3	51	26	50.9	54	
TED SIMMONS	LF	31		1,2,3,3			1					1	2				61	4	52	18	34.6	33	1
BRAD POWELL	RF	28	1	1,1,2,3,3,P3,P4,4,4,4	1	1	1P	P				1	2	4			57	4	57	29	50.9	44	
PHIL MONGER	CG	39		3,4								3	3	3	4		26	2	12	8	66.7	22	
[illegible]	CF	33										2	4				24	3	21	7	33.3	11	

Form 13-I

and team statistics for each team on one page for each game. Standard information includes date, place of game, name of team and game referees or officials.

Smith's scorebook has a unique format which provides space not only for statistics for each game, but on the same page a section where the season's cumulative statistics for each player can be entered. Thus, at the end of each game, the totals for that game can be added to the cumulative totals from the preceding page or game to provide immediate up-to-date cumulative statistics for the season, without referring to any other records.

Form 13-I is a reproduction of a partial page from this scorebook, with entries made for one game. As each area is explained in the following paragraphs, the corresponding section of the scorebook will be reproduced for clarity.

As noted in Form 13-I, positions for the starting team are pre-printed in the scorebook, and the names of the starting players and their cap numbers should be entered in the appropriate places prior to the game.

Assists

When a player is credited with an assist, enter each one in the space provided. Form 13-J shows that Beecham was credited with three assists, one in each of the second, third and fourth quarters.

Form 13-J

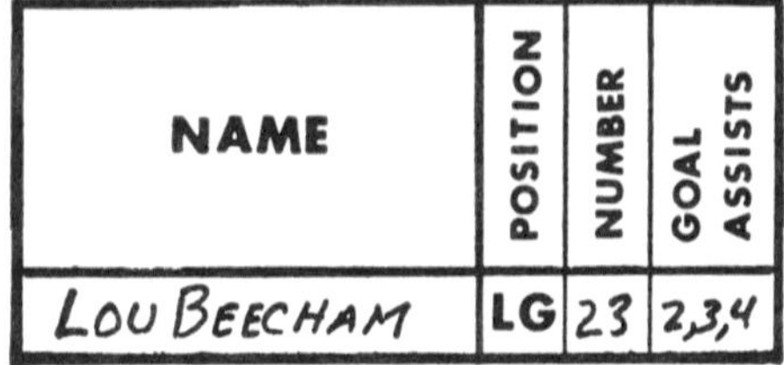

NAME	POSITION	NUMBER	GOAL ASSISTS
LOU BEECHAM	LG	23	2,3,4

Goals

The next columns in the scorebook provide space to tally each attempted Field Goal and Penalty Throw and a square to record (in the appropriate quarter of play) each goal scored.

Form 13-K shows that Powell made 8 Field Goal Attempts and 2 Penalty Throws. The numerals indicate he made 2 FGA in the first quarter, 1 in the second, 2 in the third and 3 in the fourth, and one Penalty Throw in each of the third and fourth quarters. If this detail is not desired, a simple tally of FGA and PTA can be entered, as in earlier Forms 13-B & 13-D.

For goals scored, the breakdown by quarters for Powell shows he made a FG in each of the first three quarters and a Penalty Throw in the third and fourth.

NAME	POSITION	NUMBER	GOAL ASSISTS	GOAL ATTEMPTS	GOALS SCORED: QUARTERS 1st	2nd	3rd	4th	OVERTIME 1st	2nd	3rd
BRAD POWELL	RF	28	1	1,1,2,3,3, P3,P4,4,4,4	1	1	1P	P			

Form 13-K

Playing Time

In the section where the scoring is divided into quarters, the blacked out triangles (see at right-hand side of Powell's statistics in Form 13-K) indicate the quarters in which each player was in the game. In this example, Powell played in all four quarters.

Fouls

Each violation by a player is to be tallied as the foul is called by the official. The mark is placed in the appropriate numbered column under the heading "Fouls." Form 13-L-1 is for a player who has committed three personal fouls, one in the first quarter and two in the third.

If a player commits five fouls, resulting in his removal from the game, circle the tallies (Form 13-L-2) and if he is removed because of a major foul, insert the letter "M" (Form 13-L-3) in the appropriate space.

FOULS				
1	2	3	4	5
1	3	3		

Form 13-L-1

FOULS				
1	2	3	4	5
1	3	3	4	4

Form 13-L-2

FOULS				
1	2	3	4	5
1	M			

Form 13-L-3

Note: It is strongly recommended that a "caller" or spotter be made available to assist the scorer with his official duties. The speed and accuracy with which the scoring is recorded can have an effect on the outcome of the game.

Example: Player A commits his fifth foul and table is slow in recording it. Before the desk horn is sounded to advise the official that Player A should be ejected, the ball is put back into play and Player A scores a goal. The goal counts because the official had not been notified in time to blow the whistle to stop play before the goal was scored.

Penalty Points

The scorer can tally the accumulated team fouls by marking the numbered boxes in the scorebook section labeled "Penalty Points." Form 13-M shows that Central High was charged with 9 penalties in the first quarter, 11 in the second, 5 in the third and 8 in the final period.

PENALTY POINTS	1	2	3	4	5	6	7	8	9	10	1	2	3	4	5	6	7	8	9	10	1	2	3	4	5	6	7	8	9	10
	1	1	1	1	1	1	1	1	1		2	2	2	2	2	2	2	2	2	2	3	3	3	3	3					
	4	4	4	4	4	4	4	4			2																			

Form 13-M

However, because the official timer is required to notify the official immediately when a team commits its 10th team foul, a separate form should be available to the Timer. It should be a printed or mimeographed form with pre-printed columns of numbers, from 1 to 10. There should be a minimum of four sets of the 1 to 10 columns for each team. As a team foul is recorded, the Timer merely puts a slash through the appropriate number. Form 13-N is a suitable form for this purpose.

Team A

1	1	1	1
2	2	2	2
3	3	3	3
4	4	4	4
5	5	5	5
6	6	6	6
7	7	7	7
8	8	8	8
9	9	9	9
10	10	10	10

Team B

1	1	1	1
2	2	2	2
3	3	3	3
4	4	4	4
5	5	5	5
6	6	6	6
7	7	7	7
8	8	8	8
9	9	9	9
10	10	10	10

Form 13-N

Note: The NCAA Water Polo Rules Committee approves the use of diving scorecards for use as counting cards by the Timer.

It is the duty of the Timer to see that the tally of team fouls corresponds with the number of fouls recorded in the scorebook. Thus, the scorer and Timer must work closely together to insure complete accuracy.

Goalkeeper Saves

Credit the goalkeeper with a save every time he stops or deflects a ball which, in the scorer's judgment, would have entered the goal had he not stopped or deflected it.

Form 13-O in the scorebook shows that Hinson was credited with 3 saves (including one save of a Penalty Throw) in the first quarter, 4 in the second, 1 in the third and 2 in the fourth. There is space provided for a second goalie, should a substitute be used. Space is also provided for up to three overtime periods.

GOALKEEPER SAVES					
	1 STAN HINSON	//P	////	/	//
	2				

Form 13-O

The scorebook also includes space for cumulative records of goalkeepers, showing the total saves (through the period of the report), the number of goals scored against the goalie and the average number of saves per game. Form 13-P shows this record for Hinson and for his alternate, King.

Note: The total saves per game will not be a total of the average of each goalie, but rather the result of dividing the number of saves by the number of the team's games (in this case 16). Hinson's average was computed by dividing 102 saves by 16 games, as he played in all his team's games. King played in only 9, so his average is derived by dividing 42 by 9.

Time-Outs

Each time-out should be recorded (Form 13-Q) in the period in which it occurred. Each team is entitled to three time-out periods per game, and the scorer must notify the coach and referee when a team has been charged with its third time-out. Form 13-Q shows that Central High was charged with a time-out in each of the first, second and fourth quarters.

GOALKEEPERS	GOAL SAVES	GOALS SCORED	GOAL SAVE AVERAGE
1 STAN HINSON	102	52	6.5
2 MORRIS KING	42	25	4.7
TOTALS	144	77	9.0

Form 13-P

TIME OUTS	/	/		/

Form 13-Q

Score by Periods

A space is provided for the scorer to enter the team's score for each quarter and the cumulative score at the end of each quarter. In Form 13-R, the line marked "Totals" is at the bottom of the columns for individual players and is a total of the individual performances. In Form 13-R it shows Central High scored 2 goals in the first quarter, 1 in the second, 4 in the third and 2 in the final quarter. On the line below it, the cumulative score is shown: 2 goals at the end of the first quarter, 7 at the end of the second, 7 after three periods and a total of 9 for the game.

TOTALS			2	1	4	2
SCORE BY PERIODS			2	3	7	9

Form 13-R

Running Score

Most scorebooks have space provided for maintaining a running score so that at any time during the game, the exact score can be noted.

Periodically (during a time-out, for instance) a cross-check should be made by quickly adding up all individual scoring for each team to make certain the total for all individuals equals the team total in the Running Score.

In the Running Score (Form 13-S), a diagonal line or slash should be drawn through the appropriate number (corresponding to the total number of points) after each score. A heavy vertical line can be inserted to show the score at the end of each quarter. Form S shows the Running Score for Central High, with the quarter scoring divided as in the Score by Periods in Form 13-R. Smith's scorebook has sufficient space to record up to 30 goals for each team. Form 13-S is a partial reproduction of this section.

RUNNING SCORE	1	2	3	4	5	6	7	8	9	10	11	12

Form 13-S

Team Totals

At the end of each game, all columns should be added to obtain team totals (such as for score by periods in Form 13-R).

Performance Record

One side of the Smith scorebook includes a section (Form 13-T) for recording the cumulative statistics of each player and the team at the end of each game. The form can be completed quickly by adding each player's totals for each game to his cumulative total (in the Performance Record columns) from the previous game. As an example, see the right-hand side of Form 13-I.

At the end of each game, team totals in each category should be entered at the bottom of each column. Then they are added to the cumulative team totals (represented by the totals at the bottom of the Performance Record of the previous game). These are then inserted at the bottom of the Performance Chart for the game just ended.

Then, as a cross-check for accuracy, add the individual totals in each Performance Chart column and if the team entries are accurate, the same numerical totals will result from both methods.

A condensed version of a scorebook style, the Water Polo Record Sheet, may be found included in the *Official NCAA Water Polo Rules,* available at the NCAA Publishing Service, Box 1906, Shawnee Mission, Kan., 66222

Box Scores

Each game may be summarized in a box score to show the results of the game and as many statistical performances as permitted by the style of the news media in the area.

NAME	POSITION	QUARTERS PLAYED	GOALS: ASSISTS	GOALS: ATTEMPTS	GOALS: SCORED	GOALS: PERCENT	FOULS: PERSONAL	FOULS: MAJOR
STAN HINSON	G	53						
LOU BEECHAM	LG	56	8	67	29	43.3	42	
HAL BOWMAN	RG	58	2	48	18	37.1	45	
PAUL MCGREW	CG	55	2	42	16	33.2	41	1
DAN O'CONNOR	CF	62	3	51	26	50.9	54	
TED SIMMONS	LF	61	4	52	18	34.6	33	1
BRAD POWELL	RF	57	4	57	29	50.9	44	
PHIL MONGER	CG	26	2	12	8	66.7	22	
HAROLD KING	CF	24	3	21	7	33.3	11	
TOTALS			28	350	151	43.1	292	2

(PERFORMANCE RECORD — SEASON (CUMULATIVE))

Form 13-T

At a minimum, the box score should include score by periods plus a listing of the players who scored goals (Form 13-U). Depending upon the desire or space limitations of the media, a box score also may include names of all players participating, goals scored, assists, saves, turnovers and fouls committed.

Central High	2	1	4	2 – 9
East Tech	2	1	0	1 – 4

Scoring: CH—O'Connor, Powell 5, Simmons, Beecham, Simmons, McGrew. ET—Perry 3, Smith.

Form 13-U

Records

Records should be maintained for individuals and teams in all water polo statistical categories discussed. As time and available material permits, records should be compiled in each category for single games, for a season and for careers.

Some statisticians may find useful a number of miscellaneous entries, such as most consecutive successful Field Goal Attempts, most consecutive Penalty Throws made, most consecutive games (or quarters) scoring one or more goals, etc. For teams, the most consecutive wins, most wins in a season and best season's winning percentage (both for league and overall schedules) should be listed as permanent records.

For a complete season, the cumulative statistics of each player and the team should be preserved. Most of these entries can be taken from the Performance Record (Form 13-T) for the final game of the season.

Chapter 14

Wrestling

Compared to the responsibilities in other sports, the duties of the wrestling statistician are relatively uncomplicated.

Wrestling rules provide that there be two scorers for each match, one for the home team and one for the visiting team. In a tournament, there should be a scorer and an assistant scorer. Both are responsible to the Match Timekeeper, and their chief function is to record points scored by both contestants *when signaled by the referee.*

If the two scorers are in disagreement, or if the scoreboard operator has a score posted which differs from theirs, the scorers must notify the Match Timekeeper immediately to clarify the situation.

Thus, the scorers have little responsibility in the way of decisions. They merely record points as indicated by the referee.

As a statistician, the wrestling scorer is concerned primarily with the final results of each match, the results of dual meets and tournaments, and with accomplishments in them by individuals or teams which may be noteworthy for publicity or record purposes.

For normal statistical use, summaries of various types of competition should be familiar to the statistician.

Dual Meets

The team scores in a dual meet are recorded along with the name of the winner of each individual match and his manner of victory (i.e. fall, decision, default, forfeit, disqualification, or draw).

In recording results, the weight division is indicated prior to the match results and the winning wrestler's school affiliation is noted after his name. If a wrestler is pinned, the time of the fall should be recorded. The score of the match completes the summary and, depending upon the style desired, may precede or follow the individual results.

Example: Following is a sample summary of a dual meet in a form that may be used for record purposes or for distribution to the news media:

> *Ames* 26-*Palomar* 23. 98 lb class—Smith (A) pinned Jones, 3:22; 105—Brown (P) d. Adams, 8-6; 112—Marshall (A) pinned Rocha, 2:10; 119—Johnson (P) pinned Howard, 4:14; 126—Hicks (P) pinned Feldman, 1:26; 123—Woods (A) d. Stevenson, 15-5; 138—Stewart (P) d. McBride, 9-3; 145—Garcia (A) d. Heinberg, disq.; 155—Powell (A) drew with Beecham; 167—Simmons (A) d. O'Connor, 13-3; 185—Bowman (A) d. McGrew, 12-5; Hvwt.—Hernandez (P), forfeit.

Tournaments

The same basic information is recorded for tournaments with results separated into weight divisions. Within these divisions is detailed the results of the matches by rounds, beginning with the preliminaries and ending with the finals.

Example: The following is a sample summary of tournament scoring for one weight division:

155 POUND CLASS

PRELIMINARIES—Lee (Fairmont) d. Torres (Bristol) 8-6; Snyder (Piedmont) pinned Miller (Reynolds) 2:43.

FIRST ROUND—Lee d. Anderson (Hoover) 14-6; Grant (Washington) d. Snyder 10-2; Evans (Lincoln) d. Newman (Middle Park) 10-3; Muller (Pine Crest) pinned Gardner (Hopkins) 5:17; Davis (North Springs) pinned Edwards (Columbia) 6:53; Walters (Northside) d. Latimer (Jefferson) 14-6; Green (Cedar Falls) d. Kane (Fremont) 7-1; Adams (Bisbee) pinned Dixon (Pierre) 3:10.

QUARTER FINALS—Lee d. Grant 8-6; Evans pinned Muller 4:15; Davis d. Walters 9-7; Green pinned Adams 2:27.

SEMI FINALS—Lee d. Evans 9-4; Davis pinned Green 4:20.

FINALS—Davis pinned Lee 5:17 CONSOLATION (3rd Place) Evans d. Green 3-2. (5th Place) Anderson d. Edwards 5-5, 2-2, RD

Note: The Anderson-Edwards match shows a tie in regulation time and a tie in points at the end of overtime, necessitating a Referee's Decision (RD).

When reporting Team Scoring for a tournament, the statistician should list all teams who scored points in descending order, beginning with the winner. After the name of each of the teams should appear the total points it scored in the tournament.

Example:

TEAM SCORING

Newberg 82, Lowell 58, Reynolds 48, Bisbee 43, Bowman 41, Perry 41, Fairmont 38, Columbia 35, Jefferson 34, Fremont 32, Piedmont 31, Cedar Falls 30, North Springs 29, Washington 26, Pierre 23, Bristol 11, Hoover 16, Middle Park 11, Hopkins 10, Pine Crest 9, Lincoln 9, Northside 6, Greenfield 6, Park Ridge 5, Middleton 4, Chesterton 3, Davenport 2, Roosevelt 1, Newton 1, Maplewood 1, Lowell 1, Melrose 1.

Falls and Takedowns

Many coaches wish to keep a record of the number of falls and the number of takedowns for each wrestler during the season.

This information may be taken from the individual match results (described in the section on Scoring). With the individual match scores it is a simple matter of recording the number of falls and takedowns on a season tally sheet (Form 14-A). This material also will be useful for record and for publicity purposes.

Scoring

In accordance with wrestling rules, the scorers are responsible for:

1. Recording which contestant has the down position at the start of the second and third periods.
2. Recording points scored by both contestants when signaled by the referee. The referee will signal and verbally notify the scorer when warnings or points are awarded to each contestant.
3. Constantly checking other scorers' readings.
4. Immediately advising the match timekeeper when they are in disagreement regarding the score.
5. Keeping the scoreboard operator continually advised of the official score during each match.
6. Showing the referee the scorecard at the end of each match.
7. Recording time advantage points in the final match score.

The scorers are assigned seats in the following positions:

When Individual Clocks or Stopwatches Are Used

Home Team Assistant Timekeeper	Visiting Team Assistant Timekeeper	Match Timekeeper	Visiting Team Scorer	Home Team Scorer

OPPONENTS

WRESTLER	F	T	F	T	F	T	F	T	F	T	F	T	F	T	F	T	TOTALS
ADAMS	OWINGS	II	SMITH ✓	IIII	ANDREWS ✓	III	MILLER ✓	III	JOHNSON	II	JONES ✓	~~IIII~~	WILSON	II	COLEMAN ✓	IIII	5-25
GARCIA	FERNANDEZ	I	GALT	II	CARTER ✓	~~IIII~~	HUBER	II	BRUNNER ✓	II	BELK	I	FARRELL ✓	II	KNUTSON ✓	II	4-17
ANDERSON	EDWARDS ✓	I	COOK	I	HARMON		KRAMER		STAMP ✓	I	RAY	I	OTTO ✓	II	LARSEN ✓	III	4-9
KAMPA	WILLIAMS ✓	II	PETERS ✓	I	McMillan	I	REARDON ✓	II	GILSON	II	McKEE ✓	I	DEMPSEY ✓	IIII	CASPER	I	5-14

Form 14-A

When Multiple Timer is Used

Timekeeper	Visiting Scorer	Announcer or Home Scorer

All scoring must be posted in plain view of spectators, contestants and judges. A timing device should be available and visible for the purpose of recording Time-Advantage. When not available, some other method should be devised to provide this information during the progress of a match.

Dual Meet Scoring

In dual meets, points are awarded to the team of each winning contestant, graduated according to the manner of victory, as shown in the following table:

Dual Meet Scoring Summary

Fall	6 Points	Decision (by 10 or more points)	4 points
Forfeit	6 Points	Decision (by less than 10 points)	3 points
Default	6 Points	Draw	2 points
Disqualification	6 Points		

Example: In a dual meet, Team A wins three matches by falls (18 points), one match by a decision score of 16-4 (4 points), one by a score of 8-6 (3 points), and had one draw (2 points) for a total of 27. Team B won one match by a fall (6 points), two by decisions of at least 10 points (8 points), three by decisions of less than 10 points (9 points), and had one draw (2 points) for a total of 25. Team A wins the meet, 27-25.

Thus, it is seen that the winning team in a dual meet is that one which earns the most *points,* not the team that wins the most matches.

In individual matches, the contestants are awarded points by the referee as follows:

Individual Match Scoring Summary

Takedown	2 points
Escape	1 point
Reversal	2 points
Predicament	2 points
Near-Fall	3 points
*Time Advantage	1 point

*One point is awarded for one full minute or more of net accumulated time in the advantage position. One point is the maximum that may be earned by time-advantage.

How to Keep Score

Several types of wrestling scorebooks are available, but the same basic procedure is used with each. After the spaces provided for identifying schools, coaches, date and place of contest, the individual match scoresheets appear. The scorebook used in the example is *Roderick's Wrestling Scorebook,* available at 4000 W. 19th Street, Stillwater, Oklahoma 74074 (see Form 14-B for partial reproduction of pages).

Entries should be made for the weight class, each wrestler's name, and his year in school:

CONTESTANTS
lb. Class ______________________ Yr ____________
Our ____
Their __________________________ Yr ____________

Maneuvers and Points

As the referee signals each successful scoring maneuver, the identifying symbol for that maneuver is placed in the empty square behind the box labeled "MAN'VER." Immediately below, space is provided for the number of points scored by each maneuver. Points awarded for each maneuver are tabulated in the previous section on Individual Match Scoring Summary.

Example: Form 14-C shows the results of a bout in the 155 lb. weight division. Jones scores a takedown (2 points), after which Smith escapes (1 point). Smith then makes a takedown on Jones (2 points) and Jones scores a reversal (2 points) before the end of the first period. Jones has bottom position in the second period and he escapes (1 point). Smith gets a takedown (2 points) and a near fall (3 points) before Jones is able to score a reversal (2 points). Jones is then guilty of a one-point infraction and the second period ends. Smith has bottom position in the third period and he escapes (1 point). He follows this with a takedown (2 points) and a predicament (2 points) before Jones manages an escape (1 point). After this Jones gets a takedown (2 points) and the match ends. Neither wrestler has a time-advantage. Smith is the winner of the bout, 14 points to 10, or 14-10.

Note: The letters "T" and "B" in the vertical column between the first and second periods refer to Top and Bottom position. The scorer should circle only one "T" or "B" to indicate the winner and his choice of position.

Date 2/25/72 CENTRAL HIGH Vs. EAST TECH

Coaches BOB JONES JOHN SMITH

Won by CENTRAL HIGH Score 30 To 5

Referee NED BLASS Place CENTRAL GYM

CONTESTANTS		FIRST PERIOD	SECOND PERIOD	THIRD PERIOD	TIME ADV.	BOUT SCORE	MATCH SCORE OURS	MATCH SCORE THEIRS
LB. CLASS 115 YR JR. OUR HATTA	MAN VER / POINTS	TD 2	T E 1 R 2		3:41	6	3	0
YR SR THEIR JOHNSON	POINTS / MAN VER	1 E	B 2 TD			3		

NOTES: TD--ARM DRAG; R--SWITCH; E--STANDUP

TOTAL MAN VER	OURS	THEIRS	TOTAL MAN VER	OURS	THEIRS
TD	1	1	NF		
E	1	1	P		
R	1		IF		

CONTESTANTS		FIRST PERIOD	SECOND PERIOD	THIRD PERIOD	TIME ADV.	BOUT SCORE	MATCH SCORE OURS	MATCH SCORE THEIRS
LB. CLASS 123 YR SR OUR GEORGE	MAN VER / POINTS	TD P 2 2 (FALL 2:31)				FALL	8	0
YR SOPH THEIR BROWN	POINTS / MAN VER							

NOTES: TD--SINGLE LEG

TOTAL MAN VER	OURS	THEIRS	TOTAL MAN VER	OURS	THEIRS
TD	1		NF		
E			P	1	
R			IF		

CONTESTANTS		FIRST PERIOD	SECOND PERIOD	THIRD PERIOD	TIME ADV.	BOUT SCORE	MATCH SCORE OURS	MATCH SCORE THEIRS
LB. CLASS 130 YR JR OUR SHADE	MAN VER / POINTS	TD 2 TD 1	T NF 3 E 1	E 1	1:57	9	11	0
YR SR THEIR JAMES	POINTS / MAN VER	1 E 1 E	B 2 R	1 IF		4		

NOTES: TD--DOUBLE LEG; E--SIT OUT; NF--CRADLE

TOTAL MAN VER	OURS	THEIRS	TOTAL MAN VER	OURS	THEIRS
TD	2		NF	1	
E	2	2	P		
R		1	IF		1

CONTESTANTS		FIRST PERIOD	SECOND PERIOD	THIRD PERIOD	TIME ADV.	BOUT SCORE	MATCH SCORE OURS	MATCH SCORE THEIRS
YR JR	MAN VER / POINTS	E TD 1 2	T R P 2 2			7	14	0
LB. CLASS 167 YR OUR WALKER	POINTS	2	1	E TD 1 1		6	19	5
YR SOPH THEIR KNORR	POINTS / MAN VER	6 TD TD	P B E R	1 3 TD NF	1:34	13		

NOTES: E--STAND UP; TD--UNDER ARM; E- SIT OUT; TD- SINGLE LEG

TOTAL MAN VER	OURS	THEIRS	TOTAL MAN VER	OURS	THEIRS
TD	2	3	NF		1
E	3		P		
R		1	IF		

NOMENCLAURE USED: ○ Circle Only One Top or Bottom (T B) It Shows the Winner of the Toss and his Choice

TD	Take Down 2 Pts.	E	Escape 1 Pt.	R	Reversal 2 Pts.	IF	Infraction 1 Pt.—2 Pts.

HOME CENTRAL HIGH — TEAM MAN'VERS — VISITOR EAST TECH

TD	13	P	2	DEC	6	TD	7	P	0	DEC	1
E	9	NF	2	DRAW	1	E	11	NF	1	DRAW	1
R	6	IF	1	FALL	2	R	4	IF	1	FALL	0

CONTESTANTS		FIRST PERIOD	SECOND PERIOD	THIRD PERIOD	TIME ADV.	BOUT SCORE	MATCH SCORE OURS	MATCH SCORE THEIRS
LB. CLASS 177 YR SOPH OUR LEONARDO	MAN'VER / POINTS	TD 2 (FALL 1:30)				FALL	24	5
YR JR THEIR SIMMONDS	POINTS / MAN'VER							

NOTES: TD--DOUBLE LEG; E--HALF NELSON + BAR ARM

TOTAL MAN VER	OURS	THEIRS	TOTAL MAN VER	OURS	THEIRS
TD	1		NF		
E			P		
R			IF		

CONTESTANTS		FIRST PERIOD	SECOND PERIOD	THIRD PERIOD	TIME ADV.	BOUT SCORE	MATCH SCORE OURS	MATCH SCORE THEIRS
LB. CLASS 191 YR SR OUR BEASLEY	MAN'VER / POINTS	TD 2 E 1	T TD 1		2:47	5	27	5
YR SOPH THEIR McGANCAY	POINTS / MAN'VER	2 R	B E			3		

NOTES: TD--ARM DRAG; TD--UNDER ARM + SINGLE LEG; --SIT OUT

TOTAL MAN'VER	OURS	THEIRS	TOTAL MAN VER	OURS	THEIRS
TD			NF		
			P		

LB. CLASS — OUR — YR. — THEIR — MAN'VER — T

NOTES

TOTAL MAN'VER	OURS	THEIRS	TOTAL MAN VER	OURS	THEIRS
TD			NF		
E			P		
R			IF		

P	Predicament 2 Pts.	NF	Near Fall 3 Pts.	D	Decision 3 Pts.	DO	Draw 2 Pts.	F	Fall 5 Pts.

Form 14-B

CONTESTANTS		FIRST PERIOD									SECOND PERIOD								THIRD PERIOD								TIME ADV.	BOUT SCORE	MATCH SCORE	
LB. CLASS 155 YR JR.	MAN VER		E	TD						T		TD	NF		IF				E	TD	P								OURS	THEIRS
OUR SMITH	POINTS		1	2						B		2	3		1				1	2	2						.31	14		
YR SR.	POINTS	2			2					T	1			2								1	2					10		
THEIR JONES	MAN VER	TD			R					(B)	E			R								E	TD							

Form 14-C

Time-Advantage

The offensive wrestler who has control in an advantage position over his opponent is gaining Time-Advantage. A timekeeper assigned to each wrestler records his accumulated time-advantage throughout the match. At the end of the match, the Referee subtracts the lesser time-advantage from the greater. If the difference is less than one minute, *no* point is awarded to the wrestler with the greater time-advantage. If the difference is equal to one full minute or more, one point is awarded to the wrestler with the greater time-advantage. One point is the maximum that can be awarded for the time-advantage in one match.

Example: Form 14-D shows the net time-advantage for three different matches. In the first, with only 33 seconds difference, there is no point awarded. In the other two, each of which shows more than one minute net time-advantage difference, the wrestler is awarded one point in each match.

Form 14-D

TIME ADV.	TIME ADV.	TIME ADV.
.33	1.42	2.28
	1	1

Match and Meet Score

At the end of each individual match, the score is recorded in the space provided (see Form 14-E) for both the bout just completed and the cumulative dual meet score to that point.

Form 14-E

BOUT SCORE	MATCH SCORE	
	OURS	THEIRS
14	21	18
10		

Match Summary

Below the bout scoring columns on the scorecard is a space (see Form 14-F) labeled "NOTES" for the scorer to summarize the wrestling techniques used by the home team's wrestler to accomplish his maneuvers. If the scorer does not have this technical knowledge he should request assistance in this area from a coach or competitor.

A space also is provided (Form 14-F) at the right to tally the number of maneuvers accomplished by both wrestlers during the bout.

To further summarize, at the top right of the scorecard is a section to recap each team's total maneuvers (see Form 14-G). The abbreviations indicate the type of maneuver, as follows:

TD–Takedown	P–Predicament	Dec–Decision
E–Escape	NF–Near Fall	Draw
R–Reversal	IF–Infraction	Fall

HOME Ames — TEAM MAN'VERS — VISITOR Palomar

TD	17	P	2	DEC	3	TD	9	P	1	DEC	2
E	10	NF	3	DRAW	1	E	9	NF	2	DRAW	1
R	6	IF	0	FALL	2	R	6	IF	1	FALL	2

Form 14-F

NOTES
E - Stand up
TD - Ankle pickup
TD - Ankle pickup
NF - Cradle
IF - Locked hands
E - Sitout
TD - Single leg
P - Half nelson & crotch

TOTAL MAN'VER	OURS	THEIRS	TOTAL MAN'VER	OURS	THEIRS
TD	3	2	NF	1	
E	2	2	P	1	
R		2	IF	1	

Form 14-G

Tournament Scoring

Points in individual tournament matches are awarded in the same values as in dual meets.

Summary of Tournament Match Scoring	
Takedown	2 points
Escape	1 point
Reversal	2 points
Predicament	2 points
Near Fall	3 points
*Time-Advantage	1 point

*One point is awarded for one full minute or more of net accumulated time in the advantage position. One point is the maximum that may be earned by time-advantage.

In tournaments there are three ways in which an individual wrestler may earn points for his team: (1) for placement, (2) for advancement, and (3) for winning by other than a simple decision (Tournament Points).

Placement

Individual placement points for each team are awarded as soon as they are earned. However, placement points already earned will be deducted in the case of forfeit or disqualification.

In tournaments scoring six places, the winner of each championship quarterfinal is awarded 3 points; the winner of each championship semifinal is awarded 9 additional place points; the winner of each championship final is awarded 4 additional place points.

The winner of the quarterfinal consolation match receives 3 place points; the winner of the consolation semifinals receives 4 additional place points; the winners of third and fifth places each receive 2 additional place points.

TOURNAMENT SCORING CHART

	1st	2nd	3rd	4th	5th	6th	7th	8th
Four Places	16	12	9	7				
Six Places	16	12	9	7	5	3		
Eight Places	16	12	9	7	5	3	2	1

Advancement

An *additional* point is awarded for each victory in championship and consolation eliminations except for the final first, third and fifth place matches. No points are awarded for a bye in any round.

Tournament Points

An *additional* point is awarded to each wrestler who wins any match (including final first, third and fifth place matches) by fall, default, forfeit or disqualification, or an *additional* one-half point is awarded to each wrestler who wins by a "superior" decision (by 10 points or more).

Tournament Points	
Fall	1 point
Default	1 point
Forfeit	1 point
Disqualification	1 point

Advancement

Championship bracket	1 point
Consolation bracket	½ point

Thus, wrestlers who win a place in a tournament are likely to earn more than the points assigned for that place alone. The extra points, as detailed above, are for winning matches prior to the quarterfinals and for the manner in which the matches were won.

Example: Referring to the Tournament Scoring Chart above, the champion or first-place winner in a tournament scoring six places receives 12 points. This includes 1 point for winning a quarterfinal match, 8 additional for winning his semifinal match, and 3 more for winning his final match. (In addition, he receives one advancement point for each match won in the championship eliminations prior to the quarterfinals, and any extra points won for winning by a fall or a decision won by 10 points or more, etc. in any of the matches, including the quarterfinals, semifinals or consolations.)

Example: The second-place winner in a six-place tournament is awarded a total of 9 points, which includes 1 point for a quarterfinal win and 8 for a semifinal victory. (In addition he receives 1 advancement point for each match won in the championship eliminations prior to the quarterfinals and, like the champion, extra points as earned for winning by a fall or a decision won by 10 points or more, etc.)

Example: Third place winner in a six-place tourney is the winner of the consolation eliminations. He receives a total of 7 points, 1 for quarterfinal win, 4 for a semifinal victory and 2 more for winning the consolation finals. (Again, like all place winners, he receives additional points for earlier wins in both the championship and consolation eliminations, and extra points for falls, etc.)

In tournament competition, the winner of the finals in each class is awarded first-place points, and the loser is automatically second. The winner of the final consolation match is the third-place winner and, where four places are scored, the fourth place goes to the loser in the consolation final. In six-place tournaments, the losers in the consolation and semifinals wrestle for fifth and sixth places.

Consolation competition includes all wrestlers who were defeated earlier by the quarterfinal winners (in a 32-man bracket) or the semifinal winners (in a 16-man bracket) plus the losers in the semifinal matches.

The brackets below, with wrestlers identified by numbers, illustrate the pairings and places earned in a 16-man bracket for one weight division.

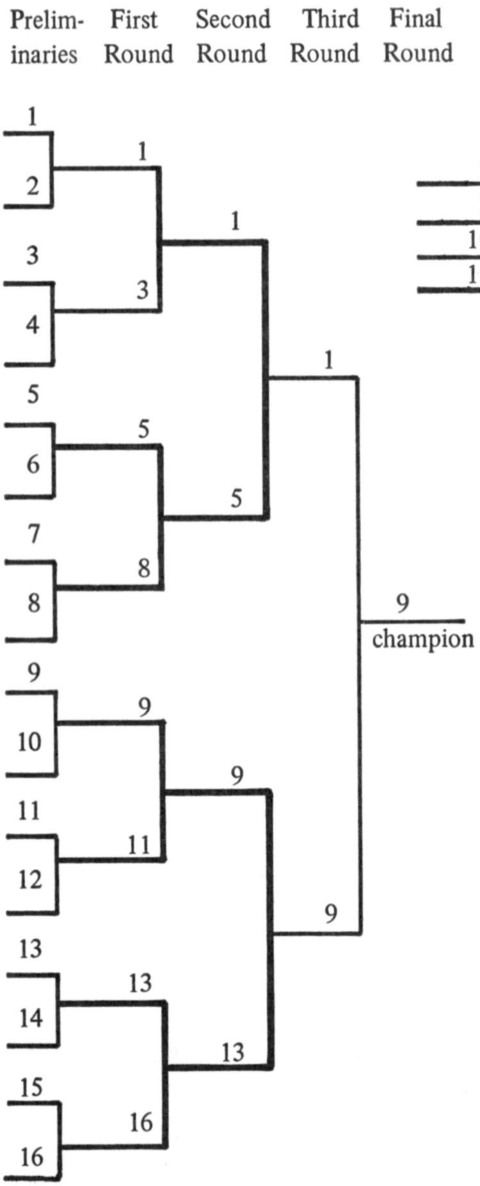

Prelim-inaries | First Round | Second Round | Third Round | Final Round

1
2
1
3
4
3
1
5
6
5
7
8
8
5
1
9
10
9
11
12
11
9
13
14
13
15
16
16
13
9
9
champion

Consolation Pairings

(6 Places)

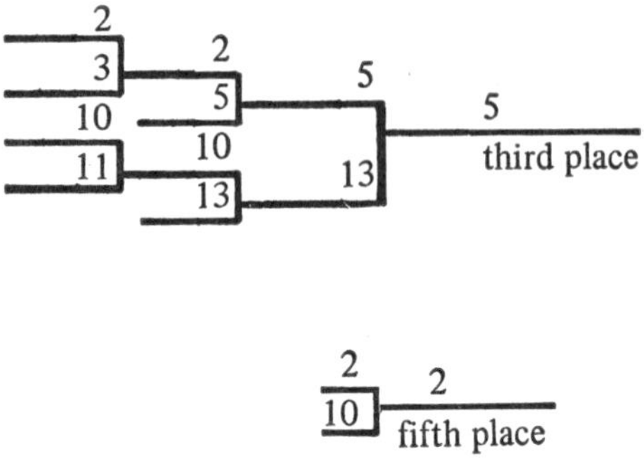

2
3
2
10
5
11
10
5
13
13
5
third place

2
10
2
fifth place

2 represents first man defeated by semifinal winner 1
3 represents second man defeated by semifinal winner 1
5 represents third man defeated by semifinal winner 1

10 represents first man defeated by semifinal winner 9
11 represents second man defeated by semifinal winner 9
13 represents third man defeated by semifinal winner 9

To convert numbers into names, here are results in the 155-pound class of a tournament with 16 men entered in the division.

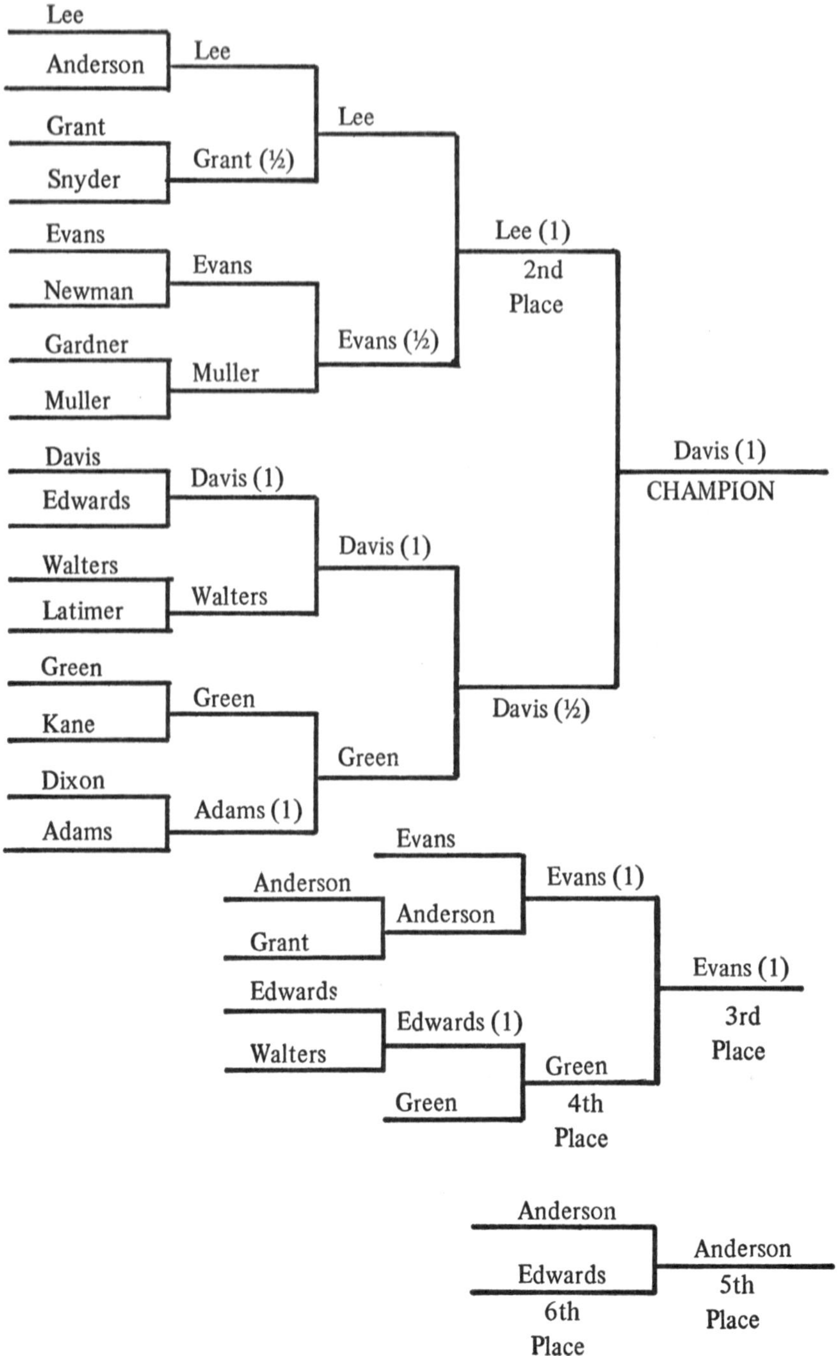

The small numerals after each wrestler's name indicate how he won his match, according to the following code: 1—for a win by fall, default, disqualification or forfeit; ½—for a win by a decision of 10 or more points. As noted earlier, these points are awarded in addition to the advancement points and placement points.

Converting these results of the 155 lb. class into points, the following table shows how each wrestler in the first three places earned points during the tournament:

WRESTLER	3 Places	4 Places	5 Places	6 Places
Davis	(15½) 9 pts = 1st 3 pts = 3 wins 3½ pts = 3 falls 1-10 pt dec.	(16½) 10 pts = lst 3 pts = 3 wins 3½ pts = 3 falls 1-10 pt dec.	(17½) 11 pts = 1st 3 pts = 3 wins 3½ pts = 3 falls 1-10 pt dec.	(18½) 12 pts = 1st 3 pts = 3 wins 3½ pts = falls 1-10 pt dec.
Lee	(10) 6 pts = 2nd 3 pts = 3 wins 1 pt = 1 fall	(11) 7 pts = 2nd 3 pts = 3 wins 1 pt = 1 fall	(12) 8 pts = 2nd 3 pts = 3 wins 1 pt = 1 fall	(13) 9 pts = 2nd 3 pts = 3 wins 1 pt = 1 fall
Evans	(8½) 3 pts = 3rd 3 pts = 3 wins 2½ pts = 2 falls 1-10 pt dec.	(9½) 4 pts = 3rd 3 pts = 3 wins 2½ pts = 2 falls 1-10 pt dec.	(11½) 6 pts = 3rd 3 pts = 3 wins 2½ pts = 2 falls 1-10 pt dec.	(12½) 7 pts = 3rd 3 pts = 3 wins 2½ pts = 2 falls 1-10 pt dec.

Penalties

When calling each infraction, the referee will stop the match (except when warning and penalizing the defensive wrestler for stalling), give the hand signal for the points or warnings, and announce the penalty. The penalty chart (Form 14-H) indicates the sequence of warnings and penalties. They are cumulative throughout the match, including overtime.

Penalty Chart

Infractions	Warning	First Penalty	Second Penalty	Third Penalty	Fourth Penalty
Illegal Holds	No	1 Pt.	1 Pt.	2 Pts	Disqualify
Technical Violations	No	1 Pt.	1 Pt.	2 Pts.	Disqualify
Stalling	Yes	1 Pt.	1 Pt.	2 Pts.	Disqualify
Unnecessary Roughness	No	1 Pt.	1 Pt.	2 Pts.	Disqualify
Abusive and/or Unsportsmanlike Conduct	No	Deduct 1 Team Point	Remove From Premises	(Removal is for duration of dual meet or tournament session only)	
Flagrant Misconduct	No	Disqualify on first offense and deduct 1 team point			
Greasy Substance on Skin Objectionable Pads and Braces, Illegal Equipment or Illegal Costume	Disqualify if not removed or corrected in allotted time				

Weight Classifications

Collegiate tournaments and dual meet competition is divided into 10 weight classes as follows:

118 lbs.	134 lbs.	150 lbs.	167 lbs.	190 lbs.
126 lbs.	142 lbs.	158 lbs.	177 lbs.	Unlimited

High School tournament and dual meet competition is divided into 12 weight divisions:

98 lbs.	119 lbs.	138 lbs.	167 lbs.
105 lbs.	126 lbs.	145 lbs.	185 lbs.
112 lbs.	132 lbs.	155 lbs.	Unlimited

Records

For purposes of records and for material which may be used in publicizing a wrestling match or tournament, individual and team records should be maintained in at least the categories listed below:

Most victories in a match, tournament, season and career.

Most consecutive victories.

Most points scored in a single match, dual meet, tournament, season and career.

Fewest points allowed in a single match, dual meet, tournament, season and career.

Most falls in a dual meet, tournament, season and career.

Fastest fall recorded.

Fewest falls incurred by individual or team in dual meet, tournament, season and career.

Most takedowns in a single match, dual meet, tournament, season and career.